The Pipe Family Letter Collection

Volume 1

The Promise of America
in Their Own Words

Joan Naomi Steiner, PhD

SCENERY HEIGHTS
Publishing

Neenah, Wisconsin (USA)

The Pipe Family Letter Collection, Vol. 1

The Promise of America in Their Own Words

ISBN: 979-8-9865709-3-8

Front cover images: John Valentine Pipe and Elizabeth Stickland Pipe

Back cover image: Aerial view of Yarcombe, Devon, England

(Privately held by Joan Naomi Steiner, Neenah, Winnebago County, Wisconsin, USA, with permission from Sarah-Jane and Neil Martin, The Belfrey at Yarcombe, Devon, England)

Scenery Heights Publications
Neenah, Wisconsin (USA)

Dedication

*To my son, Robert John Mittelstaedt, who reintroduced me
to the Pipe and Stickland families through his cousins,
Marlene Anderson Sannes and Ida Mae Rosin Frizzell,
and his aunt, Judy Mittelstaedt Anderson.*

and

*To my granddaughter, Madeline,
who will know her ancestral roots through those of her
grandfather, Robert Alan Mittelstaedt,
and her great-grandmother,
Helen Anderson Mittelstaedt, daughter of
Oliver and May Elizabeth Pipe Anderson.*

Foreword

Susan T. Moore

I was first approached by Joan Steiner to ask if I would be interested in transcribing some family letters concerning a family with connections to Devon and Somerset (England) and jumped at the chance, as I grew up and still live in this rural area and am familiar with the place names, and of course have an interest in the area.

I have been carrying out research into family and local history all my working life as a freelance researcher and have loved every minute. The commissions I have received over the years have varied widely from writing a biography of a Tudor courtier, to modern land disputes where 17th century maps need to be consulted. But what I do mostly is straightforward family history usually in the 16th to 18th centuries, with many requests for finding the 'link across the Atlantic' and the English origins of people who emigrated in the early 17th century from somewhere in England to New England or Virginia.

However, I think my favourite commissions are those where I am asked to transcribe diaries or letters. These give an insight into the characters and lives of the people concerned that cannot be matched anywhere else. I have worked on a number of naval diaries, which give an excellent idea of life aboard ship in the 19th century, the relationships between the crew and the passengers, and the places visited.

However, nothing prepared me for the intimacy and detail to be found in this collection of Pipe family letters. The collection will of course be of great interest to the wider members of the family and there are a great many references to aunts, uncles, brothers, sisters, friends and of course parents and children. But what really interested me, and will interest the wider readership, who are not necessarily related to the Pipe family, are the details of local history.

From these letters we learn of the fire in Oshkosh with a little sketch to show how it took all of Main Street and left just the Court House. Every printing house, every large store and every bank were lost. The sadness the morning after is heartfelt: "I think it the most distressing sight I ever saw with so much property burned."

Something that not everyone is aware of is just how often people crossed the Atlantic in both directions. Once in America people didn't stay there all the time. They came back to England to visit family or property. And those in England sailed to America to visit friends and family. The shipping passengers lists that are now readily available online will confirm this constant traffic to and fro.

Something that surprised me when transcribing these letters, which are mostly in the second half of the 19th century is the low level of true literacy. Yes, they could write, but the spelling was phonetic for so many of them. Although spelling was not standard in earlier centuries, by the 19th century there was little variation and there were right and wrong ways of spelling words. So, we have 'affectionate' written 'efexinant' and 'window' written 'wingo'. Words then can be a little challenging to any transcriber!

Health is something that we generally take for granted today, but in the 19th century it was very fragile and all the letters contain many confirmations that everyone is still healthy or gives details of illnesses. When a letter starts 'I hope you are well' which we may think of as a platitude, for them it was serious and a genuine question.

Finally, the details of the way farms were run both in Devon and Wisconsin are absolutely fascinating to those of us with an interest in this way of life. The comparison of weather events, the prices of wheat, the price of land are as interesting as the quantities involved. In Oshkosh we hear of 2000 bushels of wheat and 1000 of oats. Yet in Yarcombe we hear that the price of corn was very low with wheat selling at just £1 per sack. The agricultural information which can be found in these letters deserves some serious study and analysis.

Perhaps the saddest lines in the letters come from Elizabeth Stickland Pipe writing to Mr. William & Mrs. Elizabeth Coleman Jennings on 21st May 1854 concerning the drowning of her husband.

"I had a list of the passengers that was on board of the *City of Glasgow* and I saw his dear name there on the list and the steamer has not arrived which I suppose by the accounts she never will. It is supposed she was encountered ice bergs smashed to atoms and sunk with 373 passengers, 74 officers and crew. Here I am left as everyone thinks a widow with four little children."

I hope that everyone who reads this book will enjoy the details as much as I did when I was transcribing the letters, whether they are family members or those who are interested in life in the past, particularly in the farming areas of Somerset, Devon and Wisconsin.

Contents

Acknowledgements

O ver the years, Pipe descendants cared for over 105 family letters in this collection, along with several dozen framed portraits and over 100 family pictures. I especially thank the Marjorie Pipe Johnson, Marlene Anderson Sannes, and Elizabeth Pipe Hansen families. They are the guardians of these family treasures. Undoubtedly, earlier descendants found their ancestors' handwriting too difficult to read and understand. However, the letters were not discarded. These family caretakers protected ancestral voices that now have been brought back to life. Once again, their voices are heard.

I especially thank Susan Moore from Somerset, England, who professionally transcribed each letter to preserve local dialect as much as possible so that each letter writer would be heard as authentically as possible. Susan graciously met with Marlene Anderson Sannes, her daughter Sara Sannes Franson, her granddaughter Oakley, and me while we were in England to discuss, among other things, the letter collection and her transcription of the letters.

I thank Robert John Mittelstaedt who funded, in part, the transcription costs so that future generations, like himself and his daughter Madeline, will be able to read and understand the lives of their ancestors. His legacy will resonate for generations to come.

I thank Miranda Gudenian, editor of *Yarcombe Voices*, a village magazine, and Steve Horner, a local historian, for kindly helping us locate local historical sources for Yarcombe and neighboring villages. They have worked tirelessly over the years to preserve the memory of Yarcombe history, especially the Drake estate. This collection of letters builds on their work. Today, the Yarcombe Home Page website welcomes others to join its continuing research.

I thank churchwarden Geoffrey Berry for coordinating the restoration of the Stickland tombstone in St. John the Baptism Churchyard in Yarcombe. His assistance unlocked generations of Stickland family history in Yarcombe. Sarah-Jane at The Belfrey at Yarcombe, a boutique hotel, surpassed our expectations for hospitality and local information. We thank you for making our time in Yarcombe feel like a visit home! I extend special thanks to Alex from Unique Devon Tours, who made local connections, drove us safely through the hedgerows, and guided us through our ancestral villages. I thank the Parris and Meyrick families, current occupants of Birch Oak Farm and Higher Pithayne Farm, respectively, for taking time to visit with Pipe family descendants.

Several Pipe descendants read earlier versions of this book and offered valuable feedback. They include Judy Mittelstaedt Anderson, Ida Mae Rosin Frizzell, Marlene Anderson Sannes, and Robert John Mittelstaedt. Their first-hand knowledge of family matters was essential to understanding key ideas in the letters.

Pipe descendants Marlene Anderson Sannes and Judy Mittelstaedt Anderson funded various aspects of the project, especially the portrait restoration and tombstone restoration in Yarcombe. I thank Bill Casper, owner of The Hang Up Gallery of Fine Art in Neenah, Wisconsin, and Charles Dunning, a freelance photographer at Landmark Vistas in Neenah, for restoring the Pipe family portraits. As a result of their expert work, portraits are included in this book. Their work enables readers to see some of the people who wrote letters so many years ago.

I want to thank Mary Diehl and Joan Kuss, newly found descendants of Mary Ann Pipe Sinclair, who shared family pictures, Bible pages, and two letters written by Mary Ann and her brother, Edwin Pipe, in the later 1830s in England. Their mother, Charlette Jennings Pipe Pillar, kept the items as remembrances of her children.

I thank Susan Chapman for helping me scan the letter collection and for her meticulous work on the database that created the indexes for letter writers and recipients along with their locations. Any errors are mine. I am grateful to Susan for the many hours of encouraging and inspiring conversation.

I am indebted to Mike Dauplaise, president of M&B Global Solutions, for his expertise in publishing and book design. He makes his work seem easy and simple. I know it is anything but that! Thank you, Mike, for your valuable suggestions. Jeff Ash has worked tirelessly editing this manuscript. In addition, his research into my research has added a depth of understanding I would not have without his help.

I give a special thanks to Joshua Ranger, university archivist at the University of Wisconsin-Oshkosh, for his assistance in researching the town of Vinland, Winnebago County, Wisconsin. The Wisconsin Historical Society and its local affiliates. The Winneconne Historical Society and the Waupaca Historical Society, especially Waupaca Railroad Depot manager Mike Kirk, provided a foundation of original documents and family stories that others can build on as more records become available online.

I am also indebted to the town of Vinland chair, board and clerk for allowing me to research town records, especially Brooks Cemetery, where at least seven Pipe ancestors are buried, including Charlotte Jennings Pipe Pillar. Special thanks to Julie Maxwell who has helped organize and scan town records.

Because of the efforts of the people mentioned and others too numerous to mention, descendants and others interested in local history in both England and Wisconsin will get to know on a personal level many of the people who came before them.

The post office in Chard, Somerset County, England, in the later 1800s

Introduction

When did you last receive a handwritten letter? Were you quick to open it? Or did you feel apprehensive and anxious about the information contained inside?

Letter writers in the 1800s found a gentle way to communicate painful news like the loss of a loved one. A black border on the edges of an envelope announced a death. The thicker the black border, the longer the mourning period. Not only did black edging pay respect to the deceased loved one, but it also gave the recipient a forewarning. The letters in this collection include several black-edged envelopes.

Letters are personal. They reveal a writer's private thoughts, feelings, and doubts about themselves and others. Future decisions and plans can be openly discussed in the privacy of a letter to a family member or dear friend. Letters can also be transactional, relating economic, social, and political events of the day. Letters are written records that define the times. Letters also define the people who write them.

This two-volume work includes 105 original letters, many with envelopes, written between 1851 and 1914 and a transcription of each. The Pipe family, including John Valentine's brother, Thomas Pipe, and their relatives and friends wrote these letters. Taken together, the collection grants the reader a much larger view of life at this time in both England and America.

John Valentine and Elizabeth Stickland Pipe were born in southwestern England. They immigrated to America with their two children in 1850. First, they settled in New York. Then, Elizabeth and her four children headed west to Wisconsin. All the while, she and her family wrote to each other, keeping themselves informed of home events and their fast-changing lives on both sides of the Atlantic. The Pipe family letter collection is personal. The letters reveal inner thoughts and family relationships in England and America.

Return Addresses

Like GPS today, return addresses on envelopes and inside addresses on letters document locations of senders and recipients. Pipe family and friends in England wrote letters from primarily three western counties: today's East Devon, Somerset, and Dorset. For the most part, villages and family farms mentioned in the letters are scattered along the borders of these counties.

Locations in England

Elizabeth Stickland Pipe inherited properties from her Uncle John Stickland of Yarcombe, Devon, three years after the family immigrated to America. The properties identified in Uncle John Stickland's will include:

Much Hill Farm in the parish of Yarcombe aforesaid occupied by Joel King, **Combes's Pithayne** and **the allotment in Mannings Common in Yarcombe** aforesaid now in my own occupation **Whithorns otherwise Bardscombe** situate at Membury aforesaid and now in my own occupation and also **Peacross** in Membury aforesaid occupied by John Dening. (See Appendix D.)

The English counties of Devon, Somerset, and Dorset are shown in purple, yellow, and magenta, respectively, on the southwest portion of this Phillimore map. The villages and farms mentioned in the letters are mainly located here.

This is the trunk that Thomas and Elizabeth Stickland Pipe took to England in 1875. Their English family (mainly the Jennings) saved letters from the Pipes and returned the letters to the Pipes when they visited. That is the reason we have the letters today. Thomas and Elizabeth also brought back letters from friends and family who wrote to them while they were in England. The trunk transported many of the letters in the collection back to America in 1875. Today it resides in a descendant's home in Amherst, Wisconsin.

Because the Pipes were living in America, Elizabeth's husband, John Valentine Pipe, arranged for his uncle, William Jennings, who lived in Somerset County, to manage the inherited properties on behalf of Elizabeth. Business details regarding farms are frequent topics in the letters.

Birch Oak Farm is another place frequently mentioned in the letters. Both William Jennings and his sister Charlotte Jennings Pipe Pillar,

John Valentine Pipe's mother, grew up with their siblings on Birch Oak Farm. William and Charlotte's parents, John and Mary Bond Jennings, first took residence there in 1805. Birch Oak Farm was home of the Jennings family until their brother John Jennings died in 1872. Birch Oak Farm was originally located in Membury Parish, Devon. In 1884, Birch Oak Farm became part of Yarcombe Parish.

Letters reveal that William Jennings, from Birch Oak Farm, and his wife, Elizabeth Coleman Jennings, moved during their married lives. The couple first lived at Northay Farm, Whitestaunton Parish, Somerset County. Letter Number 63, dated July 9, 1870, announced the Jennings move to Forton Village, Chard, Somerset County, on "Lady Day (March 25) last." Letter Number 65, dated August 15, 1872, was written by the couple while living in Hursey Village, Burstock, Beaminster, Dorsetshire. The Jennings remained on Hursey Farm for the rest of their married lives.

Locations in America

The letter collection also documents the lives of the Pipes in America. John Valentine and Elizabeth Stickland Pipe first settled as farmers in Greece Center, Monroe County, New York, near Rochester. Thomas Pipe, brother of John Valentine, first settled in Monroe County as a farm laborer. After a short time, Thomas ventured west to the town of Vinland, Winnebago County, Wisconsin. His mother, Charlotte Jennings Pipe Pillar, also immigrated with her second husband and family to Vinland.

In 1854, John Valentine Pipe died at sea. Thomas Pipe and his mother traveled east to New York. They brought back to Vinland widowed Elizabeth Stickland Pipe and her four children. In 1855, she and Thomas married.

On a 40-acre farm in Vinland, Thomas and Elizabeth Stickland Pipe started their family. After a few years, however, they moved to the town of Farmington, Waupaca County, Wisconsin, near what is known today as the Waupaca Chain O' Lakes.

Thomas Pipe also purchased property in the Village of Waupaca, Wisconsin, and was active in business affairs. In 1875, the Pipes traveled back to England to visit family and friends and to take care of family business involving Elizabeth's properties. Letters from their Wisconsin family and friends are addressed to them in England during their seven-month visit. These letters are packed with local news.

Thomas and Elizabeth Stickland Pipe made one more move. They purchased a farm in the town of Lanark, Portage County, Wisconsin, which is known today as The Pipe House. Three more generations of Pipes would live in The Pipe House.

Overview of Chapters - Volume 1

Chapter 1 introduces Elizabeth Stickland Pipe, her first husband, John Valentine Pipe, and her second husband, Thomas Pipe, who is John Valentine's brother. All are from southwestern England. This chapter provides family background, as well as the actions that change the course of their lives. The letter collection begins in 1851, shortly after Thomas Pipe and John Valentine Pipe with his wife, Elizabeth Stickland Pipe, and two children, John Stickland and Tom, immigrate to America.

Chapter 2 includes letters dated 1851 to 1854 while the Pipe family lived in Greece Center, Monroe County, New York, near Rochester. Six letters are between the Pipes and John Valentine's aunt and uncle, William and Elizabeth Coleman Jennings. Six letters are from solicitors and agents who discuss Elizabeth Stickland Pipe's legacy from her deceased Uncle John Stickland of Yarcombe, Devon. One letter is from Robert Spiller, trustee of John Stickland's Will proved 30th July 1850. (See Appendix D.)

William Jennings receives letters from both nephews, William Jennings Pipe and Thomas Pipe. Thomas Pipe writes to John Valentine Pipe with news of an available farm in town of Vinland, Winnebago County, Wisconsin. One letter is from Elizabeth Stickland Pipe's mother in England. One is from John Valentine Pipe's mother in the town of Vinland, Winnebago County, Wisconsin. A letter from Liverpool, Lancashire County, answers an inquiry about John Valentine Pipe's whereabouts.

Chapter 3 includes letters dated 1855 to 1857 while widow Elizabeth Stickland Pipe and her four children with John Valentine Pipe are living with her brother-in-law, Thomas Pipe, in the town of Vinland, Winnebago County, Wisconsin. Elizabeth Stickland Pipe marries Thomas Pipe in 1855 in Vinland. One letter is a descendant's note on an envelope found in the original letter collection box. Six letters are between Thomas and Elizabeth Stickland Pipe and Uncle William and Aunt Elizabeth Coleman Jennings of Somerset, England. One letter is from Thomas Pipe to his Uncle John Jennings of Birch Oak Farm, Membury, Devon.

Chapter 4 includes letters dated 1858 to April 1860 while Thomas and Elizabeth Stickland Pipe and their eight children (including four from her previous marriage) are living at what would later become known as Calkins' Place in the town of Farmington, Waupaca County, Wisconsin. Eventually, Thomas Pipe's farmland extends to the shores of Sunset, Rainbow, Otter, Nessling, McCrossen, and Round lakes on today's Chain O' Lakes in Farmington. The Pipes and the Jennings exchange nine letters.

Chapter 5 includes letters dated 1860 to 1863 while Thomas and Elizabeth Stickland Pipe are living in the Village of Waupaca. The Pipes and the Jennings exchange nine letters. Included is an annuity receipt from John Stickland. Charlotte Jennings Pipe Pillar writes one letter to her brother William Jennings. Two letters are to William Jennings Pipe. Elizabeth Stickland Pipe writes to her brother-in-law William Jennings Pipe with a special request. Charlotte Jennings Pipe Pillar writes one letter to her brother and sister-in-law, William and Elizabeth Coleman Jennings. She announces the death of her daughter, Mary Ann Pipe Sinclair, in March 1860.

Original letters and surviving envelopes are included after each transcription for the reader's ease of comparing transcripts to originals. The Key Ideas include local news, especially in Yarcombe Parish, Devon, England, and in Winnebago, Waupaca, and Portage counties, Wisconsin. Marriages, births, and deaths are noted on both sides of the Atlantic and in Victoria, Australia, where Thomas Pipe's brother, William Jennings Pipe, immigrated.

An Invitation

The 105 letters in this two-volume collection tell the story of a family over 60 years and four generations. We hear from writers in their own words. Their voices at times express joy, astonishment, pain, gratitude, and wonder.

I invite you to take a seat at the dinner table. Listen to Thomas Pipe explain to his Uncle William how farming in Wisconsin differs from farming in England.

Join Elizabeth Stickland Pipe in the parlor and listen to her excitement as she vividly describes the farm that has taken her heart in the town of Lanark, Portage County.

Sit on the front porch with Grandma Pillar and enjoy the impatience of the Pipe children as they wonder when their parents will return from their trip to England.

I invite you to listen to these people. Their voices bring to life their individual personalities while they offer details of their everyday lives on both sides of the Atlantic!

Biographies

Family histories such as this work benefit from the ability to include photographs that help us match faces with names. The following pages provide a more detailed look into the backgrounds of many of the people featured in the Pipe family's letters, complete with photos to help you visualize these fascinating individuals as you read their stories.

There are several instances in which people have similar names, making it potentially challenging to keep everyone straight. You may find it useful to refer to this section on occasion as you proceed through the two volumes of this series.

Elizabeth Stickland Pipe

BIRTH
Elizabeth **STICKLAND PIPE** was christened in Yarcombe, Devon, England, on August 12, 1828. The record summary sheet notes her parents as Thomas and Elizabeth **STICKLAND**.

IMMIGRATION
Elizabeth left Liverpool, England, and arrived in New York on May 18, 1850, with her husband John Valentine **PIPE**, their two children, and her brother-in-law, Thomas **PIPE**.

MARRIAGE
On May 18, 1848, Elizabeth **STICKLAND** married John Valentine **PIPE**. John Valentine was lost at sea in March 1854. After her husband's death, Elizabeth **STICKLAND PIPE** married her brother-in-law, Thomas **PIPE**, on June 24, 1855. The date is found in Letter Number 25 written by Thomas **PIPE**. A descendant left a note in the box of letters with the incorrect date of May 4, 1855. Transcribed below is the note found in the box.

DEATH and BURIAL
Elizabeth died in 1918 at the age of 91. She is buried in Lakeside Memorial Park, Waupaca, Wisconsin, with her second husband Thomas.

NOTES
Christening Record:
Elizabeth's christening record is at Findmypast.com.

Marriage Record:
Transcription: Elizabeth keeping house for brother-in-law. Married him (in the Town of Vinland) 1855 May 4.

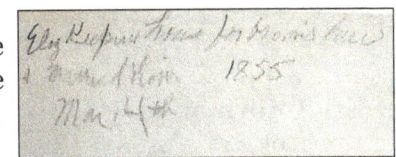

In Letter Number 25, Thomas **PIPE** states that he and Elizabeth were married on June 24, 1855.

John Valentine Pipe

BIRTH

John Valentine **PIPE** was born on February 14, 1825, likely in Donyatt in the county of Somerset, England. Donyatt is in the southwest area of England. John's parents are listed on the baptism record as John and Charlotte **PIPE**. John Valentine was baptized on March 20, 1825, as a member of an independent denomination. Below is the actual baptismal record.

MARRIAGE

John married Elizabeth **STICKLAND** on May 18, 1848, in Yarcombe, Devon, England.

IMMIGRATION

John Valentine sailed from Liverpool, England, and arrived in New York on May 18, 1850.

DEATH

In 1854, John Valentine returned to England on family business. On his return from England to his home in Greece Center, Monroe County, New York, **PIPE** sailed on the ill-fated steamship *City of Glasgow*. John **PIPE**, a cabin passenger, was one of 480 souls lost at sea in the Atlantic Ocean in March 1854.

NOTES
Baptismal Record:

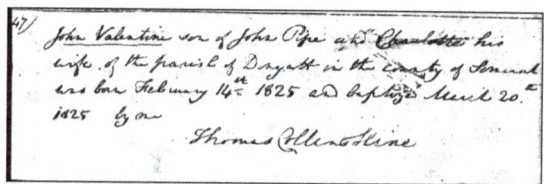

Death Information:

In the book *Let Glasgow Flourish: The Disappearance of the SS City of Glasgow* by Thomas G. Clark, John Valentine **PIPE** is listed as a cabin passenger on page 254.

John (Jack) Stickland Pipe, Elizabeth Johnson Pipe, and Edwin William Pipe

BIRTH
John (Jack) Stickland **PIPE** was born on March 1, 1848, according to his *U.S. Naturalization* application. According to his obituary, John was born in Somerset County, England. He was baptized in Membury, Devon, England, on March 26, 1848. His parents are John Valentine and Elizabeth **STICKLAND PIPE**.

Edwin Pipe stands behind his parents, Elizabeth and John (Jack) Pipe.

Elizabeth **JOHNSON PIPE** was born in October 1860 in Iola, Waupaca County, Wisconsin.

Edwin William **PIPE**, the only child of John (Jack) Stickland and Elizabeth **JOHNSON PIPE**, was born on November 12, 1882, likely in Stevens Point, Wisconsin.

MARRIAGE
John (Jack) Stickland **PIPE** married Elizabeth **JOHNSON** on April 19, 1882, in Stevens Point, Portage County, Wisconsin.

DEATH and BURIAL
John (Jack) Stickland **PIPE** died at age 65 on March 23, 1913, in Stevens Point, Portage County, Wisconsin. Elizabeth **JOHNSON PIPE** died at age 71 on March 11, 1932, in Stevens Point, Portage County, Wisconsin. Edwin William **PIPE** died at age 69 on May 20, 1951, in Stevens Point, Portage County, Wisconsin. John (Jack) Stickland **PIPE**, Elizabeth **JOHNSON PIPE**, and Edwin William **PIPE** are buried in Forest Cemetery, Stevens Point, Portage County, Wisconsin.

NATURALIZATION
John (Jack) Stickland **PIPE** applied to be a naturalized U.S. citizen, but he had died by the time his application was considered on December 1, 1913, in the Portage County Circuit Court in Stevens Point, Wisconsin.

Tom and Amelia Woodnorth Pipe

BIRTH
Tom **PIPE** was baptized on September 2, 1849, in Yarcombe, Devon, England. His parents are John Valentine and Elizabeth **STICKLAND PIPE**.

Amelia **WOODNORTH** was born, according to the *1900 U.S. Census*, in June 1852 in New York, New York. Her parents are Paul and Sarah **WOODNORTH**.

MARRIAGE
Tom **PIPE** married Amelia **WOODNORTH** on July 29, 1875, in Waupaca, Waupaca County, Wisconsin.

Tom and Amelia announced their marriage to Thomas and Elizabeth **STICKLAND PIPE** in Letter Number 88 of the Pipe family letter collection. Thomas and Elizabeth Stickland **PIPE** received the letter while they were in England visiting family and settling family business.

Tom and Amelia Pipe dressed for a costume party (above) and a young Tom Pipe (below).

DEATH and BURIAL
Tom **PIPE** died at age 82 on September 17, 1931, in Madison, Dane County, Wisconsin.

Amelia **WOODNORTH PIPE** died at age 61 on November 23, 1913, in Chippewa Falls, Chippewa County, Wisconsin.

Tom and Amelia **WOODNORTH PIPE** are buried in Lakeside Memorial Park, Waupaca, Waupaca County, Wisconsin.

Frank Pipe

BIRTH

Frank **PIPE** was born in Monroe County, New York, according to his marriage record. His tombstone gives his birth date as February 28, 1852. His parents are John Valentine **PIPE** and Elizabeth **STICKLAND PIPE**.

MARRIAGE

Frank **PIPE** married Ida May **GOFF** on October 18, 1876, in Stevens Point, Portage County, Wisconsin.

DEATH and BURIAL

Frank died at age 48 on September 4, 1900, at his brother William Edwin **PIPE**'s home, The Pipe House, in Lanark, Portage County, Wisconsin. He is buried in Lakeside Memorial Park, Waupaca, Waupaca County, Wisconsin.

Marriage Record

Transcribed

1. Date of registration: Oct. 18th 1876
2. The color: White
3. Full name of husband: Frank Pipe
4. Full name of wife previous to marriage: Ida M. Goff
5. Occupation of husband: Livery business
6. Residence of husband: Stevens Point
7. Birthplace of husband: Monroe Co., N.Y.
8. The place, town or township, and county, where the marriage was contracted: Stevens Point, Portage Co., Wis.
9. Time when the marriage was contracted: Oct. 18th 1876
10. By what ceremony contracted: Presbyterian

Mary Elizabeth Pipe

BIRTH

Mary Elizabeth **PIPE** was born in Monroe County, New York, at the beginning of March 1854, according to Letter Number 14, dated May 21, 1854. Her parents are John Valentine **PIPE** and Elizabeth **STICKLAND PIPE**. According to Williiam **JENNINGS** in Letter Number 17, dated June 14, 1854, John Valentine **PIPE** was eager to leave England and get back to his wife and children in America. Likely, in part, he wanted to be home for the birth of Mary Elizabeth **PIPE**.

Her husband, Frank Skidmore **WOODNORTH**, was born March 21, 1848, in New York. His parents are Paul Skidmore and Sarah **WOODNORTH**. Frank served as a private in Company 1, 17th Wisconsin Infantry, Union Army, Civil War. According to *Salvarsan*, he enlisted from Iola, Wisconsin, on

Mary Elizabeth Pipe with her husband, Frank Woodnorth

December 9, 1864, and mustered out on July 14, 1865.

MARRIAGE

Mary Elizabeth **PIPE** married Frank **WOODNORTH** on September 6, 1883. Letter Number 96, sent by Mary from Milwaukee, Wisconsin, to her mother, explains the reasons for their private church wedding. The letter is torn into several pieces.

DEATH and BURIAL

Mary Elizabeth died at age 77 on June 18, 1931, in Milwaukee County, Wisconsin. Frank **WOODNORTH** died at age 63 on March 3, 1911, in King, Waupaca County, Wisconsin. Both Mary Elizabeth and Frank are buried in Lakeside Memorial Park, Waupaca, Waupaca County, Wisconsin.

Thomas Pipe

BIRTH

Thomas **PIPE** was born on September 24, 1826, to John and Charlotte **JENNINGS PIPE** from Donyatt, Somerset, England. According to *Non-Conformist and Non-Parochial Registers, 1567-1936*, Thomas was baptized on November 3, 1826. (See record below.)

IMMIGRATION

Thomas left Liverpool, England, and arrived in New York on May 18, 1850.

MARRIAGE

Thomas married Elizabeth **STICKLAND PIPE** on June 24, 1855. The date is found in Letter Number 25 written by Thomas **PIPE**. A descendant left a note in the box of letters with the incorrect date of May 4, 1855. Transcribed below is the note found in the box.

DEATH and BURIAL

Thomas died on September 22, 1880, just two days before his 54th birthday. He is buried in Lakeside Memorial Park, Waupaca, Wisconsin.

NOTES
Christening Record:

> 54
>
> 9
>
> *Thomas, son of John Pipe and Charlotte his wife, of the parish of Donyatt in the county of Somerset, was born September 24th 1826, and baptized November 3: 1826. By me*
>
> *Thomas Collins Stone —*

Marriage Record:

Transcription: Elizabeth keeping house for brother-in-law Married him [in the Town of Vinland] 1855 May 4th. In Letter Number 25, Thomas **PIPE** states that he and Elizabeth were married on June 24, 1855.

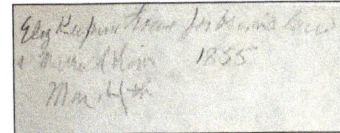

William Edwin Pipe

BIRTH
William Edwin **PIPE** was born on March 25, 1856, in Town of Vinland, Winnebago County, Wisconsin. His parents are Thomas **PIPE** and Elizabeth **STICKLAND PIPE**.

MARRIAGE
PIPE married Mary Agnes **MESSER** on November 29, 1883, in Oxford Junction, Jones County, Iowa. Their children include Mae E. **PIPE ANDERSON** (1884-1967), Mina M. **PIPE** (1886-1896), Raymond **PIPE** (1889-1977), Effie **PIPE** (1891-1896).

DEATH and BURIAL
William Edwin **PIPE** died on April 22, 1936, in Lanark, Portage County, Wisconsin. He is buried in Sheridan Cemetery, Farmington, Waupaca County, Wisconsin.

NOTES
William exchanges Letters Number 95, 97, and 98 with Thomas **MESSER**. Letter Number 104 is a tribute written to William Edwin **PIPE**.

William Pipe with his wife, Mary Agnes Messer Pipe, whose hand is on his shoulder. Seated is Margaret Messer Jeffers. Standing is Florence Pipe McCunn, mother of Florence and Ethel McCunn.

Mary Agnes Messer

BIRTH
Mary Agnes **MESSER** was born on October 19, 1865, in Fond du Lac, Wisconsin. Her parents are Thomas **MESSER** and Sarah **HUTCHINSON**. Thomas married Mary Kirkwood **NIVEN** after Sarah **HUTCHINSON**'s death in 1871.

MARRIAGE
MESSER married William Edwin **PIPE** on November 29, 1883, in Oxford Junction, Jones County, Iowa. Their children include Mae Elizabeth **PIPE ANDERSON** (1884-1967), Mina Margaret **PIPE** (1886-1896), Raymond **PIPE** (1889-1977), Effie **PIPE** (1891-1896).

DEATH and BURIAL
Mary Agnes **MESSER PIPE** died on May 13, 1938, in Lanark, Portage County, Wisconsin. She is buried in Sheridan Cemetery, Farmington, Waupaca County, Wisconsin.

Mary Messer and William Pipe wedding portrait

Mary and William Pipe's 50th anniversary portrait

Thomas Messer

BIRTH

Thomas **MESSER** is found in *Scotland Births and Baptisms, 1664-1950*. According to this record source, Thomas was born on May 4, 1831, in Legerwood, Berwickshire, Scotland, United Kingdom. On the record summary page, Thomas' parents are listed as William **MESSER** and Mary **HENDERSON**. Their residence is noted as Legerwood, Berwick, Scotland. The record summary page also shows that Thomas was christened on May 22, 1831.

NATURALIZATION

Thomas **MESSER** appears in the *Wisconsin, U.S. Naturalization Index, 1840-1970*. On November 6, 1860, in the Circuit Court, Thomas declared his intent to become a U.S. citizen in Fond du Lac, Wisconsin.

MARRIAGE

In the *Illinois, U.S., County Marriage Records, 1800-1940*, the marriage of Thomas **MESSER** and Sarah Jane **HUTCHINSON** is recorded. They married on January 12, 1865, in Marion County, Illinois. After the death of Sarah Jane **HUTCHINSON** in 1871, Thomas **MESSER** married Mary **NIVEN** on November 29, 1872, in Cook County, Illinois.

DEATH and BURIAL

Thomas died June 16, 1889, in Amherst, Portage County, Wisconsin, at the age of 58. He is buried in Sheridan Cemetery, Waupaca County, Wisconsin.

NOTES

Christening Record: The christening, along with date of birth, summary sheet is available on Findmypast.com. The record can also be obtained through The Borders Family History Society at https://bordersfhs.org.uk/legerwood.asp. Thomas **MESSNER**'s monument on FindaGrave.com states his date of birth as May 4, 1833. Since the birth record noted above states his birth year as 1831, the tombstone date is likely incorrect.

Naturalization Record: Thomas **MESSER**'s actual declaration papers are held in the University of Wisconsin-Oshkosh Archives in Oshkosh.

Sarah Jane Hutchinson

BIRTH
Sara Jane **HUTCHINSON** is found in *West Yorkshire, England, Church of England Births and Baptisms, 1813-1910*. According to this record source, Sarah Jane was born in Leeds, St. Peter, Yorkshire, England, on August 27, 1840. Her parents are noted as William and Mary **HUTCHINSON**. Sarah Jane was baptized on September 27, 1840, in Leeds, St. Peter, Yorkshire, England.

MARRIAGE
In the *Illinois, U.S., County Marriage Records, 1800-1940*, the marriage of Thomas **MESSER** and Sarah Jane **HUTCHINSON** is recorded. They married on January 12, 1865, in Marion County, Illinois.

U.S. CENSUS RECORDS
In the *1860 U.S. Census Records*, Sarah Jane aged 19 is found living in Township 1 S Range 2 E, Jefferson County, Illinois. She is listed as being born in England about 1841. Her inferred parents on the census record are William, aged 47, and Mary, aged 43, **HUTCHINSON**. Others listed on the census record include Elizabeth **HUTCHINSON,** aged 14, and Hannah **HUTCHINSON,** aged 6. In addition, the **FRANKLIN** family is listed: James **FRANKLIN,** aged 26; Angeline **FRANKLIN,** aged 18; and Josephin **FRANKLIN,** aged 1.

In the 1870 U.S. Census Records, Sarah Jane **HUTCHINSON MESSER**, aged 30, is living with her husband Thomas **MESSER**, aged 36, in the city of Fond du Lac, Wisconsin, Ward 4. They have two children: Mary, aged 4, and Margaret, aged 2. Sarah Jane's occupation is listed as keeping house. Thomas is listed as a blacksmith.

DEATH and BURIAL
Sarah Jane **HUTCHINSON MESSER** died in 1871. According to the *U.S. Find a Grave Index, 1600s to Current*, Sarah Jane **HUTCHINSON MESSER** is buried in Plot 340 in the Rienzi Cemetery in Fond du Lac, Fond du Lac County, Wisconsin.

Mary Kirkwood Niven

BIRTH
Mary **NIVEN** was born in Paisley, Scotland, on August 10, 1831.

IMMIGRATION
The *1910 U.S. Census* notes that **NIVEN** immigrated in 1871. The *1920 U.S. Census* lists **NIVEN**'s immigration date as 1870. In the *1920 U.S. Federal Census*, Mary **NIVEN MESSER** is listed as a naturalized citizen.

MARRIAGE
Mary **NIVEN** married Thomas **MESSER** on November 29, 1872, in Cook County, Illinois.

U.S. Census
In the *1905 Wisconsin, U.S. State Census, 1855-1905*, Mary **NIVEN MESSER**, aged 71, is found living in Lanark, Portage County, Wisconsin, with her brother William, aged 47, and Mary, aged 43. In the *1910 U.S. Census*, **NIVEN MESSER**, aged 78, is again found living with her brother William, aged 72. The census notes that she can read and write. In the *1920 U.S. Census*, **NIVEN MESSER** is living in Amherst, Portage, Wisconsin, with the George **JEFFERS** family. Mary is listed as 88 years old. Her relationship to George **JEFFERS** is noted as stepmother-in-law. Mary is listed as stepmother to George's wife, Margaret **JEFFERS**.

Mary Niven's husband, Thomas Messer, as a young man.

DEATH and BURIAL
Mary Kirkwood **NIVEN MESSER** died on January 30, 1926, in Portage County according to *Wisconsin, U.S. Death Records, 1872*. She is buried in Sheridan Cemetery in Farmington, Waupaca County, Wisconsin, alongside her husband, Thomas **MESSER**.

The Children of William Edwin and Mary Agnes Messer Pipe

When Mina was born in 1886, Mae Elizabeth stayed with her grandparents, Thomas and Mary **NIVEN MESSER** in Oxford, Junction City, Iowa. Thomas **MESSER** writes Letters Number 97, 98, and 99 to William Edwin **PIPE** and his two daughters, Mary Agnes **MESSER PIPE** and Margaret **MESSER JEFFERS**, describing Mae Elizabeth, who is nicknamed "Toots."

Mae Elizabeth PIPE (1884-1967) and her sister, Mina Mary PIPE (1886-1896)

Above on the left is Raymond PIPE (1889-1977) at about 11 years old. On the right is his cousin, Harry PIPE (1886-1908), whose parents are Tom and Amelia WOODNORTH PIPE. The little girl on the right is Effie PIPE (1891-1896) at age 8½ months. Effie died of diphtheria, as did her sister, Mina (in the top photo). Both are buried in Lakeside Memorial Park, Waupaca, Waupaca County, Wisconsin.

This 1950s-era aerial view of the Pipe farm also shows Pipe School, the small, white building on the far left, where William Pipe's children attended.

Raymond writes a letter to his cousin Harry in June 1897 while attending Pipe School:

Sheridan, Wis
June 2th, 1897

Dear Harry

How are you getting along. Don't you remember when you swung on the barn and kicked the basket outdoors. I have got on that coat your mamma sent up by Papa and Mae. You come up some day and we will go fishing down to your house when Papa goes after her. I am going to your house. We have got 57 little chickens and not one

[page 2]
dead. And 3 little calves, their names Spot, Cherry and Strawberry. Don't you think they are pretty ones. Papa and Mae got home just before the rain storm that night. Mae was sorry that she was not home that day you rode up with Mr Burleson. Mamma is making me a new [?] waistor. I mean to, [?] there is only fifteen today with the teacher. Mamma is better, she went up to Granda Messers yesterday to see her. Didn't we have an awful rain, I must stop printing for this time. Write me a letter. From RP [Raymond Pipe]

———————

Harry **PIPE** died in 1908 with tuberculosis. He is buried at Lakeside Memorial Park, Waupaca, Waupaca County, Wisconsin.

Raymond's letter to Harry, Page 1

write from Raymond.

SHERIDAN WIS
JUNE 2TH 1898.

DEAR HARRY.

HOW = ARE = YOU = GETTING = A = LONG =
DONT = YOU = REMEMBER = WHEN =
YOU = SWONG = IN = THE = BARN =
AND = KICKED = THE = BASKET, OUT =
DOORS. I = HAVE = GOT = ON =
THAT = COAT = YOUR = MAMMA =
SENT = UP = BY = PAPA = AND =
MAE, = YOU = COME = UP = SOME =
DAY = AND = WE = WILL = GO = A =
FISHING = MAMMA = IS =
GOING = DOWN = TO = YOU =
HOUSE = WHEN = PAPA =
GOES = AFTER = HER = I =
AM = GOING = TO. = YOUR = HOUSE
WE = HAVE = GOT = 57 = LITTLE
CHICKENS = AND = NOT = ONE =

Raymond's letter to Harry, Page 2

DEAD = AND- 3=LITTLE=CALVES=
THERE = NAMES = IS = SPOT = CHERRY
= STRAWBERRY = DONT = YOU =
THINK = THEY = ARE = PRETTY = H
O NES, = PAPA = AND = MAE = GOT =
H HOME = JEST = BE=FOR = THE =
RAIN = STORM, = THAT = KNIGHT =
MAE = WAS = SORRY = THAT =
SHE = WAS = NUT = HOME = THAT =
DAY = YOU = RODE = UP = WITH =
MR = BURLESON = MAMMA = IS =
MAKING = ME = A = KNEW = WATSR =
OR = I = MEEN = TO = THERE = IS =
ONLY = FIFTEEN = TO = DAY =
WITH = THE = TEACHER =
MAMMA = IS = BETTER = SHE =
WENT = UP = TO = GRANDA =
MESSES = YESTERDAY = TO =
SEE = HER. = DIDENT
DIDENT = WE = HAVE = A =
AWFUL = RAIN = I = MUST
STOP = PRINTING = FOR =
THIS = TIME = WRITE =
ME = A LONG = LETTER = RUM
RA

The Florence Ida Pipe and John Niven McCunn Daughters

PARENTS' BIRTH
Florence Ida **PIPE** was born on January 5, 1860, in Farmington, Waupaca County, Wisconsin. Her parents are Thomas and Elizabeth **STICKLAND PIPE**.

John Niven **McCUNN** was born on December 10, 1858, in Glasgow, Lanark, Scotland. He traveled to America via Canada with his widowed mother in 1870. They made their home in Portage County, Wisconsin, where his older brother James **McCUNN** had settled.

MARRIAGE
Florence **PIPE** married John Niven **McCUNN** on October 25, 1884, in Waupaca County, Wisconsin.

Ethel and Florence in Dunfermline, Scotland, circa 1900.

CHILDREN

• Ethel May **McCUNN** born May 5, 1885 (Sheridan, Waupaca County, Wisconsin), died April 30, 1996, age 110 (Connecticut)

• Florence Vera **McCUNN** born March 14, 1887 (Green Bay, Brown County, Wisconsin), died February 15, 1979, age 91 (Boston, Suffolk County, Massachusetts)

• Walter Thomas **McCUNN** born November 4, 1888 (Green Bay, Brown County, Wisconsin), died March 3, 1963, age 74 (Boston, Suffolk County, Massachusetts)

Florence and Ethel **McCUNN** wrote Letters Number 100 and 102 to their grandmother, Elizabeth **STICKLAND PIPE**.

Ethel May, 1915 in
U.S., Consular Certificates 1908-1918

PARENT'S DEATH and BURIAL

Florence **PIPE McCUNN** died at age 29 on January 10, 1889, in Green Bay, Brown County, Wisconsin. She is buried in Woodlawn Cemetery, Allouez, Brown County, Wisconsin. John Niven **McCUNN** died at age 78 on January 13, 1937, in Danbury, Connecticut. His burial location is unknown.

NOTE: John Niven **McCUNN** owned and taught at Green Bay Business College from 1887 to 1901. He was elected to the Green Bay Common Council in 1893. McCunn and his family left Green Bay in 1897, when he was appointed as U.S. consul in Dunfermline, Scotland. In 1908, he was appointed to U.S. consul in Glasgow, Scotland, serving there until 1921. McCunn then was U.S. consul in Georgetown, (British) Guyana, and finally in Yarmouth, Nova Scotia, Canada, retiring in 1924. McCunn lived in Ridgefield, Connecticut, after retiring.

Mae Elizabeth Pipe

BIRTH
Mae Elizabeth **PIPE** was born on October 23, 1884, in Lanark, Portage County, Wisconsin. Her parents are William Edwin **PIPE** and Mary Agnes **MESSER**.

MARRIAGE
Mae E. **PIPE** married Oliver L. **ANDERSON** on May 21, 1903, in Farmington, Waupaca County, Wisconsin.

Their children include: William Kenneth **ANDERSON** (1905-1976); Floyd Andrew **ANDERSON** (1906-1951); Genevieve **ANDERSON NEUSEN** (1911-2003); Agnes **ANDERSON ROSIN** (1913-2009); Margaret E. **ANDERSON BIEVER** (1920-2009); Helen **ANDERSON MITTELSTAEDT** (1924-2005).

DEATH and BURIAL
Mae Elizabeth **PIPE ANDERSON** died on May 19, 1967, in Waupaca, Waupaca County, Wisconsin. Her husband died on December 23, 1941, in Lanark, Portage County, Wisconsin. Mae Elizabeth **PIPE ANDERSON** and her husband are buried in Sheridan Cemetery, Farmington, Waupaca, Wisconsin.

NOTES
Source for Mae Elizabeth **PIPE ANDERSON**'s birth and death information and husband's death information: *Oshkosh Northwestern* newspaper, Oshkosh, Wisconsin, Monday, May 22, 1967, Page 22, accessed via newspapers.com digital database. Marriage record is located at Ancestry.com.

Oliver Anderson

BIRTH

Oliver **ANDERSON** was born on June 20, 1878, in Farmington, Waupaca County, Wisconsin. His parents are Andrew **ANDERSON** and Christina **WILSON**.

MARRIAGE

Oliver **ANDERSON** married Mae Elizabeth **PIPE** on May 21, 1903, in Farmington, Waupaca County, Wisconsin. Their children include: William Kenneth **ANDERSON** (1905-1976); Floyd Andrew **ANDERSON** (1906-1951); Genevieve **ANDERSON NEUSEN** (1911-2003); Agnes **ANDERSON ROSIN** (1913-2009); Margaret E. **ANDERSON BIEVER** (1920-2009); Helen **ANDERSON MITTELSTAEDT** (1924-2005).

DEATH and BURIAL

Oliver **ANDERSON** died on December 23, 1941, in Lanark, Portage County, Wisconsin. He is buried in Sheridan Cemetery, Farmington, Waupaca County, Wisconsin.

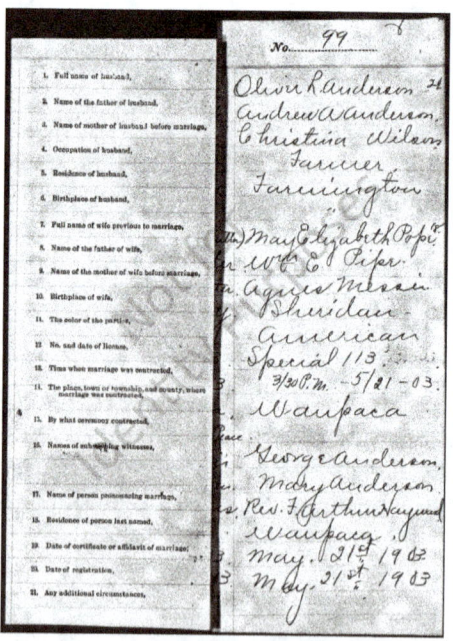

Oliver Anderson and Mae Pipe's marriage record

Raymond Pipe

BIRTH
Raymond **PIPE** was born on May 19, 1889, in Lanark, Portage County, Wisconsin. His parents are William Edwin **PIPE** and Mary Agnes **MESSER PIPE**.

MARRIAGE
Raymond **PIPE** married Florence Estelle **ANDERSON** on December 2, 1916. Raymond and Florence **PIPE**'s children include William Edwin **PIPE** "Bud" (1917-1998), Marjorie **PIPE JOHNSON** (1919-2019), and Carla Jane **PIPE** (1932-1997).

DEATH and BURIAL
Raymond **PIPE** died on November 10, 1977, in Waupaca, Waupaca County, Wisconsin. He is buried in Sheridan Cemetery, Farmington, Waupaca County, Wisconsin.

Raymond Pipe's wife, Florence Anderson Pipe (left), with her cousin, Irma Ester Gibbons Dunham.

Raymond Pipe, Mae Elizabeth Pipe, Margaret Jeffers Timm, and Agnes Jeffers Larson

BIRTH
Agnes **JEFFERS** was born on February 20, 1895, and Margaret **JEFFERS** was born in 1899. Their parents are George Nicholas **JEFFERS** (1866-1955) and Margaret **MESSER** (1868-1944). Mae **PIPE** is noted on this picture as being 16 years old.

MARRIAGE
Agnes married Charles Waldemar **LARSON** on June 25, 1924, in Menominee County, Michigan. Margaret **JEFFERS** married William **TIMM** on March 14, 1924, in Chicago.

DEATH
Agnes **JEFFERS LARSON** died on February 14, 1979, in Waupaca, Waupaca County, Wisconsin. Charles died on December 19, 1957, in Cuba

(Clockwise from top) Raymond Pipe, Mae Elizabeth Pipe, with their cousins Agnes Elizabeth Jeffers Larson, Margaret Mary Jeffers Timm

City, Grant County, Wisconsin. Margaret **JEFFERS TIMM** died on November 28, 1985, in Kent, King County, Washington. Her husband died on March 29, 1988, in Seattle, King County, Washington.

BURIAL
Agnes and her husband are buried in Sheridan Cemetery in Farmington, Waupaca County, Wisconsin. Margaret and her husband are buried in Miller-Woodlawn Memorial Park in Bremerton, Kitsap County, Washington.

NOTES
Source for Margaret **JEFFERS TIMM** death information: *Kitsap Sun* newspaper, Bremerton, Washington, Saturday, November 30, 1985, Page 4, accessed via newspapers.com digital database.

Source for William **TIMM** death information and wedding date to Margaret **JEFFERS**: *Kitsap Sun* newspaper, Bremerton, Washington, April 1, 1988. Page 10, accessed via newspapers.com digital database.

Effie Agnetta Pipe Alexander

BIRTH
Effie Agnetta **PIPE** was born on March 11, 1863, in Waupaca, Waupaca County, Wisconsin. Her parents are Thomas **PIPE** and Elizabeth **STICKLAND PIPE**.

Taylor **ALEXANDER** was born at Buena Vista, Portage County, Wisconsin, on August 23, 1863. His parents are John and Jane McIndoe **ALEXANDER**. John was born in Glasgow, Scotland. Jane McIndoe was born in Kippen, Stirling, Scotland.

MARRIAGE
Effie Agnetta **PIPE** married Taylor **ALEXANDER** at The Pipe House in Lanark, Portage County, Wisconsin, on June 15, 1887.

Effie Pipe Alexander with her niece, Mae (Toots) Elizabeth Pipe, circa 1885

CHILDREN
Effie Agnetta **PIPE ALEXANDER** and Taylor **ALEXANDER** had four children: Florence (1888-1947), McIndoe "Mac" John (1890-1982), Jennings Wellington (1897-1965), and Neil (1903-1910).

DEATH and BURIAL
Effie Agnetta **PIPE ALEXANDER** died at age 44 on January 19, 1908, in Wausau, Marathon County, Wisconsin. Taylor **ALEXANDER** died at age 72 on April 19, 1936, in Wausau, Marathon County, Wisconsin. Both Effie Agnetta and Taylor are buried in Pine Grove Cemetery, Wausau, Marathon County, Wisconsin.

William Jennings

BIRTH

William **JENNINGS** was born in Membury, Devon, England, and baptized on May 31, 1812, in Yarcombe Parish, Devon. His parents are noted as John, a yeoman, and Mary **BOND JENNINGS** from Membury who married on December 11, 1799.

SIBLINGS

William **JENNINGS** had five known siblings: Edwin **JENNINGS**, born in 1800; Charlotte **JENNINGS PIPE PILLAR**, baptized on January 31, 1802; John **JENNINGS**, baptized on November 13, 1803; Thomas **JENNINGS**, born in 1805; and Mary Ann **JENNINGS DOMMETT**, baptized on January 11, 1811. All were baptized in Yarcombe Parish, Devon.

MARRIAGE

William married Elizabeth **COLEMAN** on July 21, 1844, in Whitestaunton, Somerset, England.

CHILDREN

William and Elizabeth gave birth to their daughter Mary Ann, who was baptized on August 24, 1845, in Whitestaunton Parish. The record notes: "Xmas day Admitted into Church."

William and Elizabeth gave birth to their son John, who was baptized on May 19, 1853, at Whitestaunton. On June 15, 1853, the infant died and was buried in Whitestaunton, Somerset. The record shows the family living at Northay Farm.

William and Elizabeth gave birth to their daughter Ellen (Nelly), who was baptized on June 26, 1855, at Whitestaunton.

CENSUS RECORDS

1841 UK Census finds William, aged 25, living with his mother, Mary **BOND JENNINGS,** who is aged 71. William is also living with his brother John, aged 35; his sister Mary Ann, aged 25; Honor **WARD**, aged 25 and daughter of Matthew **WARD**; John **PIPE**, aged 15; Mary **PIPE**, age 11; and William **PIPE**, aged 7.

1851 UK Census finds William and Elizabeth **COLEMAN JENNINGS** living on Northay Farm with their 5-year-old daughter Mary Ann. William is noted as a farmer with 70 acres and eight laborers.

William Jennings's broken tombstone (left) lies in the St. John the Baptist churchyard in Broadwindsor, West Dorset, England.

1861 UK Census finds William and Elizabeth **COLEMAN JENNINGS** living on Northay Farm with their 15-year-old daughter Mary Ann and their 6-year-old daughter Ellen. A nephew and a niece, William and Mary **DOMMETT**, respectively, are living with the family along with a servant. William is noted as a farmer with 200 acres employing seven laborers and two boys. They live next door to Richard **COLEMAN**, Elizabeth **COLEMAN JENNINGS**' father.

1871 UK Census finds William and Elizabeth **COLEMAN JENNINGS** living in the village of Forton in the parish of Chard. William at age 57 is listed as a retired farmer.

1881 UK Census find William and Elizabeth **COLEMAN JENNINGS** living in Hursey Village. They have a servant, Mary **BARTLETT**, who is 15 years old. William is listed as a farmer with 28 acres and one laborer.

<u>DEATH and BURIAL</u>
William died in 1890 at the age of 78. William was buried on April 30, 1890, in St. John the Baptist Churchyard in Broadwindsor, West Dorset. He is buried with his wife, Elizabeth **COLEMAN**; his daughter, Mary Ann; and her husband, William Clement **DAVY**. His daughter, Ellen (Nelly), is buried in Union Cemetery in Calgary, Alberta, Canada. His infant son, John, is buried in St. Andrew Churchyard in Whitestaunton, Somerset.

Record citations and links to actual records for the individuals in this section are held in a database at https://www.germanbohemianwisconsin.com/.

The John Valentine and Elizabeth Stickland Pipe Family

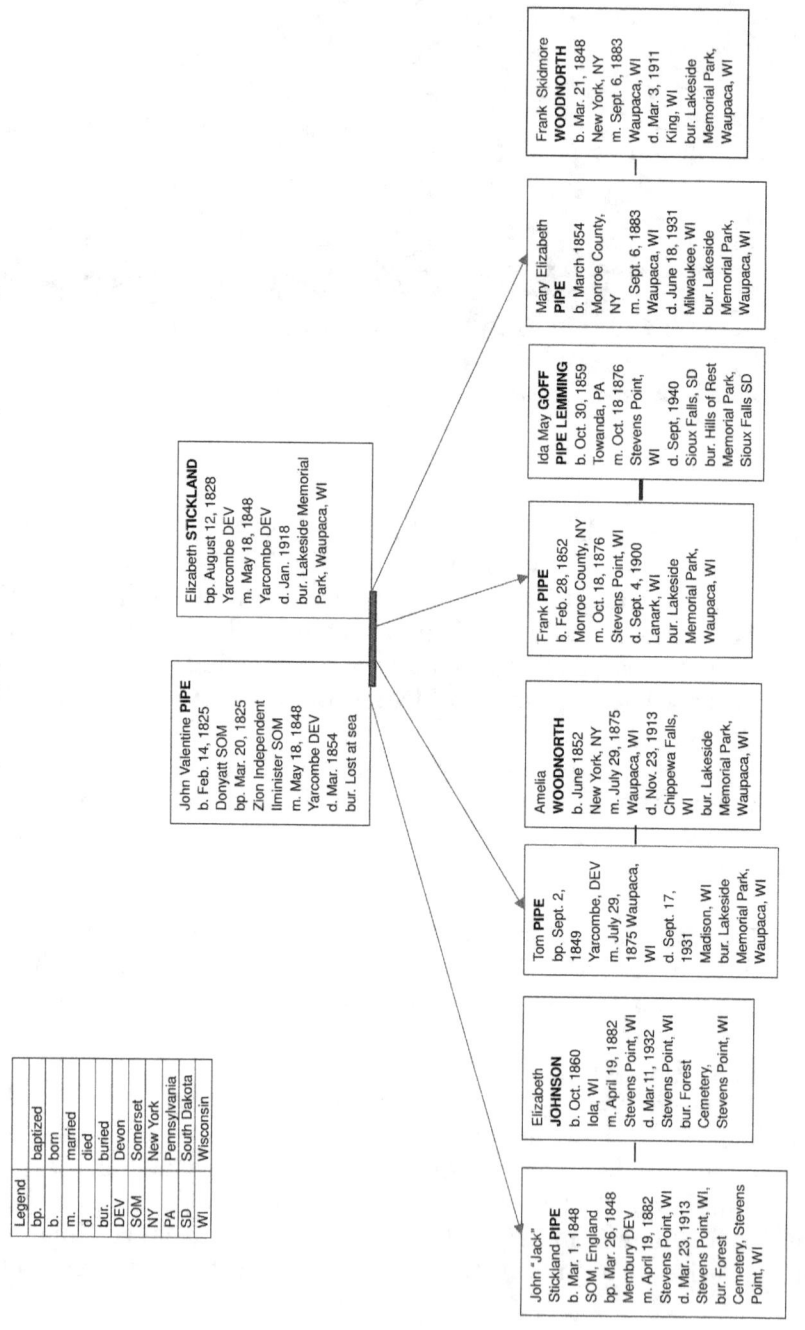

Legend	
bp.	baptized
b.	born
m.	married
d.	died
bur.	buried
DEV	Devon
SOM	Somerset
NY	New York
PA	Pennsylvania
SD	South Dakota
WI	Wisconsin

Elizabeth STICKLAND
bp. August 12, 1828
Yarcombe DEV
m. May 18, 1848
Yarcombe DEV
d. Jan. 1918
bur. Lakeside Memorial
Park, Waupaca, WI

John Valentine PIPE
b. Feb. 14, 1825
Donyatt SOM
bp. Mar. 20, 1825
Zion Independent
Ilminister SOM
m. May 18, 1848
Yarcombe DEV
d. Mar. 1854
bur. Lost at sea

Frank Skidmore WOODNORTH
b. Mar. 21, 1848
New York, NY
m. Sept. 6, 1883
Waupaca, WI
d. Mar. 3, 1911
King, WI
bur. Lakeside
Memorial Park,
Waupaca, WI

Mary Elizabeth PIPE
b. March 1854
Monroe County,
NY
m. Sept. 6, 1883
Waupaca, WI
d. June 18, 1931
Milwaukee, WI
bur. Lakeside
Memorial Park,
Waupaca, WI

Ida May GOFF PIPE LEMMING
b. Oct. 30, 1859
Towanda, PA
m. Oct. 18 1876
Stevens Point,
WI
d. Sept, 1940
Sioux Falls, SD
bur. Hills of Rest
Memorial Park,
Sioux Falls SD

Frank PIPE
b. Feb. 28, 1852
Monroe County, NY
m. Oct. 18, 1876
Stevens Point, WI
d. Sept. 4, 1900
Lanark, WI
bur. Lakeside
Memorial Park,
Waupaca, WI

Amelia WOODNORTH
b. June 1852
New York, NY
m. July 29, 1875
Waupaca, WI
d. Nov. 23, 1913
Chippewa Falls,
WI
bur. Lakeside
Memorial Park,
Waupaca, WI

Tom PIPE
bp. Sept. 2,
1849
Yarcombe, DEV
m. July 29,
1875 Waupaca,
WI
d. Sept. 17,
1931
Madison, WI
bur. Lakeside
Memorial Park,
Waupaca, WI

Elizabeth JOHNSON
b. Oct. 1860
Iola, WI
m. April 19, 1882
Stevens Point, WI
d. Mar.11, 1932
Stevens Point, WI
bur. Forest
Cemetery,
Stevens Point, WI

John "Jack" Stickland PIPE
b. Mar. 1, 1848
Membury DEV
bp. Mar. 26, 1848
SOM, England
m. April 19, 1882
Stevens Point, WI
d. Mar. 23, 1913
Stevens Point, WI,
bur. Forest
Cemetery, Stevens
Point, WI

Prepared by ST Moore and JN Steiner

The Thomas and Elizabeth Stickland Pipe Family

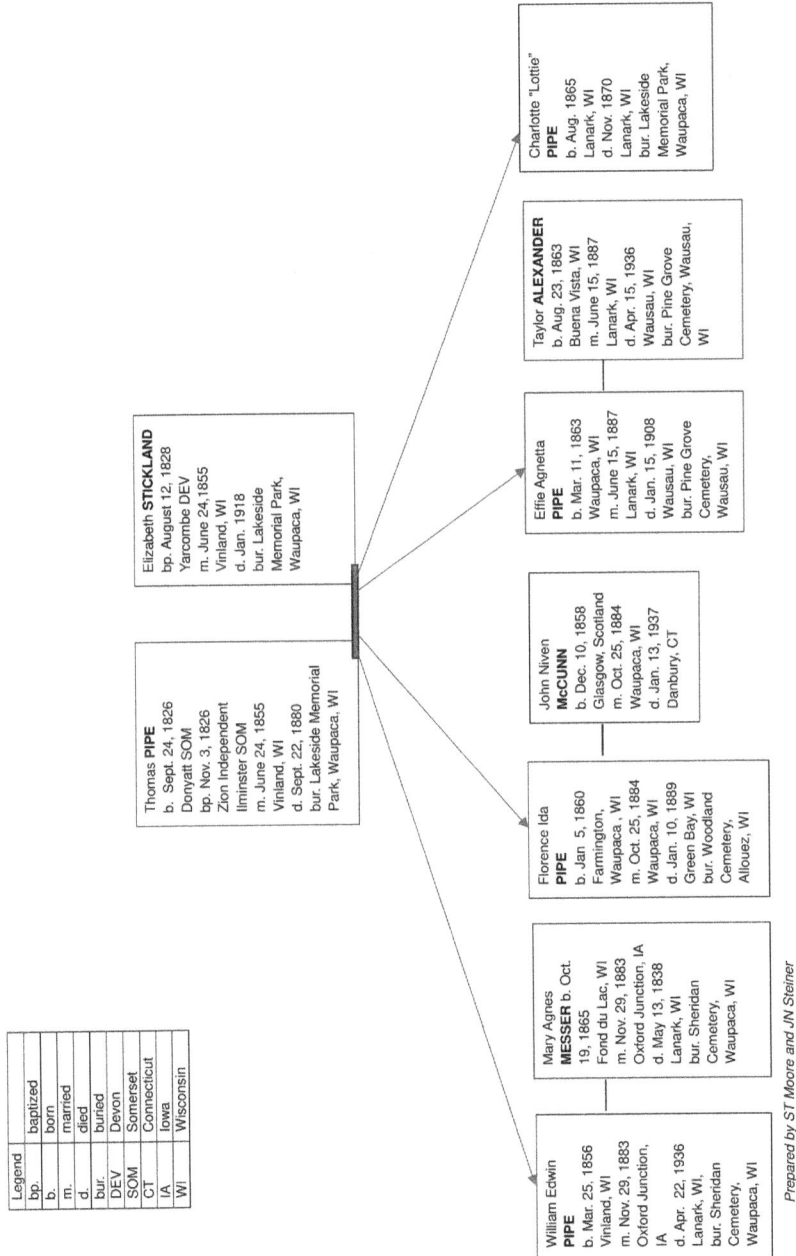

Legend	
bp.	baptized
b.	born
m.	married
d.	died
bur.	buried
DEV	Devon
SOM	Somerset
CT	Connecticut
IA	Iowa
WI	Wisconsin

Thomas **PIPE**
b. Sept. 24, 1826
Donyatt SOM
bp. Nov. 3, 1826
Zion Independent
Ilminster SOM
m. June 24, 1855
Vinland, WI
d. Sept. 22, 1880
bur. Lakeside Memorial
Park, Waupaca, WI

Elizabeth **STICKLAND**
bp. August 12, 1828
Yarcombe DEV
m. June 24,1855
Vinland, WI
d. Jan. 1918
bur. Lakeside
Memorial Park,
Waupaca, WI

William Edwin
PIPE
b. Mar. 25, 1856
Vinland, WI
m. Nov. 29, 1883
Oxford Junction,
IA
d. Apr. 22, 1936
Lanark, WI,
bur. Sheridan
Cemetery,
Waupaca, WI

Mary Agnes
MESSER b. Oct.
19, 1865
Fond du Lac, WI
m. Nov. 29, 1883
Oxford Junction, IA
d. May 13, 1838
Lanark, WI
bur. Sheridan
Cemetery,
Waupaca, WI

Florence Ida
PIPE
b. Jan. 5, 1860
Farmington,
Waupaca, WI
m. Oct. 25, 1884
Waupaca, WI
d. Jan. 10, 1889
Green Bay, WI
bur. Woodland
Cemetery,
Allouez, WI

John Niven
McCUNN
b. Dec. 10, 1858
Glasgow, Scotland
m. Oct. 25, 1884
Waupaca, WI
d. Jan. 13, 1937
Danbury, CT

Effie Agnetta
PIPE
b. Mar. 11, 1863
Waupaca, WI
m. June 15, 1887
Lanark, WI
d. Jan. 15, 1908
Wausau, WI
bur. Pine Grove
Cemetery,
Wausau, WI

Taylor **ALEXANDER**
b. Aug. 23, 1863
Buena Vista, WI
m. June 15, 1887
Lanark, WI
d. Apr. 15, 1936
Wausau, WI
bur. Pine Grove
Cemetery, Wausau,
WI

Charlotte "Lottie"
PIPE
b. Aug. 1865
Lanark, WI
d. Nov. 1870
Lanark, WI
bur. Lakeside
Memorial Park,
Waupaca, WI

Prepared by ST Moore and JN Steiner

Charlotte Jennings Pipe Pillar: The Story of a Pioneer Woman

From a London Workhouse in the Late 1820s to an 80-Acre Farm in Wisconsin in 1855

*Charlotte Jennings Pipe and her
second husband, James Pillar[1]*

Charlotte **JENNINGS PIPE PILLAR** could be called the matriarch of the **PIPE/STICKLAND/PILLAR** families. Letters Number 11 and 36 in the **PIPE** family letter collection convey her strength of character, her wisdom of age and experience, and her deeply rooted Christian faith. Charlotte likely developed these qualities by overcoming hardships that include living in a Victorian London workhouse with her first husband and three children and later facing his abandonment. Her letters do not reveal these past circumstances. Research into her life does. Her past difficulties serve as the foundation for her wisdom and unrelenting faith.

When Charlotte **JENNINGS PIPE PILLAR** found herself in an abusive relationship with her second husband, she mustered the strength in 1867 to challenge him with a divorce in Winnebago County Circuit

Court in Wisconsin. Her divorce was granted. The financial settlement allowed her to live out the rest of her life comfortably and with dignity.

According to her obituary, Charlotte **JENNINGS PIPE** brought nine children into the world. Only seven children have been located to date: five with her first husband, John **PIPE** and two with James **PILLAR**. The only child who outlived her is William Jennings **PIPE** who settled in Australia. Charlotte died on January 2, 1882, in Oshkosh, Wisconsin. William Jennings **PIPE** died 24 days after his mother on January 26, 1882, in Melbourne, Victoria, Australia.

Descendants of Charlotte **JENNINGS PIPE PILLAR** can be proud of their ancestor. She served as a role model for her children. She continues to give strength to the descendants who read about her life. What follows is Charlotte's family background along with that of her first husband, John **PIPE**.

The JENNINGS and BOND Family

The John and Mary **BOND JENNINGS** family of Birch Oak Farm, Yarcombe, Devon, England:

John **JENNINGS** was a yeoman from the parish of Membury (later Yarcombe), Devon. He married Mary **BOND** from the parish of Membury, Devon, on December 12, 1799.[2] Their children include:

- Edwin **JENNINGS** was born in 1800 as estimated in the *1851 Census of England*.[3]
- Charlotte **JENNINGS** was christened in Yarcombe, Devon, on January 31, 1802.[4]
- John **JENNINGS** was christened in Yarcombe, Devon, on November 13, 1803 (pictured at right).[5]

John Jennings[6]

- Thomas **JENNINGS** was born in 1805 as estimated in the *1851 Census of England.*[7]
- Mary Ann **JENNINGS** was christened in Yarcombe, Devon, on January 11, 1811.[8] Mary Ann married William **DOMMETT**.[9]
- William **JENNINGS** was christened in Yarcombe, Devon, on May 31, 1812.[10] William married Elizabeth **COLEMAN**.[11] William and Elizabeth **COLEMAN JENNINGS** write and receive many of the letters in the **PIPE** family letter collection. *(See Indexes of Letters.)*

The PIPE and HORSEY Family

The James and Alice **HORSEY PIPE** family of Donyatt and Sea Somerset, England:

James **PIPE** was a yeoman and wick yarn maker (for candles) from the parishes of Donyatt and Sea, Somerset, England. He married Alice **HORSEY** from Donyatt, Somerset, on February 20, 1794.[12] Their children include:
- Elizabeth Horsey **PIPE** was born December 31, 1794, and baptized on February 5, 1795, in Ilminster, Somerset.[13]
- Joseph **PIPE** was born December 31, 1795, and baptized on June 5, 1796, in Broadway, Somerset.[14]
- James **PIPE** was born July 16, 1799, and baptized on October 10, 1800, in Ilminster, Somerset.[15]
- John **PIPE** (Sr.) was born on August 8, 1801, baptized on June 29, 1802, in Ilminster, Somerset.[16]
- Edward **PIPE** was born on September 29, 1803, and baptized on December 22, 1803, in Broadway, Somerset.[17]
- Orlando **PIPE** was born on January 3, 1806, and baptized on April 28, 1806, in Broadway Meeting Independent, Broadway Somerset.[18] Orlando died on May 2, 1856, in Somerset.[19]

The PIPE and JENNINGS Family

- Charlotte **JENNINGS** married John **PIPE** Sr. in Membury, Devon, on April 24, 1823.[20]

Charlotte **JENNINGS** and John **PIPE** Sr. children include:

- John Valentine **PIPE** was born February 14, 1825, in Donyatt, Somerset.[21] John Valentine died in March 1854 when the *City of Glasgow* sank in the Atlantic Ocean.[22]
- Thomas **PIPE** was born September 24, 1826, in Donyatt, Somerset.[23] Thomas died on September 22, 1880, and is buried in Lakeside Memorial Park in Waupaca, Wisconsin.[24]
- Mary Ann **PIPE** was born in 1830, according to London Workhouse records.[25] Mary Ann **PIPE** was baptized in Yarcombe, Devon.[26] She is found in the *1851 Census for England* working as a domestic servant for Rector Hyde and his family in Donyatt, Somerset.[27] She married George Washington **SINCLAIR**.[28]
- Edwin Jennings **PIPE** was born in July 1832, according to London Workhouse records.[29] He was baptized on April 9, 1837, in Yarcombe, Devon.[30] Edwin was buried on September 26, 1840, at the age of 8. He is buried in Donyatt, Somerset.[31]
- William Jennings **PIPE** was born in May 1833, according to London Workhouse records.[32] He was baptized on April 9, 1837, in Yarcombe, Devon.[33] William died on January 26, 1882, and is buried in Melbourne General Cemetery in Parkville, Melbourne City, Victoria, Australia.[34] William exchanges several letters with family: Letters Number 6, 38, 44, 77, and 91.

William Jennings Pipe[35]

~ 46 ~

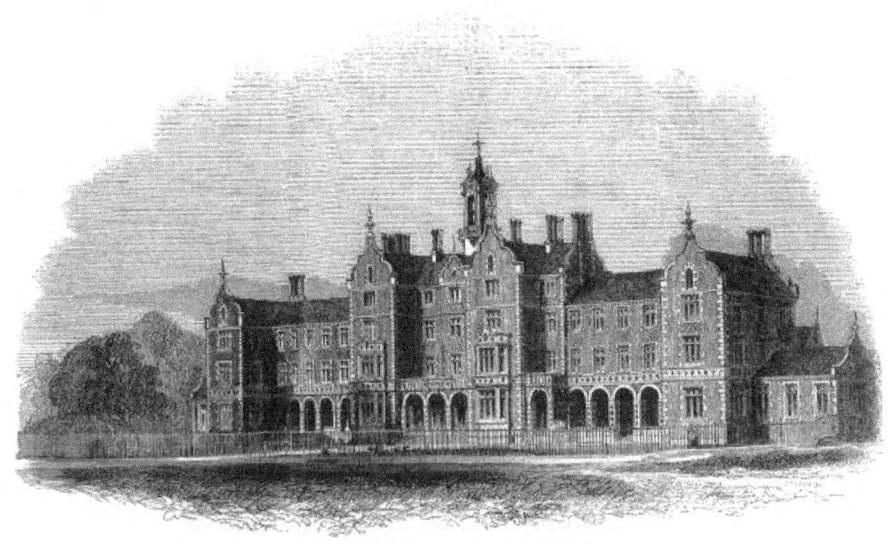

VIEW OF THE KENSINGTON UNION WORKHOUSE

Architect Thomas Allom's design for the Kensington and St. Mary's Abbots Workhouse on Marloes Road in London, circa 1847. For more information, go to https://www.workhouses.org.uk/kensington.

Kensington Workhouse in London

In 1826, John **PIPE** Sr. rented a farm called Boroughshot Farm from Major **BRICE** in the parish of Uplyme, Devon, near Axminster, Devon, for 85 pounds a year and taxes. **PIPE** Sr. paid the rent for two years, but thereafter, he did not. This offense put the **PIPE** family in the St. Mary's Abbot Workhouse in London.[36]

On January 4, 1834, Charlotte and John **PIPE** Sr. are found in an affidavit in the *St. Mary Abbots Poor House Records in Kensington and Chelsea, London, England, Poor Law Records*. Charlotte **JENNINGS** and John **PIPE** are residing with three of their five children: Mary Ann, age 4; Edwin, age 2; and William, age eight months at St. Mary, Abbots Workhouse/Poor House, Kensington and Chelsea, London.[37]

In 1834 the **PIPE** family was ordered to leave the London workhouse required by a change in Poor House Laws. They were to enter a workhouse in their home parish of Uplyme. (The name of the workhouse for their parish is Axminster Union Workhouse. This is likely where they were assigned.)[38]

John **PIPE** Sr. is found in *Axminster Board of Guardians Minutes (1836-1838)* in 1836. Charlotte twice brought forth charges of abandonment and requested support for her family. Below is an excerpt from a report on the matter by present-day researcher, Susan Moore from Somerset:

> 13 Oct 1836 • Axminster Board of Guardians. Minutes (1836-1838) The Clerk was also directed to write to the Overseers of the Poor of Uplyme requesting them to pay to Charlotte **PIPE**, the wife of John **PIPE**, a pauper of that Parish, (who had deserted her) at the Rate of 3s per week towards the support of her children from the 1st day of February last [1836] to the commencement of the operation of the union.[39]

According to Moore's report, admission records for Axminster Union Workhouse have not survived. Therefore, it is unknown whether the family ever entered the Axminster Union Workhouse.[40]

1841 Census in England

The *1841 Census in England* finds Thomas and John Valentine **PIPE** working on their uncles' farms. Thomas **PIPE**, age 15, is living with Orlando **PIPE**, age 34, who is John **PIPE** Sr.'s brother.[41] The *1846 Poll Book* locates Orlando in Donyatt, Somerset, leasing Wheadons Farm.[42]

John Valentine **PIPE**, age 15, is found living in Membury, Devon, with his Uncle William **JENNINGS**, age 25; John Valentine's sister, Mary Ann, age 11; and his brother, Willam, age 7. William **JENNINGS'** mother and the other children's grandmother, Mary **BOND JENNINGS**, age 71, is also living in the household. William's brother, John **JENNINGS**, age 35, and Honor **WARD**, age 25, are also listed on the *1841 Census in England* for the William **JENNINGS** household. (Census records round up ages to the next five years.)[43]

Charlotte **JENNINGS PIPE** (age 35) and James **PILLAR** (age 30) are found living with 12 other people ranging from ages 2 months to 40 years old. Charlotte **JENNINGS PIPE** and James **PILLAR** are both listed as servants employed by Puddington Lodge in Witheridge, Devon.[44] The picture on the left below is Puddington Lodge. The picture on the right below shows the servants' quarters behind the house, where Charlotte and James would have lived.

Puddington Lodge (left)[45] and the building housing the servants' quarters (right).[46]

Charlotte **JENNINGS PIPE** and James **PILLAR** were married in May 1843 at St. Peter's Church, Tiverton, Devon, with their religion noted as Anglican.[47]

1851 Census in England

The 1851 Census in England was taken on Sunday evening, March 30, 1851. The **PILLAR** family is living at Mount Pleasant Inn in Nomansland, Devon. Charlotte **JENNINGS PIPE** and James **PILLAR** are found with their two children: James, age 7 and Elizth (Elizabeth), age 2. The census record shows that James **PILLAR** is a farmer and an innkeeper.[48]

The two pictures on the left were taken in the late 1800s and early 1900s, and are displayed inside the inn today. The picture above was taken in April 2025.[49]

Charlotte JENNINGS PIPE and James PILLAR children

The **PILLAR**s had two children who were born in England.

James **PILLAR** Jr. was baptized in Witheridge, Devon, on March 17, 1844.[50] He later served as a private in Company B of the 21st Infantry of Wisconsin during the Civil War. James mustered in on August 14, 1862, and was killed in the Battle at Chickamauga in Georgia on September 29, 1863.[51]

Elizabeth **PILLAR** was born on February 13, 1849, according to her tombstone. She married Jacob F. **BOWRON** in Winnebago County, Wisconsin, on November 27, 1867. Elizabeth **PILLAR BOWRON** died on December 9, 1915, and is buried in Brooks Cemetery in town of Vinland, Winnebago County, Wisconsin.

1851 Residents of Wisconsin

Charlotte **JENNINGS PIPE PILLAR** and James **PILLAR** first resided in Wisconsin on December 16, 1851 (according to 1867 divorce papers).[52] Charlotte testified that she had received a legacy of $250 from her deceased uncle. (See Appendix E for Will of John Bond of Atherstone, gent., proved 18 May 1854.) She also had savings "which she had earned with her own labor, the sum of one hundred pounds sterling" (likely earned at Puddington Lodge). She stated she put the legacy and her savings toward buying an 80-acre farm in the Town of Vinland, Winnebago County, Wisconsin.

A warranty deed dated August 1, 1855, supports Charlotte's testimony. The deed shows Jabus **WILKINSON** and his wife Susan are grantors and James **PILLAR** is grantee of 80 acres in Section 19, Township 19 (Vinland) Range 17. Conditions state that James **PILLAR** will pay **WILKINSON** on or before the 1st day of May 1857 the sum of 250 dollars with interest at the rate of 10% per annan from the 1st day of May 1855.[53]

1860 U.S. Census

Ellen St. Clair (**SINCLAIR**), age 3, is found living with the **PILLAR** family in the *1860 U.S. Census*. Ellen is the daughter of the deceased Mary Ann **SINCLAIR**. Charlotte's descendants state she also provided a temporary home for Ellen's brothers, William and baby Jonathon, although they are not shown in the census. (See Letter Number 59, dated 14 February 1868.)[54]

1867 Divorce Proceedings between James and Charlotte PILLAR

- Divorce is granted.
- $175 per year is ordered paid to Charlotte **JENNINGS PIPE PILLAR** commencing March 7, 1867, and continuing for the rest of her life, which was 15 years.

- For security of payment, the court required a lien be put on the farm if James **PILLAR** neglects to pay. Agreement is dated June 27, 1868.
- Among others, Elizabeth **PILLAR BOWRON** testified against her father. Thomas **PIPE** was a character witness for James **PILLAR**.

Charlotte Jennings **PIPE PILLAR** received $175 per year for the rest of her life, which was 15 years. The table below shows her approximate settlement over 15 years converted into today's value using an online calculator:

Year(s)	Amount	Value Today	Notes Charlotte lived 15 years
Commencing 1867	$175 per year	$3,992.38	https.//www.westegg.com/inflation/
1867-1882+	$2,625 over 15 years	$59,885.70	Total payments over 15 years

James **PILLAR** married Eliza **MORGAN**, who was born in England.[56] James was 30 years older than Eliza, about the age of his eldest daughter, Elizabeth **PILLAR BOWRON**. Eliza **MORGAN PILLAR** died on April 29, 1891.[57]

Charlotte **JENNINGS PIPE PILLAR** died on January 2, 1882, at the home of her daughter Elizabeth **PILLAR BOWRON** in Oshkosh, Wisconsin. She is buried with her daughter Elizabeth and the **BOWRON** family in Brooks Cemetery, town of Vinland, Winnebago County, Wisconsin.[58]

James **PILLAR** died from "general debility" on December 16, 1892, at age 81. **PILLAR**'s daughter Elizabeth testified at the probate hearing that he had asthma and shingles with lesions on his arm and leg. James is buried in Brooks Cemetery with his second wife, Eliza **MORGAN PILLAR**.[59]

Conclusion

Pioneer woman Charlotte **JENNINGS PIPE PILLAR** overcame many financial hardships in life. She buried all but one of her nine children. Life challenges and her struggles to overcome them built her strong, unshakable character. She serves as a role model for her descendants today.

---

1 Privately held by Elizabeth Pipe Hansen [ADDRESS FOR PRIVATE USE,] Amherst, Wisconsin, 2025. (This picture was found unlabeled in the Pipe family letter box. Descendants believe the couple is the Pillars. Any further information would be appreciated.)

2 "England, Devon and Cornwall, Marriages, 1660-1912", *Family Search* (https://www.familysearch.org/ark:/61903/1:1:QGYS-QFCM : Thu Mar 07 21:12:23 UTC 2024), Entry for John Jennings, Yeoman and Mary Bond, 11 Dec 1799.

3 "England and Wales, Census, 1851", *FamilySearch* (https://www.familysearch.org/ark:/61903/1:1:SGGB-BJ3 : Fri Jul 12 03:54:01 UTC 2024), Entry for Edwin Jennings and Mary Jennings, 1851.

4 "England, Births and Christenings, 1538-1975", database, *Family Search* (https://www.familysearch.org/ark:/61903/1:1:N56Z-29F : 4 February 2023), Charlotte Jennings, 1802.

5 "England, Births and Christenings, 1538-1975", database, *FamilySearch* (https://www.familysearch.org/ark:/61903/1:1:N56Z-85Y : 4 February 2023), John Jennings, 1803.

6 Privately held by Elizabeth Pipe Hansen [ADDRESS FOR PRIVATE USE,] Amherst, Wisconsin, 2025.

7 "England and Wales, Census, 1851", *FamilySearch* (https://www.familysearch.org/ark:/61903/1:1:SGGB-WXH : Sun Mar 10 09:20:11 UTC 2024), Entry for Thomas Jennings and Sarah Jennings, 1851.

8 "England, Births and Christenings, 1538-1975", database, *FamilySearch* (https://www.familysearch.org/ark:/61903/1:1:J73W-NB8 : 4 February 2023), Mary Ann Jennings, 1811.

9 "England and Wales, Census, 1851", *FamilySearch* (https://www.familysearch.org/ark:/61903/1:1:SGGL-47R : Fri Jul 26 14:54:08 UTC 2024), Entry for William Dommett and Mary Ann Dommett, 1851.

10 "England, Births and Christenings, 1538-1975", database, *FamilySearch* (https://www.familysearch.org/ark:/61903/1:1:NB7L-M6T : 4 February 2023), William Jennings, 1812.

[11] "England, Somerset, Church Records, 1501-1999", database, *Family Search* (https://www.familysearch.org/ark:/61903/1:1:6DMP-J42Z : 10 August 2022), William Jenning, 1844.

[12] "England, Somerset, Church Records, 1501-1999", database, *Family-Search* (https://www.familysearch.org/ark:/61903/1:1:6DM2-RK7K : 10 August 2022), James Pipe, 1794.

[13] "England, Births and Christenings, 1538-1975", database, *FamilySearch* (https://www.familysearch.org/ark:/61903/1:1:JWDD-538 : 4 February 2023), Elizabeth Horsey Pipe, 1795.

[14] "England, Births and Christenings, 1538-1975", database, *FamilySearch* (https://www.familysearch.org/ark:/61903/1:1:NYBZ-X8R : 4 February 2023), Joseph Pipe, 1796.

[15] "England, Births and Christenings, 1538-1975", database, *FamilySearch* (https://www.familysearch.org/ark:/61903/1:1:NYBZ-2YW : 4 February 2023), James Pipe, 1800.

[16] "England, Births and Christenings, 1538-1975", *FamilySearch* (https://www.familysearch.org/ark:/61903/1:1:NPJ7-CJ5 : 4 February 2023), John Pipe, 1802.

[17] "England, Births and Christenings, 1538-1975", database, *FamilySearch* (https://www.familysearch.org/ark:/61903/1:1:NPJQ-VZZ : 4 February 2023), Edward Pipe, 1803.

[18] "England, Births and Christenings, 1538-1975", database, *FamilySearch* (https://www.familysearch.org/ark:/61903/1:1:NPJQ-2NY : 4 February 2023), Orlando Pipe, 1806.

[19] "England, Deaths and Burials, 1538-1991", *FamilySearch* (https://www.familysearch.org/ark:/61903/1:1:J8PH-N4S : Fri Jul 12 22:26:54 UTC 2024), Entry for Orlando Pipe, 2 May 1856.

[20] "England Marriages, 1538–1973", *FamilySearch* (https://www.familysearch.org/ark:/61903/1:1:N2JB-YVH : Wed Apr 16 06:46:35 UTC 2025), Entry for John Pipe and Charlotte Jennings, 24 Apr 1823.

[21] "England, Births and Christenings, 1538-1975", database, *FamilySearch* (https://www.familysearch.org/ark:/61903/1:1:NPJ7-CLK : 4 February 2023), John Valentine Pipe, 1825.

[22] Thomas G. Clark, *Let Glasgow Flourish: The Disappearance of the SS City of Glasglow* (www.distinctivepress.com, 2024), 254.

[23] "England, Births and Christenings, 1538-1975", , *FamilySearch* (https://www.familysearch.org/ark:/61903/1:1:J3Z1-QXN : 4 February 2023), Thomas Pipe, 1826.

[24] "Find a Grave Index", *FamilySearch* (https://www.familysearch.org/ark:/61903/1:1:QVGM-9JDF : Tue Apr 01 14:45:51 UTC 2025), Entry for Thomas Pipe.

25 Susan Moore, "Investigate John PIPE and the poor house records of Uplyme," John PIPE. Kensington & Chelsea. MDX. Poor Law Examination. Kensington & Chelsea RO MS58/56/29 [Anc; Kensington & Chelsea, London, England, Poor Law Records, 1695-1921] p. 2; Report prepared for Joan Naomi Steiner [ADDRESS FOR PRIVATE USE], March 2025; copy privately held by Joan Naomi Steiner [ADDRESS FOR PRIVATE USE,] 2025.

26 "England, Devon, Parish Registers (Devon Record Office), 1529-1974", *FamilySearch* (https://www.familysearch.org/ark:/61903/1:1:6NXB-VR3J : Mon Mar 11 00:31:19 UTC 2024), Entry for Mary Ann Pope [Pipe] and John, 1830.

27 "England and Wales, Census, 1851", *FamilySearch* (https://www.familysearch.org/ark:/61903/1:1:SGPS-LJT : Mon Jul 22 01:38:56 UTC 2024), Entry for William Hyde and Emma Hyde, 1851.

28 "Wisconsin, Marriages, 1836-1930", database, *FamilySearch* (https://www.familysearch.org/ark:/61903/1:1:XR2Z-JP1 : 29 February 2024), Mary Ann Sinclair in entry for Henry Smillie, 1881.

29 Moore, "Investigate John PIPE and the poor house records of Uplyme," 2.

30 "England, Births and Christenings, 1538-1975", *FamilySearch* (https://www.familysearch.org/ark:/61903/1:1:N56Z-4Y3 : 4 February 2023), Edwin Jennings Pipe, 1837.

31 "England, Deaths and Burials, 1538-1991", *FamilySearch* (https://www.familysearch.org/ark:/61903/1:1:J8PH-F49 : Sun Mar 10 02:56:05 UTC 2024), Entry for Edwin Jennings Pipe, 26 9 1840.

32 Moore, "Investigate John PIPE and the poor house records of Uplyme," 2.

33 "England, Births and Christenings, 1538-1975", database, *FamilySearch* (https://www.familysearch.org/ark:/61903/1:1:N56Z-JMZ : 4 February 2023), William Jennings Pipe, 1837.

34 "Australia, Cemetery Inscriptions, 1800-1960", *FamilySearch* (https://www.familysearch.org/ark:/61903/1:1:FLJ4-8ZP : Fri Feb 14 21:00:34 UTC 2025), Entry for William Jennings Pipe, 26 January 1882.

35 Privately held by Elizabeth Pipe Hansen [ADDRESS FOR PRIVATE USE,] Amherst, Wisconsin, 2025.

36 Moore, "Investigate John PIPE and the poor house records of Uplyme," 4.

37 *Ibid.* 2.

38 *Ibid.* 2

39 *Ibid.* 6.

40 *Ibid.* 7.

[41] 1841 census of England for Membury, Devon, England, Chardstock, Book 6, 6, p.5, John Pipe; digital image. Ancestry,com (https://www.ancestry.com) : accessed November 17, 2025.

[42] *1846 Register of Electors Entitled to Vote at Elections*, Ilminster, Donyatt Orlando Pipe; digital image. Ancestry.com (https://www.ancestry.com) : accessed November 17, 2025.

[43] 1841 census of England for Donyatt, Somerset, England, Ilminster, Book 13, p.19, Thomas Pipe; digital image. Ancestry,com (https://www.ancestry.com) : accessed November 17, 2025.

[44] "England and Wales, Census, 1841", *FamilySearch* (https://www.familysearch.org/ark:/61903/1:1:MQT2-VD5 : Tue Jan 28 23:02:50 UTC 2025), Entry for Gerard Bolton and Alice Wellman, 1841.

[45] Privately held by Joan Naomi Steiner [ADDRESS FOR PRIVATE USE,] Neenah, Wisconsin, 2025.

[46] *Ibid.*

[47] "England and Wales, Marriage Registration Index, 1837-2005," database, *FamilySearch* (https://familysearch.org/ark:/61903/1:1:2DZD-KXS : 22 May 2014), James Pillar, 1843; from "England & Wales Marriages, 1837-2005," database, *findmypast* (http://www.findmypast.com : 2012); citing 1843, quarter 2, vol. 10, p. 450, Tiverton, Devon, England, General Register Office, Southport, England.

[48] 1851 census for Tiverton, Devon, England, Barnstable, Folio 402, p. 7, James Pillar; digital image. Ancestry,com (https://www.ancestry.com) : accessed November 17, 2025.

[49] Privately held by Joan Naomi Steiner [ADDRESS FOR PRIVATE USE,] Neenah, Wisconsin, 2025.

[50] "England, Devon Bishop's Transcripts, 1558-1887", *FamilySearch* (https://www.familysearch.org/ark:/61903/1:1:Q2CY-5V3C : Fri Mar 08 20:59:58 UTC 2024), Entry for James Pillar and James Pillar, 17 Mar 1844.

[51] "United States, Census, 1860", *FamilySearch* (https://www.familysearch.org/ark:/61903/1:1:MW9V-H6C : Mon Jul 08 23:58:01 UTC 2024), Entry for James Pillar and Charlotte Pillar, 1860.

[52] "United States, Civil War Soldiers Index, 1861-1865", *FamilySearch* (https://www.familysearch.org/ark:/61903/1:1:FS3R-GJ8 : Thu Feb 13 00:00:04 UTC 2025), Entry for James Pillar, from 1861 to 1865.

[53] Winnebago County, Wisconsin, Deed Book 10:488, Jabus and Susan Wilkinson & James Pillar, 1 May 1855; Register of Deeds Office, Oshkosh.

[54] "United States, Census, 1860", *FamilySearch* (https://www.familysearch.org/ark:/61903/1:1:MW9V-H6C : Mon Jul 08 23:58:01 UTC 2024), Entry for James Pillar and Charlotte Pillar, 1860.

55 Winnebago County, Wisconsin, Winnebago Circuit Court, divorce file 2958 (1867), Charlotte Pillar v. James Pillar, final decree; Winnebago County Circuit Court. Digital image. University of Wisconsin Oshkosh Archives.

56 "United States, Census, 1870", FamilySearch (https://www.familysearch.org/ark:/61903/1:1:MNSF-NGF : Wed Jan 22 13:29:22 UTC 2025), Entry for James Pillar and Eliza Pillar, 1870.

57 "Wisconsin, Death Index, 1820-1907", *FamilySearch* (https://www.familysearch.org/ark:/61903/1:1:VJGT-DFC : Tue Feb 18 20:35:47 UTC 2025), Entry for Eliza Pillar, 29 Apr 1891.

58 "Find a Grave Index", *FamilySearch* (https://www.familysearch.org/ark:/61903/1:1:QVVC-S1ML : Wed Apr 02 15:59:14 UTC 2025), Entry for Charlotte Jennings Pillar.

59 "Wisconsin, Death Index, 1820-1907", *FamilySearch* (https://www.familysearch.org/ark:/61903/1:1:VJGT-DFZ : Tue Feb 18 23:34:29 UTC 2025), Entry for James Pillar, 16 Dec 1892.

The John Jennings and Mary Bond Family
of Birch Oak Farm

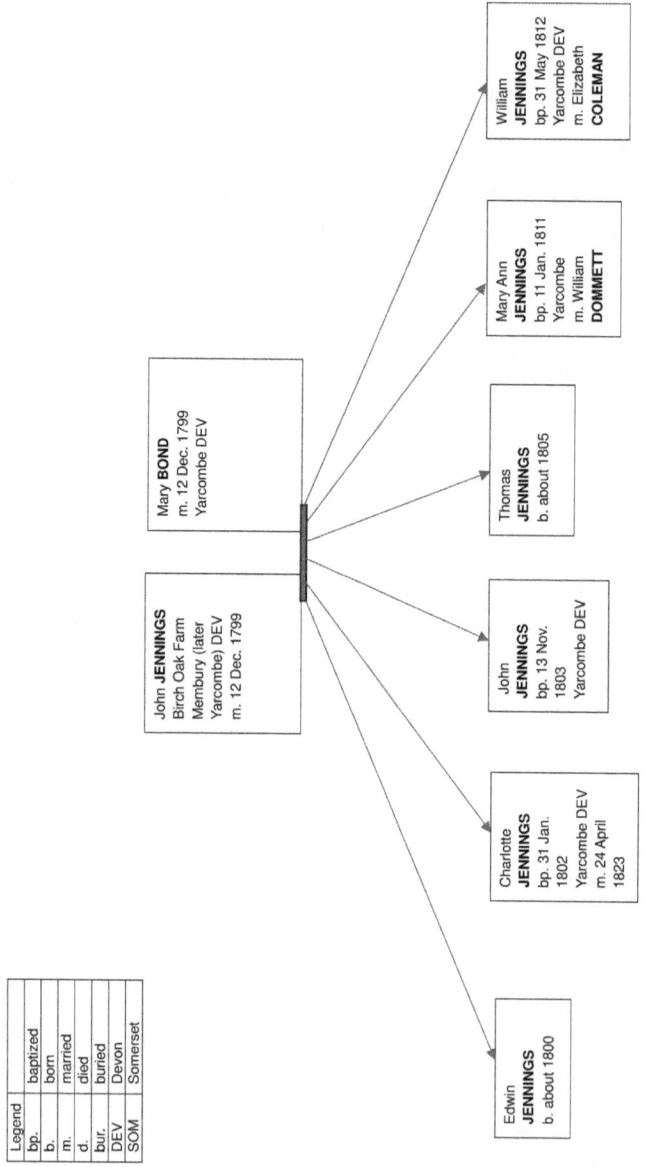

Legend
bp.	baptized
b.	born
m.	married
d.	died
bur.	buried
DEV	Devon
SOM	Somerset

John JENNINGS
Birch Oak Farm
Membury (later
Yarcombe) DEV
m. 12 Dec. 1799

Mary BOND
m. 12 Dec. 1799
Yarcombe DEV

Edwin
JENNINGS
b. about 1800

Charlotte
JENNINGS
bp. 31 Jan.
1802
Yarcombe DEV
m. 24 April
1823

John
JENNINGS
bp. 13 Nov.
1803
Yarcombe DEV

Thomas
JENNINGS
b. about 1805

Mary Ann
JENNINGS
bp. 11 Jan. 1811
Yarcombe
m. William
DOMMETT

William
JENNINGS
bp. 31 May 1812
Yarcombe DEV
m. Elizabeth
COLEMAN

Prepared by ST Moore and JN Steiner

The James and Alice Horsey Pipe Family

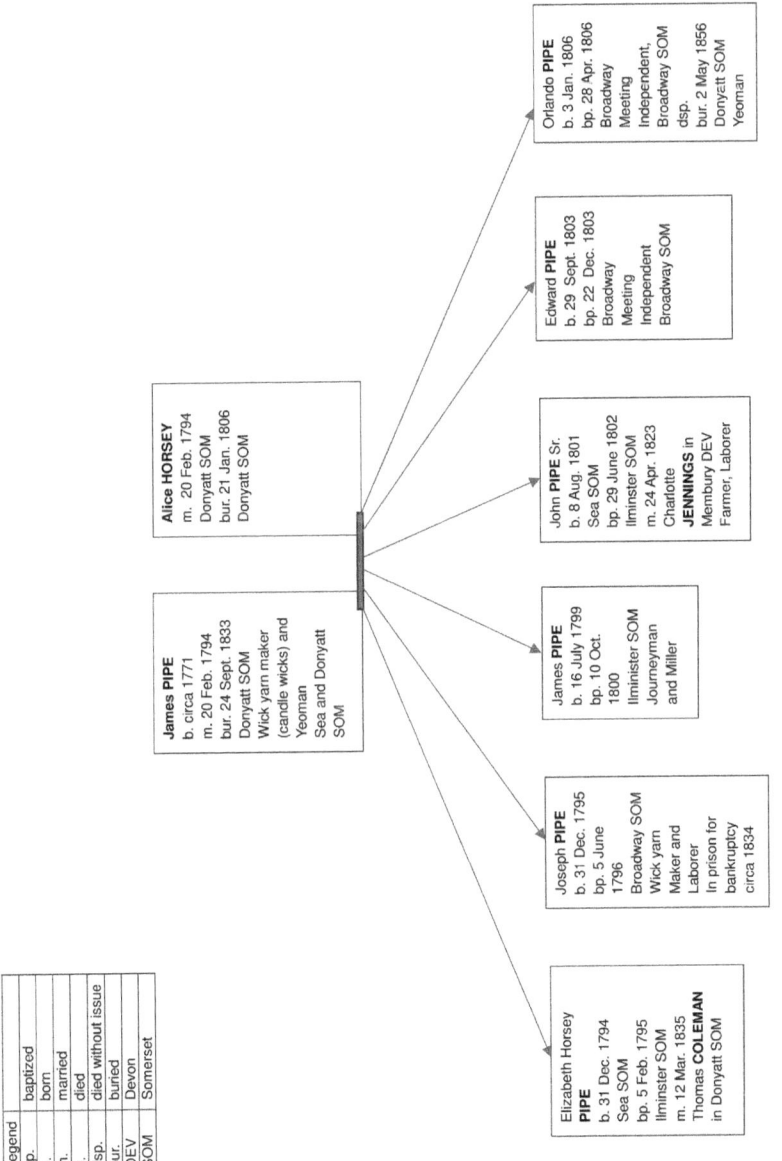

Legend	
bp.	baptized
b.	born
m.	married
d.	died
dsp.	died without issue
bur.	buried
DEV	Devon
SOM	Somerset

James PIPE
b. circa 1771
m. 20 Feb. 1794
Donyatt SOM
bur. 24 Sept. 1833
Donyatt SOM
Wick yarn maker
(candle wicks) and
Yeoman
Sea and Donyatt
SOM

Alice HORSEY
m. 20 Feb. 1794
Donyatt SOM
bur. 21 Jan. 1806
Donyatt SOM

Elizabeth Horsey
PIPE
b. 31 Dec. 1794
Sea SOM
bp. 5 Feb. 1795
Ilminster SOM
m. 12 Mar. 1835
Thomas **COLEMAN**
in Donyatt SOM

Joseph **PIPE**
b. 31 Dec. 1795
Broadway SOM
bp. 5 June
1796
Wick yarn
Maker and
Laborer
In prison for
bankruptcy
circa 1834

James PIPE
b. 16 July 1799
Ilminster SOM
bp. 10 Oct.
1800
Ilminster SOM
Journeyman
and Miller

John **PIPE** Sr.
b. 8 Aug. 1801
Sea SOM
bp. 29 June 1802
Ilminster SOM
m. 24 Apr. 1823
Charlotte
JENNINGS in
Membury DEV
Farmer, Laborer

Edward **PIPE**
b. 29 Sept. 1803
bp. 22 Dec. 1803
Broadway
Meeting
Independent
Broadway SOM

Orlando **PIPE**
b. 3 Jan. 1806
bp. 28 Apr. 1806
Broadway
Meeting
Independent,
Broadway SOM
dsp.
bur. 2 May 1856
Donyatt SOM
Yeoman

Prepared by S T Moore and J N Steiner

The John Sr. and Charlotte Jennings Pipe Family

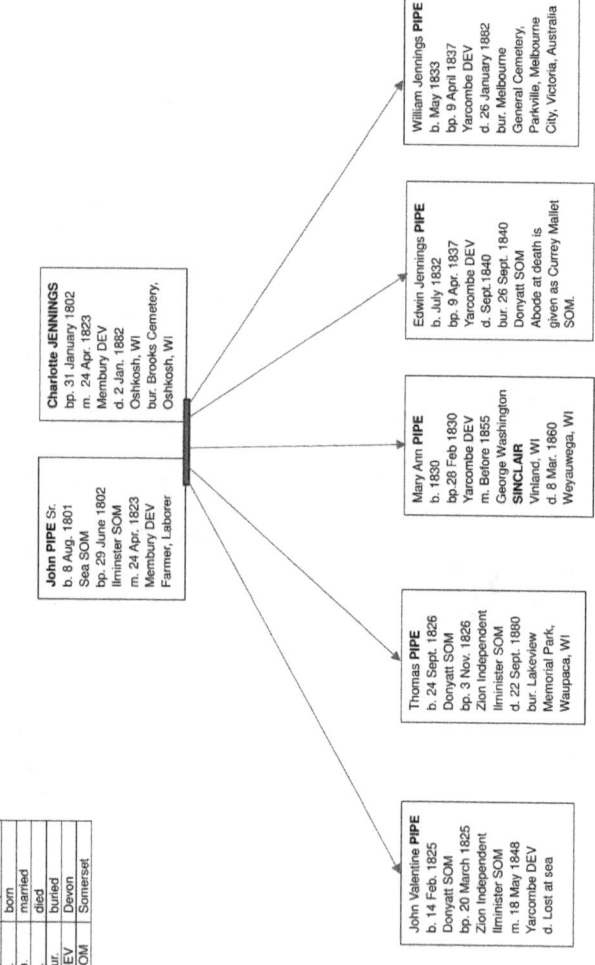

Legend

bp.	baptized
b.	born
m.	married
d.	died
bur.	buried
DEV	Devon
SOM	Somerset

John PIPE Sr.
b. 8 Aug. 1801
Sea SOM
bp. 29 June 1802
Ilminster SOM
m. 24 Apr. 1823
Membury DEV
Farmer, Laborer

Charlotte JENNINGS
bp. 31 January 1802
m. 24 Apr. 1823
Membury DEV
d. 2 Jan. 1882
Oshkosh, WI
bur. Brooks Cemetery,
Oshkosh, WI

John Valentine PIPE
b. 14 Feb. 1825
Donyatt SOM
bp. 20 March 1825
Zion Independent
Ilminster SOM
m. 18 May 1848
Yarcombe DEV
d. Lost at sea

Thomas PIPE
b. 24 Sept. 1826
Donyatt SOM
bp. 3 Nov. 1826
Zion Independent
Ilminster SOM
d. 22 Sept. 1880
bur. Lakeview
Memorial Park,
Waupaca, WI

Mary Ann PIPE
b. 1830
bp. 28 Feb 1830
Yarcombe DEV
m. Before 1855
George Washington
SINCLAIR
Vinland, WI
d. 8 Mar. 1860
Weyauwega, WI

Edwin Jennings PIPE
b. July 1832
bp. 9 Apr. 1837
Yarcombe DEV
d. Sept.1840
bur. 26 Sept. 1840
Donyatt SOM
Abode at death is
given as Currey Mallet
SOM.

William Jennings PIPE
b. May 1833
bp. 9 April 1837
Yarcombe DEV
d. 26 January 1882
bur. Melbourne
General Cemetery,
Parkville, Melbourne
City, Victoria, Australia

Prepared by ST Moore and JN Steiner

St. John the Baptist Church in Yarcombe, Devon, England

Four Generations

The Stickland Family Tombstone

Introduction

The history of St. John the Baptist Church in Yarcombe, Devon, England, reaches back to the 1300s, according to *The Church of St. John the Baptist, Yarcombe, Devon* by Donald Tapster (1928-2012), who was a reader in the church for 37 years. Tapster details renovations of this scared space over generations. As I walk through the churchyard, I wonder about the generations of Yarcombe people, especially the Stickland family, who were baptized, married, and buried in St. John the Baptist Churchyard. I have included in blue Elizabeth **STICKLAND PIPE**'s relationship to family members identified.

This leaning tombstone in St. John the Baptist Churchyard in Yarcombe, Devon, England, marks the burial spot for the John Stickland family of Hay Farm.

On the north side of the churchyard, a leaning tombstone bears the name of John **STICKLAND** of Hay (Farm) who died on December 9, 1809, at the age of 61. In *Devon, England, Church of England Deaths and Burials, 1813-1920*, John **STICKLAND**'s baptism was recorded on June 2, 1746. His parents are listed as John and Mary **STICKLAND (great-grandparents)**. Although there is a slight discrepancy in age (65 from church records and 61 from the tombstone), this likely is the John **STICKLAND** of Hay Farm who is buried in the family plot with the leaning tombstone.

John STICKLAND (grandfather) of Hay Farm (1746-1809)

STICKLAND married Betty (Elizabeth) **SMITH (grandmother)** on October 25, 1791, in St. John the Baptist Church. John is listed as a "Bachelor," and Betty is listed as "likewise Spinster." The vicar is identified as William Palmer. Witnesses to the wedding are Robert **SPILLER** and Joan **SPILLER**. Their marriage record is found in the *Marriage Register Book for Parish of Yarcombe in the County of Devon*. John died on December 9, 1809, and is remembered on the **STICKLAND** Family Tombstone.

The Will of John **STICKLAND** (grandfather) (1746-1809) is found in *England & Wales Prerogative Court of Canterbury Wills, 1384-1858* dated 28 February 1806 and proved 22 June 1810. (See Appendix A.) **STICKLAND** bequeaths to his son John **STICKLAND** (uncle) (his heirs and assigns) "for ever all my messuage (buildings) and lands which I have in fee simple within the parish of Yarcombe aforesaid or elsewhere." Fee simple is a real estate term that means John **STICK-LAND** (grandfather) (1746-1809) owned lands and buildings, maintained them, and paid taxes on them.

Guardians, trustees, and joint executors of John **STICKLAND**'s will are identified as joint executors in trust:

- Robert **SPILLER** of Underdown Farm (Yarcombe, Devon) (See Letter Number 9.)
- Henry **SPILLER** of Knightshayne Farm (Yarcombe, Devon)
- Robert **SMITH** of Stockland (Devon)

John STICKLAND (uncle) (1794-1850)

John **STICKLAND** (uncle) (1794-1850), who inherited all his father's buildings and lands, was baptized in St. John the Baptist Church on June 24, 1794, according to *Devon, England, Church of England Baptisms, Marriages, and Burials*. John's parents are listed as John and Elizabeth **STICKLAND** (grandparents). *St. John the Baptist Church Burial Record* notes his burial date as April 18, 1850. His name does not appear on the family tombstone. John **STICKLAND** (uncle) (1794-1850) likely had his own family plot that is no longer marked with a tombstone.

John **STICKLAND**'s (uncle) (1794-1850) left all his lands and buildings to his nephew, Thomas (brother), son of his brother, Thomas **STICKLAND** (father). John **STICKLAND**'s (uncle) will, proved 30 July 1850, is found in *England & Wales, Prerogative Court of Canterbury Wills, 1384-1858*. (See Appendix D.)

Thomas STICKLAND *(brother) (1831-1853)*

Thomas **STICKLAND** (brother) died of natural causes at age 21 in 1853. Thomas did not have any children. According to John **STICKLAND**'s (uncle) will (proved 30 July 1850), Elizabeth Stickland **PIPE** and Mary **STICKLAND** (sister), inherit all lands and buildings (See Appendix D). Thomas **STICKLAND**'s name does not appear on the family tombstone.

Other Family Members Identified on the Stickland Tombstone

In the will of the elder John **STICKLAND** (grandfather) (1746-1809), other children are identified. Their baptisms at St. John the Baptist Church are all found in *Devon, England, Church of England Baptisms, Marriages, and Burials, 1538-1812*. They all appear on the family tombstone:

- Mary (aunt) (1792-1810) was baptized on November 28, 1792. Mary's parents are listed as John and Elizabeth **STICKLAND** (grandparents). Mary died on October 12, 1810, just seven weeks before her 18th birthday.

- Elizabeth (aunt) (1795-1812) was baptized on September 8, 1795. Elizabeth's parents are listed as John and Elizabeth **STICKLAND** (grandparents). Elizabeth died in 1812 at age 17. Elizabeth is not cited on the spreadsheet of parish deaths on the Yarcombe Home Page (http://www.yarcombe.net/AncestralSearches.html), but she is listed on the family tombstone.

- Thomas (father) (1798-1836) was baptized on September 16, 1798. Thomas's parents are listed as John and Elizabeth **STICKLAND** (grandparents). Thomas was buried on September 1, 1836, at age 38 in St. John the Baptist Churchyard. His death is recorded in the *England & Wales Civil Registration Death Index, 1837-1915*. His name was recently revealed after the tombstone was cleaned and straightened.

- Robert (uncle) (1801-1831) was baptized on April 3, 1801. Robert's parents are listed as John and Elizabeth **STICKLAND** (grandparents). Robert died on April 25, 1831, at age 30. The will of Robert STICKLAND was proved on 19 March 1832, according to *England & Wales, Prerogative Court of Canterbury Wills, 1384-1858*. (See Appendix B.)

Any posthumous child or children were also provided for in the will. No other children have been located at the time of this writing.

Thomas STICKLAND (1798-1836) and Elizabeth WALL (father and mother)

Thomas **STICKLAND** (father) (1798-1836), son of John (1746-1809), married Elizabeth **WALL** (mother) from Chard on May 13, 1824, according to *Chard, Somerset, England Marriages* (D/P/CHARD 2/1/17).

Thomas and Elizabeth **WALL STICKLAND**'s (parents) children are found in *England, Select Births and Christenings, 1538-1975* and *Devon, England, Church of England Deaths and Burials, 1813-1920*:

Elizabeth Wall Stickland Bartlett

- **John STICKLAND** (brother) (1826-1905), pictured below with his wife, was baptized in St. John the Baptist Church in Yarcombe, Devon, England, on January 12, 1826, according to *England, Select Births and Christenings, 1538-1975.* He was

married in St. John the Baptist Church in Yarcombe, Devon, on April 15, 1847, to Elizabeth **MATHEWS**, whose father is listed as John **MATHEWS** (Yeoman). **STICKLAND**'s father is listed as Thomas **STICKLAND** (Yeoman). John is listed as a "bachelor of age" from Yarcombe. Elizabeth is listed as a "spinster of age" from Yarcombe. Witnesses to the wedding are John **WALE** (**WALL**) and Gary (?) **MATHEWS**. **STICKLAND**'s burial date of June 10, 1905, is found in *Devon, England, Church of England Deaths and Burials, 1813-1920*. He is buried in the Anglican Church of Holy Cross Churchyard in Highampton, Devon.

Two of John and Elizabeth **MATHEWS STICKLAND**'s children are pictured below, Annie (left, shown in 1875) and Emily:

Annie **STICKLAND** (niece) writes Letter Number 80 to her Uncle Thomas and Aunt Elizabeth **STICKLAND PIPE**. The picture on the right is her sister, five-year-old Emily **STICKLAND** (niece).

- Elizabeth **STICKLAND PIPE** (1828-1918) was christened in Yarcombe, Devon, England, on August 12, 1828. The record summary sheet notes her parents as Thomas and Elizabeth **STICKLAND**. In May 1848, Elizabeth **STICKLAND** married John Valentine **PIPE** (pictured in the middle on the next page) in St. John the Baptist Church in Yarcombe. Elizabeth left Liverpool, England, and arrived in New York on May 18, 1850, with

Elizabeth
Stickland Pipe

John
Valentine Pipe

Thomas
Pipe

her husband John Valentine **PIPE**, their two children, 2-year-old John Stickland and infant Tom, and her brother-in-law, Thomas **PIPE**. John Valentine **PIPE** was lost at sea in March 1854. After her husband's death, Elizabeth **STICKLAND PIPE** married her brother-in-law, Thomas **PIPE**, in the Town of Vinland, Winnebago County, Wisconsin, on June 24, 1855. Elizabeth **STICKLAND PIPE** died in 1918 at age 91. She is buried in Lakeside Memorial Park, Waupaca, Wisconsin, with her second husband Thomas. (See Chapter 1.)

- **Thomas STICKLAND (brother)** (1831-1853) was baptized on August 14, 1831, in Pendomer, Somerset, England. **STICKLAND** married in the Anglican church of The Blessed Virgin Mary, Buckland St. Mary, Somerset, on June 5, 1851, Jemima Maria Shire **WYATT**, whose father is listed as John **WYATT** (Yeoman). **STICKLAND's** father listed on the marriage record is Thomas **STICKLAND** (Yeoman). Thomas is listed as a 20-year-old bachelor from Yarcombe. Jemina is listed as a "spinster of full age" from Buckland, St. Mary, Somerset. Witnesses to the wedding are Levi **DOBLE** and Elizabeth Shire **WYATT**. **STICKLAND's** burial date, found in the *Devon, England, Church of England Deaths and Burials, 1813-1920,* is May 27, 1853, at age 22. Thomas is buried in St. John the Baptist Church in Yarcombe, Devon. His name does not appear on the family tombstone.

Mary **(sister)** (1834-Unknown) was born in 1834 in Pendomer, Somerset. Mary writes Letters Number 81, 84, and 86 to her sister Elizabeth **STICKLAND PIPE** in Chapter 8.

Conclusion

The Stickland family tombstone has been cleaned and straightened. Visitors can now read the tombstone and get to know Elizabeth **STICKLAND PIPE**'s paternal great-grandparents, grandparents, aunts and uncles, parents, and siblings who worked, prayed, loved, and died in Yarcombe. The **STICKLAND** family tombstone stands tall among other past generations of Yarcombe people who built and renovated St. John the Baptist Church in the heart of the beautifully expansive and historic Yarcombe community.

Mary Stickland

Note: To date, Elizabeth **STICKLAND PIPE**'s direct line of ancestors has been traced back to John **STICKLAND**, who married Mary **COSSENS (COSSINS)** on December 26, 1703, in St. John the Baptist Church in Yarcombe, Devon. They had 6 known children. John **STICKLAND**, born March 8, 1710, is the direct ancestor of John **STICKLAND** (1791-1809) of Hay Farm. The **COSSENS (COSSINS)** family is noted as being one of the substantial landowners along with the **DRAKE** family, who owned a large Estate in Yarcombe, according to Ruth Everitt's book *From Monks to Millennium: A History of Yarcombe Parish.*

Prepared by Dr. Joan Naomi Steiner on July 21, 2025. Record citations and links to the actual records are held in a database at https://www.germanbohemianwisconsin.com/. Parish records are available at Findmypast.com. Many records are also kept in the parish chest located in St. John the Baptist Church.

Photo courtesy of A. G. Real & Son Monumental Masons of Honiton

In

Memory of John Stickland

of Hay in this Parish who died Dec 9, 1809

Aged 61 Years

(Continued on next page)

Also of

Mary & Elizabeth Daughters of the

Above by Elizabeth His Wife

Mary Died Oct 12 1810 Aged 18 Years

Elizabeth Died July (?)0 1812

Aged 17 Years

A tender Husband of two Daughters dear

Are now bereft of life lie sleeping here

We trust our loss is their eternal gain

To be with Christ and free from grief & pain.

Also of

Robert Stickland Son of the

Above Who Died April 25 1831

Aged 30 Years

Son of John & Elizabeth Stickland

Also of Thomas Stickland

Son of the above Died Sept 1st 1836

Aged 38 years

A Husband kind a friend so dear

A tender Father layeth here

In Love he lived in peace he died

His Life was be gd but God denied

The Stickland Family Tombstone in St. John the Baptist Churchyard
in Yarcombe, Devon

All events occurred in Yarcombe, Devon, unless stated otherwise.

Prepared by ST Moore and JN Steiner

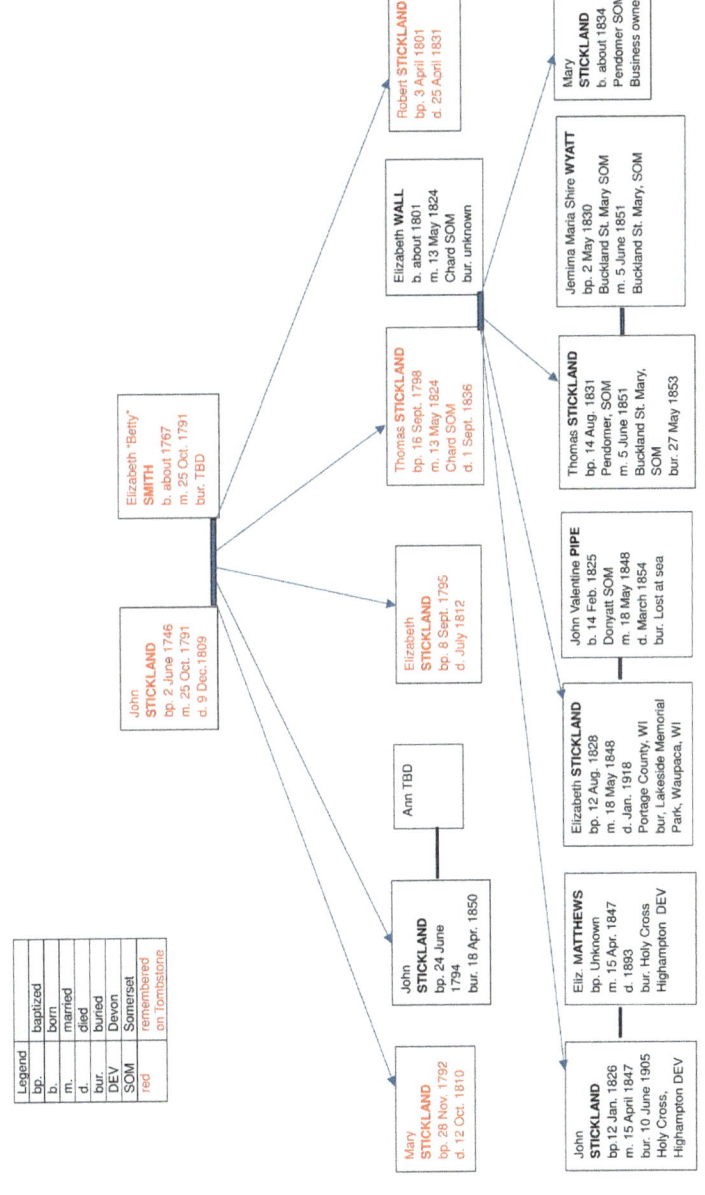

Legend	
bp.	baptized
b.	born
m.	married
d.	died
bur.	buried
DEV	Devon
SOM	Somerset
red	remembered on Tombstone

John
STICKLAND
bp. 2 June 1746
m. 25 Oct. 1791
d. 9 Dec.1809

Elizabeth "Betty"
SMITH
b. about 1767
m. 25 Oct. 1791
bur. TBD

Robert STICKLAND
bp. 3 April 1801
d. 25 April 1831

Elizabeth WALL
b. about 1801
m. 13 May 1824
Chard SOM
bur. unknown

Mary
STICKLAND
b. about 1834
Pendomer SOM
Business owner

Thomas STICKLAND
bp. 16 Sept. 1798
m. 13 May 1824
Chard SOM
d. 1 Sept. 1836

Jemima Maria Shire WYATT
bp. 2 May 1830
Buckland St. Mary SOM
m. 5 June 1851
Buckland St. Mary, SOM

Elizabeth
STICKLAND
bp. 8 Sept. 1795
d. July 1812

Thomas STICKLAND
bp. 14 Aug. 1831
Pendomer, SOM
m. 5 June 1851
Buckland St. Mary, SOM
bur. 27 May 1853

John Valentine PIPE
b. 14 Feb. 1825
Donyatt SOM
m. 18 May 1848
d. March 1854
bur. Lost at sea

Ann TBD

Elizabeth STICKLAND
bp. 12 Aug. 1828
m. 18 May 1848
d. Jan. 1918
Portage County, WI
bur. Lakeside Memorial
Park, Waupaca, WI

Mary
STICKLAND
bp. 28 Nov. 1792
d. 12 Oct. 1810

John
STICKLAND
bp. 24 June
1794
bur. 18 Apr. 1850

Eliz. MATTHEWS
bp. Unknown
m. 15 Apr. 1847
d. 1893
bur. Holy Cross
Highampton DEV

John
STICKLAND
bp.12 Jan. 1826
m. 15 April 1847
bur. 10 June 1905
Holy Cross,
Highampton DEV

Lithograph of the City of Glasgow *by Edward Duncan*

Chapter 1

How the Sinking of the City of Glasgow *in 1854*
Changed the Lives of One Early Settler's Family
in the Town of Vinland, Winnebago County, Wisconsin

Chapter 1 introduces Elizabeth Stickland Pipe, her first husband, John Valentine Pipe, and her second husband, Thomas Pipe, who is John Valentine's brother. All are from southwestern England. This chapter provides family background, as well as the actions that change the course of their lives. The letter collection begins in 1851, shortly after Thomas Pipe and John Valentine Pipe's wife, Elizabeth Stickland Pipe, and two children, John Stickland and Tom, immigrate to America.

**John Valentine Pipe
circa 1848**

**Elizabeth Stickland Pipe
circa 1875**

**Thomas Pipe
circa 1875[1]**

Introduction

The ill-fated steamship *City of Glasgow* embarked from Liverpool, England, on March 1, 1854. The *City of Glasgow* is presumed to have struck an iceberg and sunk while crossing the North Atlantic Ocean, taking 480 souls.[2] News of this catastrophic event reached the town of Vinland, Winnebago County, Wisconsin, where Thomas Pipe had to have felt ripples of change that would alter his life forever because onboard the *City of Glasgow* was his brother, John Valentine Pipe, a cabin passenger.

According to family letters, in 1854 John Valentine Pipe traveled from Greece Center, Monroe County, New York, to Devon and Somerset, England, to settle some family business. His wife and children remained in Greece Center.

Looking Back

Both brothers, Thomas Pipe[3] and John Valentine Pipe,[4] were born in Donyatt in the county of Somerset, England, in 1826 and 1825, respectively. In May of 1848, John Valentine married Elizabeth Stickland.[5] Elizabeth was christened on August 12, 1828, in Yarcombe, Devon, England.[6] While living in England, John Valentine and Elizabeth brought two children into the world: John Stickland[7] and Tom.[8]

In early 1850, Thomas Pipe and John Valentine Pipe's family traveled to Liverpool, England. They boarded the ship *Empire State* and set sail for America to begin their new lives. The family appears on the passenger list: Thomas Pipe, age 23; John Pipe, age 25; Elizabeth (nee Stickland), age 22; John Stickland, age 2; and Tom, noted as an infant. The Pipe family arrived in New York on May 18, 1850. Below is an excerpt from the passenger list for the ship *Empire State* listing the Pipe family members.[9]

Both brothers are found in the *1850 U.S. Census* as living in Greece Center, Monroe County, New York. The census was taken in September 1850. Listed below is Thomas Pipe, age 24. He is working as a farm laborer for John Davis (age 54) who was born in New York. The Davis entry includes the following members: John's wife, age 50; his son Edwin Frank, age 22; and his daughter Mary, age 22. Truman Stoddard (age 16) is also listed as a laborer living with the family. The value of the Davis farm listed in the 1850 Census is $7,680.[10]

John V. Pipe and his family are found in the *1850 U.S. Census* as farmers in Greece Center, Monroe County, New York. The excerpt below shows that John, age 25, is working as a farmer. His wife Elizabeth is age 23. John L. (S.) is 2 years old, and Tom is 10 months old.[11] (Baby Tom was only 7 months old when the family arrived in New York after making the trip across the Atlantic Ocean.)

Thomas Pipe Moves Westward to Wisconsin

Thomas Pipe left Greece Center, New York, after September, 1850, and before November 8, 1853. Thomas is found in naturalization records in Winnebago County, Wisconsin, where he made his Declaration of Intent to become a citizen of the United States on November 8, 1853.[12] Below is his Declaration of Intent:

John Valentine Pipe Travels Across the Atlantic Ocean

Letter Number 11, dated February 5, 1854, reveals that John Valentine left Greece Center, Monroe County, New York, for England before February 5 to settle family business. C. Pillar (Charlotte Jennings Pipe Pillar), Thomas and John Valentine's mother, had also immigrated to Vinland with her second husband and family. In the letter, Charlotte identifies herself as a sister who lives in Vinland. She writes to her siblings in England. The letter is transcribed, in part, below:

Transcription of Letter Number 11:

> Vinland Feb 5/ 1854
>
> My dear Brother and Sister
>
> Tom [Thomas Pipe] has just such a letter from Elizabeth [Stickland Pipe] saying my dear John [Valentine Pipe] left her for England and this I say I trust he is arrived same to you [siblings] and that he will settle everything comfortable and [re]turn safe to his dear wife [Elizabeth Stickland Pipe] and children [John Stickland, Tom, and Frank]. I can only comfort him by prayer to an all wise and good God.[13]

Sadly, John Valentine Pipe is lost at sea on his return.

According to Letter Number 19, Elizabeth Coleman Jennings remarks that Thomas Pipe and his mother, Charlotte Jennings Pipe Pillar, had traveled from Vinland, Wisconsin, to Greece Center, New York, to assist John Valentine's family and offer comfort for their great loss. In Letter Number 20, Thomas Pipe tells his Uncle John Jennings, who lives in

Devon, England, that Elizabeth Stickland Pipe and her four children, John Stickland, Tom, Frank, and Mary Elizabeth, in December 1854 returned with Thomas and his mother, Charlotte Jennings Pipe Pillar, to the town of Vinland. Letter Number 21 is a note written later by a descendant that has been transcribed and gives some details of their marriage:

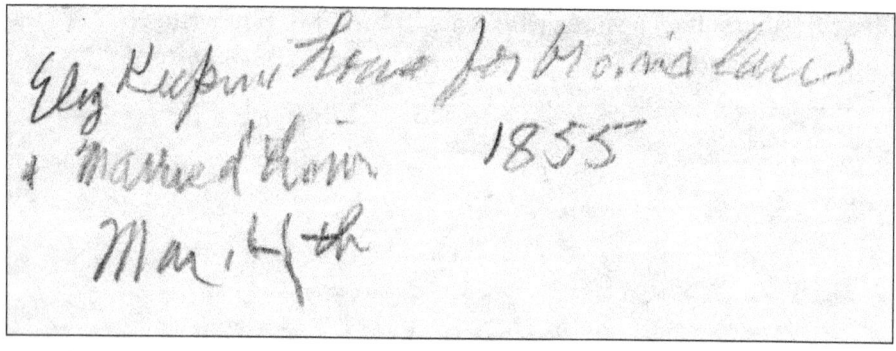

Transcription of Letter Number 21:

> Elizabeth [Stickland Pipe] is keeping house for her brother-in-law [Thomas Pipe] and married him 1855 May 4.[14]

In Letter Number 25, however, Thomas Pipe states he and Elizabeth Stickland Pipe were married on June 24, 1855.

Thomas and his brother's wife Elizabeth, now his wife, and John Valentine Pipe's children, now his stepchildren, are found in the *1855 Wisconsin Census* for Vinland.[15]

In the *1855 Wisconsin Census* shown on the next page, Thomas Pipe is head of household in Vinland. We see four males and two females in his household. The four males include John Valentine Pipe's sons who were born in England, John S (Stickland), and Tom, and his son, Frank,[16] who was born in New York. Thomas is the fourth male.

The two females in the *1855 Wisconsin Census* are Elizabeth Stickland Pipe and John Valentine's daughter, Mary Elizabeth,[17] who also was born in New York.

The Thomas Pipe family made their home in Vinland for the next several years. During this time, Thomas established his farm. While living in Vinland, he and his wife gave birth to William Edwin.[18] Daughter Florence was born in 1860 in Farmington, Waupaca County, Wisconsin.[19] Thomas is said to have loved and cared for his brother's children as he did his own.

The Thomas Pipe Family Moves to Waupaca County

By 1860 Thomas and his family moved to Waupaca County, Wisconsin. Perhaps they wanted to start their lives anew. They certainly must have been drawn to Waupaca's pristine beauty with what is today called the Chain O' Lakes. The *1860 U.S. Census* below shows that Thomas is a farmer with $4,000 in real estate property and $400 in personal property.[20]

In July/August of 1863, Thomas Pipe registered for the U.S. Civil War draft in Waupaca.[21] He is listed as a 37-year-old resident of Waupaca. Below is the record that shows his registration:

Looking Ahead

Although the Thomas Pipe family left Vinland and moved to the town of Farmington, Waupaca County, Wisconsin, in the late 1850s, more than 170 years ago, their memory is still alive today, especially in the hearts of several Vinland residents.

In December 2023, Thomas Pipe's great-great-grandson purchased a home in Vinland. At the time, he did not know his ancestors had once lived in Vinland. He remarked to his family that Vinland just felt like home to him. He only recently learned that his great- great-grandfather, Thomas Pipe, and his great-great-great grandmother, Charlotte Jennings Pipe Pillar, had chosen Vinland for their home in the early 1850s. Vinland is indeed a place that he and his family now call home. Learning about his ancestors has given him a deeper understanding of his sense of place and his endearing feelings for his new home in Vinland.

Note:

An earlier version of this chapter was written for the town of Vinland's 175th Anniversary.

[1] Privately held by Marlene Sannes [ADDRESS FOR PRIVATE USE,] Amherst, Wisconsin.

[2] Thomas Clark, *Let Glasgow Flourish: The Disappearance of the SS City of Glasgow* (Distinctive Press: Monee, Illinois, 2019) 254-264.

[3] "England, Births and Christenings, 1538-1975", database, *FamilySearch* (https://www.familysearch.org/ark:/61903/1:1:J3Z1-QXN : 4 February 2023), Thomas Pipe, 1826.

[4] "England, Births and Christenings, 1538-1975", database, *FamilySearch* (https://www.familysearch.org/ark:/61903/1:1:NPJ7-CLK : 4 February 2023), John Valentine Pipe, 1825.

[5] Yarcombe Parish (Yarcombe, England). Parish Registers p. 24, Pope [Pipe]-Stickland marriage (1848); Southwest Heritage Trust: https://www.findmypast.com/transcript?id=GBPRS%FDEV%FMar%2F224687%2F27T-AB=THIS . (accessed August 23, 2025).

[6] "England, Devon, Parish Registers (Devon Record Office), 1529-1974", FamilySearch (https://www.familysearch.org/ark:/61903/1:1:6NXB-RP2X : Thu Mar 07 00:41:50 UTC 2024), Entry for Elizabeth Stickland and Thomas, 1828.

[7] "Wisconsin, County Naturalization Records, 1807-1992", *FamilySearch* (https://www.familysearch.org/ark:/61903/1:1:6FNC-6QRM : Sun Mar 10 18:14:37 UTC 2024), Entry for John Stickland Pipe, 1 Dec 1913. [Birth listed as March 1, 1848]

[8] "England and Wales, Birth Registration Index, 1837-2008," database, *FamilySearch* (https://familysearch.org/ark:/61903/1:1:2XSF-ZNV : 1 October 2014), Tom Pipe, 1849; from "England & Wales Births, 1837-2006," database, *findmypast* (http://www.findmypast.com : 2012); citing Birth Registration, Chard, Somerset, England, citing General Register Office, Southport, England.

[9] *Registers of Vessels Arriving at the Port of New York from Foreign Ports, 1789-1919*. Microfilm publication M237, rolls 1-95; NAID: 6256867; Records of the U.S. Customs Service, 1745 - 1997, Record Group 36; National Archives at New York, NY; Ancestry.com. *New York, U.S., Arriving Passenger and Immigration Lists, 1820-1850* [database on-line]. Lehi, UT, USA: Ancestry.com Operations Inc, 2003; (accessed August 23, 2025).

[10] Seventh Census of the United States, 1850; (National Archives Microfilm Publication M432, 1009 rolls); Records of the Bureau of the Census, Record Group 29; National Archives, Washington, D.C.; Ancestry.com. *1850 United States Federal Census* [database on-line]. Lehi, UT, USA: Ancestry.com Operations, Inc., 2009. Images reproduced by FamilySearch; (accessed August 23, 2025).

[11] Ibid. Seventh Census of the United States, 1850.

[12] Privately held by Marlene Sannes [ADDRESS FOR PRIVATE USE,] Amherst, Wisconsin.

[13] Ibid.

[14] Ibid.

[15] Jackson, Ron V., Accelerated Indexing Systems, comp. *Wisconsin Census, 1836-1890*. Compiled and digitized by Mr. Jackson and AIS from microfilmed schedules of the U.S. Federal Decennial Census, territorial/state censuses, and/or census substitutes; Ancestry.com. *Wisconsin, U.S., Compiled Census and Census Substitutes Index, 1836-1890* [database on-line]. Lehi, UT, USA: Ancestry.com Operations Inc, 1999; (accessed August 23, 2025).

[16] Findagrave.com, digital images (https://www.findagrave.com/memorial/103002750/Frank Pipe: accessed 25 August 2025), photograph, gravestone for Frank Pipe (February 1852- 1900), Waupaca, Waupaca County, Wisconsin.

[17] "United States, Census, 1880", FamilySearch (https://www.familysearch.org/ark:/61903/1:1:MNH8-W62 : Sun Jan 19 19:21:25 UTC 2025), Entry for Thomas Pipe and Elizebeth Pipe, 1880.[Mary Elizabeth Pipe was born in New York about 1854.]

[18] "Many Attend Funeral," *The Stevens Point Journal*, 29 April 1936, citing p. 9. [William Pipe was born on March 25, 1856.]

[19] Findagrave.com, digital images (https://www.findagrave.com/memorial/83139880/florence_ida-mccunn: accessed 24 August 2025), photograph, gravestone for Florence Pipe McCunn (5 January 1860 – 10 January 1889), Allouez, Brown County, Wisconsin.

[20] "United States, Census, 1860," *FamilySearch* (https://www.familysearch.org/ark:/61903/1:1:MW9D-2W1 : Tue Jul 09 00:30:09 UTC 2024), Entry for Thos Pipe and Elizabeth Pipe, 1860.

[21] National Archives and Records Administration (NARA); Washington, D.C.; *Consolidated Lists of Civil War Draft Registration Records (Provost Marshal General's Bureau; Consolidated Enrollment Lists, 1863-1865)*; Record Group: *110, Records of the Provost Marshal General's Bureau (Civil War)*; Collection Name: *Consolidated Enrollment Lists, 1863-1865 (Civil War Union Draft Records)*; NAI: *4213514*; Archive Volume Number: *3 of 3*; Ancestry.com. *U.S., Civil War Draft Registrations Records, 1863-1865* [database on-line]. Lehi, UT, USA: Ancestry.com Operations, Inc., 2010; (accessed August 23. 2025).

Chapter 2

Greece Center, Monroe County, New York
1851 - 1854

Chapter 2 includes letters dated 1851 to 1854 while the Pipe family lived in Greece Center, Monroe County, New York, near Rochester. Six letters are between the Pipes and John Valentine's aunt and uncle, William and Elizabeth Coleman Jennings. Six letters are from solicitors and agents who discuss Elizabeth Stickland Pipe's legacy from her deceased Uncle John Stickland of Yarcombe, Devon. One letter is from Robert Spiller, trustee of John Stickland's Will proved 30th July 1850. (See Appendix D.)

William Jennings receives letters from both nephews, William Jennings Pipe and Thomas Pipe. Thomas Pipe writes to John Valentine Pipe with news of an available farm in town of Vinland, Winnebago County, Wisconsin. One letter is from Elizabeth Stickland Pipe's mother in England. One is from John Valentine Pipe's mother in the town of Vinland, Winnebago County, Wisconsin. A letter from Liverpool, Lancashire County, answers an inquiry about John Valentine Pipe's whereabouts.

The letters reveal that John Valentine Pipe sailed to England to settle his wife's inheritance from her uncle, John Stickland. John Valentine Pipe sailed the *City of Glasgow* on his return. He was one of 480 souls lost at sea when the ship disappeared. The chapter ends with grief-stricken family on both sides of the Atlantic scrambling to figure out what to do.

Letter Number 1

Date: 18 March 1851
Writer: Edwin Scranton
Recipient: William Jennings
Sent from: Rochester, Monroe County, New York, USA
Sent to: Northay Farm, Whitestaunton, Chard,
                 Somerset County, England

Key Ideas

- Edwin Scranton tells Willam Jennings that John Valentine and Elizabeth Stickland Pipe came to his office to appoint William Jennings as their attorney.
- William Jennings is to collect a £300 legacy left for Elizabeth Stickland Pipe at Dommett & Canning, Solicitors in Chard, Somerset. (See Appendix D.)
- In an earlier letter Mr. Dommett told John Valentine and Elizabeth Stickland Pipe they must make out a deed of release and go to the foreign counsel in New York and hand it to them to claim the legacy.
- Edwin Scranton, however, advises that this would be expensive and not very safe. Instead, he recommends Mr. Dommett prepare the power of attorney for William Jennings so he can act on the Pipes' behalf. The power of attorney is enclosed with the letter.
- Edwin Scranton advises William Jennings to consult someone in England who can advise him. He tells William to follow that person's directions.
- William Jennings can execute the deed of release after he receives the total amount of money coming to John Valentine and Elizabeth Stickland Pipe.
- William Jennings is to inform Edwin Scranton immediately when he receives the money owed to the Pipes. Edwin Scranton will receive the draft for the amount and send it to the Pipes.
- Another option is for William Jennings to buy a draft on a New

York bank at some town near him in England.

- Edwin Scranton says that John Valentine and Elizabeth Stickland Pipe live about nine miles from Rochester, New York. The Pipes will call on Scranton occasionally until he hears from William Jennings regarding this matter.
- Edwin Scranton tells William Jennings to contact him immediately if there is any problem.

———————

Rochester State of
New York March 18, 1851

Mr Jennings

Dear Sir

Mr. & Mrs. [John Valentine & Elizabeth Stickland] Pipe, living [in Greece Center, Monroe County, New York] near this city [Rochester, Monroe County, New York] have come to my office and this day constituted you their attorney to collect of William Dommett Esq. a legacy left for them, and which they have received word is ready to be paid. Mr. Dommett [Solicitor of Dommett & Canning in Chard, Somerset, England] wrote them that they must make out a Deed and go to New York and execute it before the Foreign Consul and send it to him. But as this would be very expensive, and would not be as safe for them, I have advised them to send you a power of attorney to act for them. Which power of attorney accompanies this letter. On receiving these papers, it may be well for you to consult some person who can direct you aright, and follow his advice. You can execute the Deed, after having received the money for Mr. & Mrs. [John Valentine & Elizabeth Stickland] Pipe. After receiving the amount coming to them you will immediately inform me how much it is. And I will get them a draft on you for the amount due them, and send it forward for payment, unless you can buy a draft on New York at some town near you of which you must inform me. Mr. & Mrs. [John Valentine & Elizabeth Stickland] Pipe reside about 9 miles from the city and will occasionally call on me until I hear from you. If there is any difficulty in collecting the amount inform me at once

Awaiting your reply I am your obedient servant.

Edwin Scranton

Letter Number 1, Page 1

Rochester State of
New York, March 18, 185_

Wm Jennings

Dear Sir—

Mr. & Mrs. Pipe, living near this city have come to my office and this day constituted you their attorney to collect of William Dommet Esq. a legacy left for them, and which they have received word is ready to be paid. Mr. Dommet wrote them that they must make out a Deed and go to New York and execute it before the foreign Consul, and send it to him. But as this would be very expensive, and would not be at safe for them, I have advised them to send you a power of Attorney to act for them. Which power of Attorney accompanies this Letter. On receiving these papers, it may be well for you to consult some person who can direct you aright, and follow his advise. You can execute the Deed, after having received the money for Mr. and Mrs. Pipe. After receiving the amount coming to them, you will immediately inform me, how much it is, and I will get their Draft on you for the amount due them, and send it forward for payment, unless you can buy a Draft on New York at some town near you— of which you must inform me. Mr. & Mrs. Pipe reside about 9 miles from this city, and

Letter Number 1, Page 2

will occasionally call on me untill I hear
from you. If there is any difficulty in collecting the amt. inform me at once —
Awaiting your reply I am your ob't serv'

Edwin Scranton

1851

Letter Number 2

Date: 30 June 1851
Writer: Edwin Scranton
Recipient: William Jennings
Sent from: Rochester, Monroe County, New York, USA
Sent to: Northay Farm, Whitestaunton, Chard, Somerset County, England

Key Ideas

- Edwin Scranton receives a letter dated May 4 from Dommett & Canning with a deed of release enclosed.
- The deed of release is for the £300 legacy that was left for John Valentine's wife, Elizabeth Stickland Pipe. They are to sign the deed of release and execute it properly and return it to Dommett & Canning in Chard, Somerset.
- Dommett & Canning will send the money to the Pipes when they draw for that amount payable in a London bank.
- William Jennings has not acknowledged Edwin Scranton's letter. He does not know if William Jennings will act on behalf of John Valentine and Elizabeth Pipe.
- Edwin Scranton sends William Jennings the deed of release and a draft on Dommett & Canning for the total amount due.
- John Valentine and Elizabeth Stickland Pipe do not want William Jennings to give the deed of release to Dommett & Canning until the whole £300 is paid. Once the deed of release is given to Dommett and Canning, the Pipes have no claim to any money left in the legacy.
- Edwin Scranton tells William Jennings the Pipes require him to hold the deed of release until the whole legacy is paid.
- William Jennings can buy a draft for a bank in New York City for the amount he receives and send it to the Pipes in care of Edwin Scranton.
- In a postscript, Edwin Scranton states the Pipes conclude to forward the draft of £100.

- The deed of release remains with Edwin Scranton until he hears from William Jennings.
- Edwin Scranton asks William Jennings if he has gotten his power of attorney recorded.

———————

Rochester, New York, June 30, 1851

William Jennings

Dear Sir – I duly received a letter from Messrs. Dommett and Canning under date 4th May enclosing a Deed of Release of all claim by John [John Valentine] Pipe and wife [Elizabeth Stickland Pipe] to the legacy left her – and requesting that they would sign it and execute it properly and return it to them. That on their receiving it they would send them £100 if they have draft for that amount payable in London etc. I have waited some time expecting that you would acknowledge the receipt of my letter, and say whether you received the papers, and would act for Mr. & Mrs. [John Valentine & Elizabeth Stickland] Pipe or not. Not hearing from you I now send you the Deed of Release and also a Draft on Messrs. Dommett & Canning for £100. Mr. & Mrs. [John Valentine & Elizabeth Stickland] Pipe do not wish you to give the Deed of Release to Messrs. Dommett & Canning until <u>the whole £300 is paid</u> because, as soon as this Deed of Release of Legay is put into their hands, and is once on record, they have no claim for anything except as against Messrs. D. & D. You are therefore required by them to hold this paper until all of the £300 is paid you. If they pay you £100 you can send it to Mr. [John Valentine] Pipe, to my care, by buying a draft on some house in N. [New] York City. Let me hear from you at your earliest convenience.

Mr. William Jennings	Your obedient servant
White Stanton	Edwin Scranton
Somerset, England	

P.S. On second thought Mr. & Mrs. [John Valentine & Elizabeth Stickland] Pipe conclude to forward the draft for £100 and let the release remain with me until they hear from you. They are a great way off, and do not wish to take any steps to make their claim less certain than it is now. The Deed of Release is in my hands properly signed and executed, acknowledge etc., and we wait your reply. We want the whole £300 and interest.

Yours etc.
E.S.

Have you got your Power of Attorney recorded and if you have is not that sufficient to empower you to convey.
E.S.

Letter Number 2, Page 1

Letter Number 2, Page 2

P.S. On second thought,
Mr. teller Pipe conclude to
forward the Dft for £100, &
let the release remain with
me untill they hear from.
you. They are a great way
off, and do not with to take
any steps to make their clam
less certain than it is now.
The Deed of Release is in my
hands properly signed and
executed, acknowledged &c.
and we wait your reply.
We want the whole £300
and interest. Yours &c
E. J.

Letter Number 2, Page 3

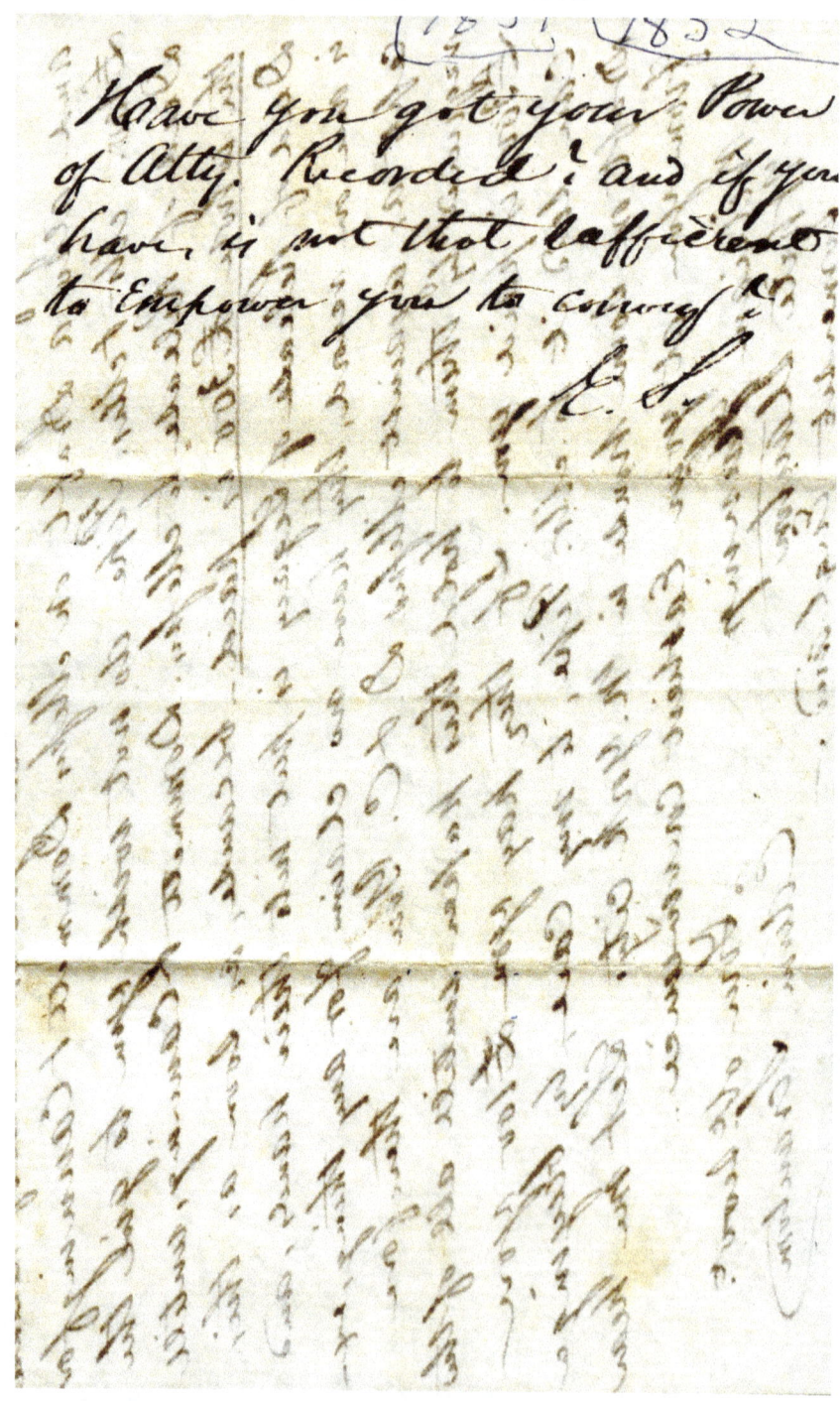

Letter Number 3

Date:	19 August 1851 [stamped 5 September 1851]
Writer:	Edwin Scranton
Recipient:	William Jennings
Sent from:	Rochester, Monroe County, New York, USA
Sent to:	Northay Farm, Whitestaunton, Chard, Somerset County, England

Key Ideas

- Messrs. Dommett & Canning will pay the legacy when the deed of release is received.
- John Valentine Pipe requires that the deed of release be turned over only when the legacy is paid in full.
- William Jennings is the legally constituted attorney representing John Valentine Pipe. William Jennings is authorized to sign papers on behalf of John Valentine and Elizabeth Stickland Pipe.
- William Jennings will receive the money. He is to remit the money to John Valentine Pipe by drafting a New York bank.
- William Jennings is to retain enough for his trouble and expenses.
- The deed of release will be sent to New York agents, Messrs. Phillip Speyer & Co. They will obtain needed signatures of the Governor and the Consul. Then, Edwin Scranton will forward the deed of release to William Jennings.
- The deed of release will be given to Messrs. Dommett & Canning when paid in full.
- The deed of release will be held until full payment is received.
- John Valentine Pipe needs to receive all the money at once to buy a farm.

Rochester Aug 19, 1851

Wm Jennings

Dear Sir, Your letter of July 19th to J. [John Valentine] Pipe is received. Mr. [John Valentine] Pipe has just brought it to me and by it we find that Messrs. Dommett & Canning will, on receiving the Deed [of Release], pay over the money to you. It is the instructions of Mr. [John Valentine] Pipe, and he requires it, that you should not deliver up the Deed <u>until all is paid</u>. In this we do not intend to doubt the veracity or responsibility of Messrs. D&C, but we do not wish to weaken our claim or change it from its present situation. We want it <u>paid</u>, and then we are willing to pass the deed [of release], and not till then. It is singular to us that any Draft at all should be called for from us. <u>You</u> are <u>legally</u> constituted Attorney to John [Valentine] Pipe, and the paying of the money to you, and your receipt for the same is the same to Messrs. Dommett & Canning as if signed by John [Valentine] & Eliz [Elizabeth Stickland] Pipe. We hope therefore to have the money paid to you, and not be required to draw draft, payable in London. After receiving the money, or any part of it, you will please remit it to Mr. J. [John Valentine] Pipe to my care. You can obtain a draft from some responsible Bank payable in New York at 3- or 4-days sight. We expect that you will retain sufficient to pay you for your trouble and expenses. The Deed [of Release] has been sent to my Agents in New York – Messrs. Philip Speyer & Co – who will obtain the necessary signatures of our Governor and the Consul to it – and will then forward it to you, by my directions. On receiving it, you will please direct a letter to me of your success in obtaining the money, and if Messrs. D&C refuse to pay over a part you can hold the Deed [of Release] until all is paid. It is Mr. [John Valentine] Pipe's wish to receive it all at once as he is waiting to buy him a farm, and a part of it would not do. Awaiting your reply, I am

Your obedient servant
Edwin Scranton

Letter Number 3, Page 1

Rochester Aug 19. 1857.

Wm Jennings

Dear Sir – Your letter of July 19th.
to J. Pipe is rec'd. Mr Pipe has just brought it to
me, and by it we find that Messrs. Dommett & Canning will, on receiving the Deed, pay over the money
to you. It is the instructions of Mr. Pipe, and he
requires it, that you should not deliver up
the Deed, untill all is paid. In this, we do
not intend to doubt the veracity or responsibility
of Messrs. D. & C. but we do not wish to weaken our
claim, or change it from its present situation.
We want it paid, and then we are willing to
pass the Deed, and not till then. It is singular
to us that any Draft at all should be called
for from us. You are legally constituted attorney
for John Pipe, and the paying of the money to
you, and your receipt for the same, is
the same to Messrs Dommett & Canning, as if
signed by John & Eliz. Pipe. We hope, therefore
to have the money paid to you, and not be required
to draw drafts payable in London. After receiving the money, or any part of it, you will
please remit it to Mr. J. Pipe to my care. You
can obtain a draft from some responsible Bank
payable in New York at 3 or 4 days sight. We
expect that you will retain sufficient to
pay you for your trouble and expense. (over

Letter Number 3, Page 2

New York — Messrs. Philip Speyer &c. — Who will obtain the necessary signatures of our Governor and the Consul to it — and will then forward it to you, by my directions. On receiving it, you will please direct a letter to me of your success in obtaining the money, and if Messrs. D. & C. refuse to pay over a part, you can hold the Deed untill all is paid. It is Mr. Pipers with to receive it all at once, as he is waiting to buy him a farm, and a part of it would not do. Awaiting your reply, I am

Your obt servant

Edwin Scranton

Letter Number 3, Envelope Front

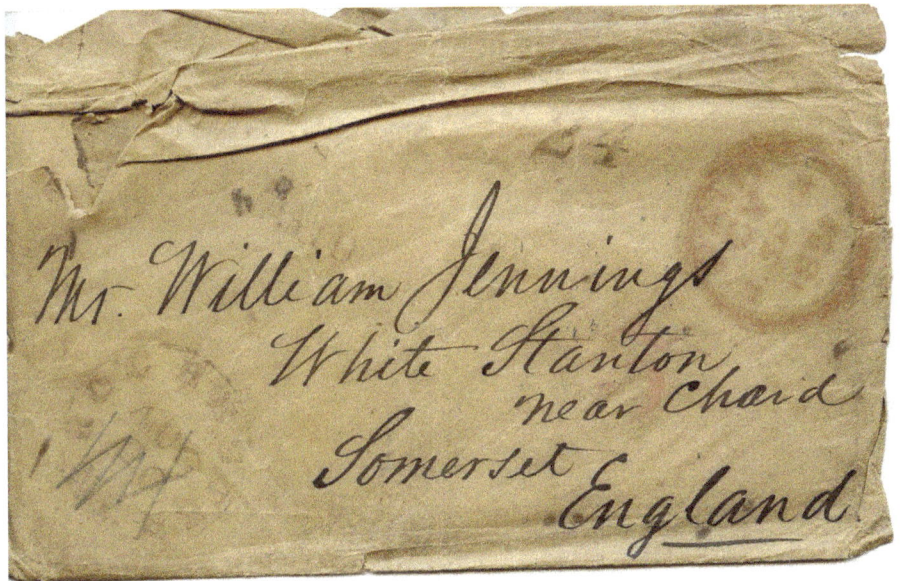

Letter Number 3, Envelope Back

Letter Number 4

Date:	21 October 1851
Writer:	John Valentine & Elizabeth Stickland Pipe
Recipient:	William Jennings
Sent from:	North Greece, Monroe County, New York, USA
Sent to:	Northay Farm, Whitestaunton, Chard, Somerset County, England

Key Ideas

- John Valentine and Elizabeth Stickland Pipe announce that they have received the legacy papers and signed them.
- They ask William Jennings to send the signed papers to Mr. Scranton.
- The Pipes tell William Jennings that they will pay him for his time and expenses.
- They give their love to Elizabeth Coleman Jennings and ask William Jennings to tell her that a letter to her will follow.
- They tell William Jennings that a longer letter will follow.
- The Pipes hope that Mrs. Jennings (Elizabeth Coleman Jennings) and daughter Mary Ann Jennings are well and report that the two Pipe children have colds.
- Elizabeth Stickland Pipe asks whether John Valentine's brother, William Jennings Pipe, is coming to America.

North Greece October 21ˢᵗ/[18]51

Dear Uncle

We received the Legacy and signed it and was glad to do so and we shall I suppose the next letter receive this morning we shall thank you to send it as Mr. Scranton stated in his letter when you send the money we should wish you to pay all the expenses you have <u>been</u> to and what you charge for your trouble. We will write you a long letter next as we are afraid it will <u>weigh</u> too heavy. Please to give my love to Mrs. [Elizabeth Coleman] Jennings and say I shall write a letter to her before long, hope she is well likewise little Mary Ann [Jennings] and we are well with the exception of the two children and they have very bad colds which I think will soon wear off.

From your affectionate nephew I remain

J. E. [John and Elizabeth] Pipe
North Greece
Monroe County
State New York
North America

Have you heard anything if John's brother [William Jennings Pipe] is coming to America or not?

Letter Number 4, Page 1

North Greece October 21st /51

Dear Uncle/

We received the Legacy
and Signed it and was
glad to do so and we shall
I suppose the next letter receive
the money we shall thank
you to send it as Mr Scranton
Stated on his letter when
you send the money we
should wish you to pay
all the expences you have
been too and what you charge
for your trouble we will
write you a long letter next

As we are afraid it will weigh
too heavy please to give my love
to Mrs Jennings and tell say
I shall write a letter to her before
long hope she is well likewise
little mary ann and we are well
with the exception of the two Children
and they have very bad cold's which
I think will soon were off from

Your ever affectionate Nephew & Neice

J & C Pipe

North Grace
Morris County
State New York
North America

directions
for
Mr Swanton

they have you heard any
thing of fathers brother is
coming to America or
not

Letter Number 5

Date:	26 February 1852
Writer:	Edwin Scranton
Recipient:	William Jennings
Sent from:	Rochester, Monroe County, New York, USA
Sent to:	Northay Farm, Whitestaunton, Chard, Somerset County, England

Key Ideas

- Edwin Scranton reminds William Jennings that John Valentine and Elizabeth Stickland Pipe, a long time ago, arranged for their legacy to come to him with instructions on how to receive the money and how to transfer it to them.
- Scranton, along with John Valentine and Elizabeth Stickland Pipe, have been expecting the money for months. Neither party has heard from William Jennings.
- John Valentine Pipe requested Edwin Scranton to write William Jennings for the money immediately.
- Scranton reminds William Jennings that spring is at hand. The Pipes are anxious for the money so they can buy land and permanently settle down.
- John Valentine Pipe has also requested Edwin Scranton to write to Dommett & Canning with the purpose of arriving at the truth of this matter.
- Scranton again tells William Jennings to send the money to him without delay by draft of John Valentine Pipe.

Rochester, February 26, 1852

Mr. Wm. Jennings

Dear Sir

Mr. & Mrs. John [Valentine] Pipe through me a long time ago arranged a legacy coming to them to fall into your hands, instructing you how to receive it, and how to transmit the money. They and myself have for some time been expecting the amount sent forward, and Mr. [John Valentine] Pipe says that some months ago in answer to a letter received from you, he instructed you to forward the money to me. Nothing having been heard of it, or from you since, Mr. [John Valentine] Pipe requested me today to write you and request your immediate answer. The spring is near at hand, and they are anxious to get their money and buy some land and settle down permanently. He has also requested me to write to Messrs. Dommett & Canning, which I shall also do, with a view to arrive at the truth of these matters. Let me hear from you without further delay, and send the money by draft as before instructed, payable to the order of John [Valentine] Pipe and <u>send it to me</u>.

Yours truly
Edwin Scranton

Back is blank except for heading "Legacy in England 1852"

Letter Number 5, Page 1

Rochester Feby. 26 1852.

Mr. Wm Jennings.

Dear Sir. Mr & Mrs. John Pipe
thro' me, a long time ago, arranged a legacy coming
to them to fall into your hands, instructing you
how to receive it, and how to transmit the
money. They and myself have for some time
been Expecting the amount sent forward – and
Mr. Pipe says that some months ago, in answer to a letter recd from you, he instructed
you to forward the money to me. Nothing
having been heard of it, or from you since,
Mr. Pipe requested me to-day to write you
and request your immediate answer.
The Spring is near at hand, and they
are anxious to get their money and buy
some land and settle down permanently.
He has also requested me to write to Messrs.
Dormot & Canning, which I shall also do,
with a view to arrive at the truth of these
matters. Let me hear from you without
further delay – and send the money by Draft
as before instructed – payable to the order of John
Pipe – and send it to me.

Yours truly,
Edwin Scrantom

Letter Number 4, Page 2

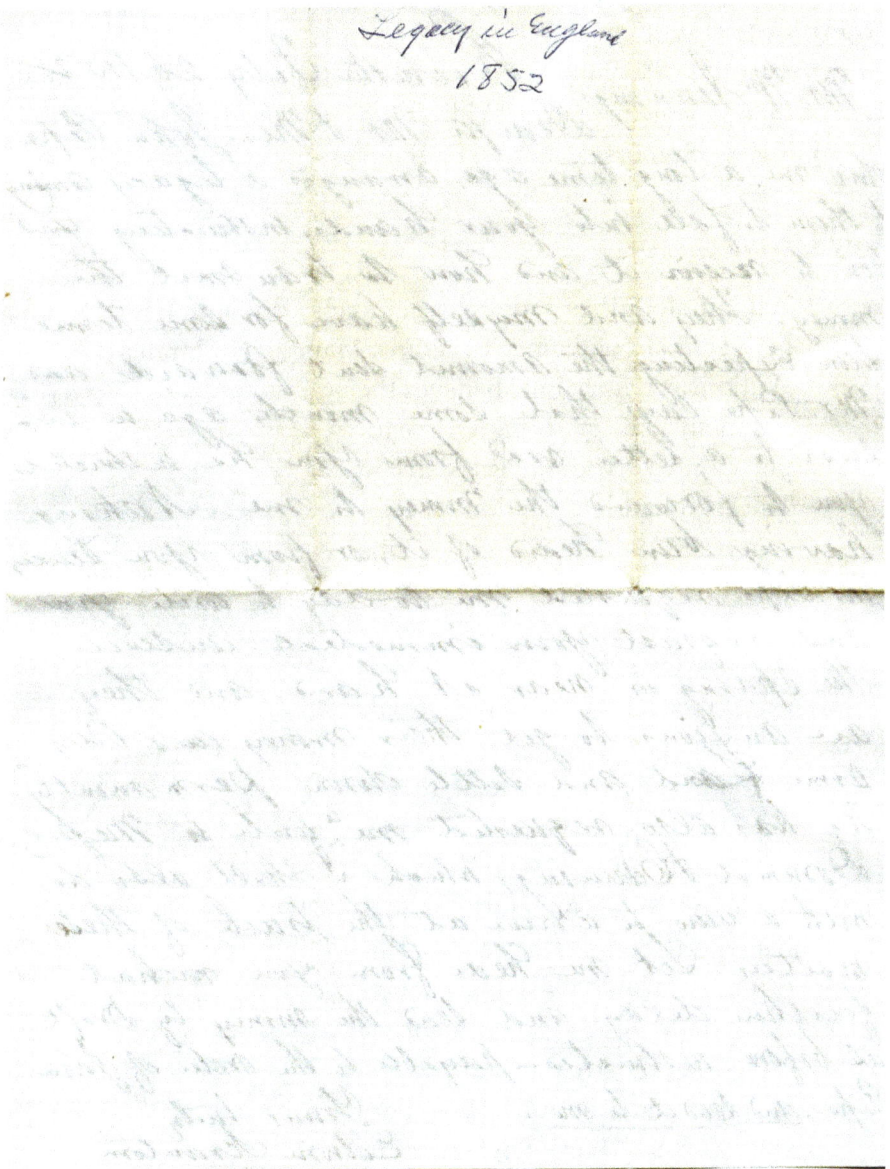

Legacy in England
1852

Letter Number 6

Date: March 1853
Writer: William Jennings Pipe
Recipient: William Jennings
Sent from: Fort Manoel, Manoel Island, Gżira, Republic of Malta
Sent to: Northay Farm, Whitestaunton, Chard,
                    Somerset County, England

Key Ideas

- William Jennings Pipe tells his uncle, William Jennings, that his regiment will move from Fort Manoel on March 30.
- William Jennings Pipe believes the regiment will try to take Sevastopol, Crimea, from the Russians.
- The regiment left London on February 14. William Jennings Pipe recounts his unit's journey to Malta.
- William gives his mailing address as Direct Corporal Pipe, Coldstream Guards, Malta.
- William says that he cannot get any newspapers or books to read.
- William Jennings Pipe asks his uncle not to tell his mother about his whereabouts. He feels the information would make her uneasy.
- William Jennings Pipe is a corporal in the Coldstream Guards.
- He gives an account of the leadership. General Lord Ragland is in command of the expedition. Prince George, the Duke of Cambridge, commands the cavalry.

William Jennings Pipe built a distinguished career in law enforcement in Victoria, Australia. In 1880 as a Senior Constable, Pipe was appointed by the Governor to be a Crown Lands Bailiff in and for the colony of Victoria.

Fort Manoel Malta

March 1853

<u>Dear Uncle [William Jennings]</u>

I now with the greatest of pleasure take my pen to write you a few lines to you wishing ~~that~~ they may find you in a perfect state of health as I am glad to say it leaves me at present. I expect you will open this letter with no very good feeling, perhaps I should be the same but it is no use as we wish for forgiveness so we must forgive, but there is thought you have put in my head which I should not have dreamed of else, and now I ~~should~~ scorn the very thought of such a thing I heard of it but if you think such a thing would not put it into every one's mouth if I am neglectful I am not such a rogue as that to think of drawing the money again. I now enclose the form. I intended to have sent it at Chichester [West Sussex, England] but we were so very busy before coming away and now I return it by the first mail. Mother I have not sent to since I had a letter from her a long time ago nor do I think I shall till we know where we are going if we are to be engaged before I send to her I shall write and leave a letter with some of my comrades in case I should lose my life, we shall be moved from here about the 30th of this month I expect and if so before you get this letter

I believe they intend to take Sebastopol [Sevastopol Crimea] from the Russians, if so we may go there, if we don't go there, very likely we shall go to Calafat [Argentina] and meet the main body of the enemy. We left London on the 14th February for Chichester [West Sussex, England] where we remained until the 22nd when we proceeded to Southampton [Hampshire, England] and embarked on board the *Orinoco*, set sail 23rd, crossed the front of the Bay of Biscay 25 and 26 passed Gibraltar 28th and Algiers opposite on the coast of Africa the same time and arrived at Malta 10 o'clock am 4th March and disembarked the same day. The living is cheaper than in England, fruits and wines and spirits is very cheap, spirits 1s per bottle Black and White wine 4d per bottle, Marsella equal to our sherry 9d per bottle, oranges 8 a penny, figs as cheap, potatoes are dear, bread about 5 pence per loaf, I think one of the young Godwins is in the 13th regiment but whether they make part of the expedition I do not know, give my best respects to Aunt Mary

Ann [Jennings Dommett] and Uncle John [Jennings] and all else that take an account in my fate if ever I should return again I shall come and see you if not you will hear of it by some means or other if you answer this letter direct Corporal Pipe Coldstream Guards Malta or elsewhere but if you will not forgive me I shall not expect an answer. Perhaps Uncle John [Jennings] will write if you tell him my address for letters or anything is very acceptable here for there is no books or anything of the sort for information and it seems very dull, and I scarcely well know what to do to pass the time away. I hope we shall go to Turkey and do what there is to be done and come home again if we live so to do There is about 1200 thousand troops here now and we expect so many more but news I can tell you none for you have more in England from newspapers, here we can get no newspapers. If you write to Mother you need not mention it to her that we are come away or else Perhaps she will be rather uneasy whether it is right or not but you must know I heard John [Valentine Pipe] was in England if so and did not write I shall never write to him any more.

The Greek insurgents are rising again in Corfu and Zante [Greece] and in the Turkish possessions as well but how for right I do not but if so there will a plenty to do for a short time to come but I hope everything will end for the best. Lord Ragland is in command of the expedition I believe and they say a very able General which I hope is the case. Prince George the Duke of Cambridge the command of the cavalry it is a colonel of our own regiment will have command of our brigade and a fine officer he is too as can be [torn] now I must conclude with my best wishes to you and [torn] in that Quarter

From your ever well [torn] nephew William [Jennings] Pipe
You as soon as you can send
[Written later, Nephew William (Jennings) Pipe at War 1853]

Mr. [William] Jennings
Northay Farm
Whitestaunton
Near Chard
Somerset
England

Letter Number 6, Page 1

Fort Manuel Bretta
March 1853

Dear Uncle

I now with the greatest
of pleasure take my pen to write a few lines to you wishing that
they may find you in a perfect state of health as I am glad to say
it leaves me at present. I expect you will open this letter with a
very good feeling perhaps I should be the same but it is no use
as we wish for forgiveness so we must forgive but there is
thoughts you have put in my head which I should not have
dreamed of else, and now I should scorn the very thought
of such a thing I heard of it but if you think such
a thing I would not put it into any ones mouth if I am
unplotful I am not such a rogue as that to think of Drawing
the money again I now inclose the form I intended to have
sent it at Chichester, but was in so very hurry before I came
away and now I return it by the first mail Mother I have
not sent to since I had a letter from her a long time ago
nor do I think I shall till we know where we are going
if we are to be engaged before I send to her I shall write
and leave a letter with some of my Comrades if in case I should
loose my life so we shall she moved from here about the 30 of
this month I expect and so before you get this letter

Letter Number 6, Page 2

a believe they intend to take Sebastopool from the Russians
if so wee may go there if wee donot go there very likely wee shall
go to Tibilt and meet the maine body of the enemy. We left
London on the 8th February for Chichester where we remained
until the 22nd when we proceeded to Southampton and embarked
on Board the Orinoco Sat April 23rd Crossed the front of the Bay of Biscay
24 & 25 passed Gibralter 27th And Algiers reposits on the Coast of
Africa the same time and arrivd at Malta 10 oclock A.M. 4th Chen
and Disembarked the same day. The living is cheaper than in England
Fruits and Wines and spirits is very cheap Spirits 1s per bottle Black
& White wine 4d per bottle Marsells equal to our Sherry 9d per bottle
Oranges 8 a penny Figs are cheap Potatoes are dear, Bread about 5 p per pr
loaf I think one of the Young Godwins is in the thirteenth Regiment
but where they make Part of the expedition I dont know give my
best respects to Aunt Mary Ann Uncle John and all else that has any
account in my fate if ever I should return again I shall come and see
you if not you will hear of it by some means or other if you answer this
letter Direct Corpl W Pipe Coldstream Guards Malta or else where
but if you will will not forgive me I shall not expect an answer Perhaps
Uncl John will write if you tell him my adress for letters or any thing
is very exceptible here for there is no books or any thing of the sort for information
and it seems very dull and I scarcely well know what to Do before
the time away I hope wee shall go to Turkey and do what there is to be done
and come home again if wee live so to Do there is about 1400
thousand Troops here now and wee expect so many more but news I can
tell you none for you can have more in England from Newspapers here we
can get no Newspapers, If You write to. Mother you need not mention
it to her that wee are come away or else Perhaps She will be rather uneasy
wether it is right or not but you must know I heard John was in
England if so and did not write I shall never write to him any more

Letter Number 6, Page 3

The Greek insurgents are rising again in Corfue and Zant and in the Turkish
possessions as well but how far unright I do not but if so there will a plenty
to Do for a short time to come but I hope every thing will end for the best
- Lord Raglans is in Command of the expedition I believe and they say a very
old General which I hopes the case since Down the Duke of Cambridge
the command of the Cavalry it is a colonel of our own Regiment
will have Command of our Brigade and a fine Officer he is he is
Co... he and now I must conclude with my Best wishes to you

...else in that Quarter— from You ever well... greatest
I would leave ... to see from You
& You as soon as you can send   Nephew   William Pipe

Letter Number 6, Envelope

Nephew William Pipe at home
(53)
Mr Jennings
Nothing Farm
Whitelackington
Mr Chard
Summerset   England

Letter Number 7

Date: 24 June 1853
Writer: John Valentine & Elizabeth Stickland Pipe
Recipient: William Jennings
Sent from: Cataract House, Greece Center, Monroe County, New York, USA
Sent to: Northay Farm, Whitestaunton, Chard, Somerset County, England

Key Ideas

- John Valentine Pipe tells his uncle, William Jennings, that he has not yet bought a farm. He traveled to Winnebago County, Wisconsin, in spring 1853 to see the land in Vinland. He will likely purchase his land in Vinland.
- He explains that property prices in New York have gone up. The cost of land is about as expensive as in England. Land costs less in Wisconsin.
- John Valentine Pipe reports his mother Charlotte Jennings Pipe Pillar and his brother Thomas Pipe are well. He was hoping to visit William Coleman, Elizabeth Coleman Jennings' brother, since he was only 50 miles from him. However, weather did not permit the trip.
- John Valentine Pipe's family had the measles this spring.
- John Valentine Pipe has sold his butchery business to George Salter. The Pipes have a three-year lease on a tavern which Elizabeth Stickland Pipe operates. John Valentine Pipe shears sheep and plans to buy cattle again.
- The Pipes have lost their license to run the tavern. John Valentine Pipe reports that the county is becoming more aligned with the temperance movement.
- John Valentine Pipe asks how Tom Stickland and his wife, Mary (Jemima Maria Shire Wyatt), are getting along.
- In a note on the bottom of the letter, John Valentine Pipe writes he just received a letter regarding the death of Tom Stickland. He requests the details of his death and final arrangements.

Elizabeth continues

- Elizabeth Stickland and John Pipe visited Charlotte Jennings Pipe Pillar and report that the Pillars will buy some land.
- Elizabeth Stickland Pipe says that Thomas is likely to take a wife. She describes her as a "first rate industrious good girl." The girl is English and immigrated a week before they did.
- The Pipes saw Joel Knight while visiting Vinland.
- Robert Knight lives about one half mile from John Valentine and Elizabeth Stickland Pipe in Monroe County, New York.
- Elizabeth Stickland Pipe states that John Valentine Pipe likes Wisconsin. She thinks they will be going west in September when their three-year lease is up at the Cataract House, Monroe County, New York.
- John Valentine Pipe had sold his butchering business and leased a tavern, likely called Cataract House, for three years.

––––––––––––

[Greece City, New York, 24 June 1853, from nephew John V [Valentine] Pipe added after the letter was written.]

Dear Uncle [William Jennings]

I must beg to be forgiven this time for being so rightful about writing. I hope it will not happen so again. I am very much obliged to you for the trouble you have taken for me. I must return the compliment if ever I get a chance, I have not bought any farm yet, I have been to [Vinland] Wisconsin this spring to see the country which I have now made up my mind that is the best place for a person to go with a little property for land is betting nearly as high here [Monroe County, New York] as in England, it is raised five pounds to the acre since we came here, there is about as much difference between this and the west [Wisconsin] as there is in England. Here everything seems to be getting up although the sheep that we used to buy for one dollar now sell for two and most everything else in proportions, 7 of September last I hired [rented] this tavern for three years and sold out the butchering business to George Salter, we have done a very good business ever since till now they are getting so very temperate inn this country and now they have taken the lishous [licence] away so we leave at the year end. Elizabeth tends to the tavern. I have been sheep shearing this last three weeks and now I am going on buying cattle again, so we manage to do a good business one and the other. I found mother and T [Thomas] Pipe

and all the two well and doing well I thought to have seen Mr. W. Colman I guess I was within 50 miles of him but the road was so very bad there was not getting about on account of being so much wet weather. I suppose sheep shearing is over with you, wool is worth two shillings English money here but it is finer and better in quality than yours. I shear one sheep the other day his fleece weighed 13 ½ lbs and his whole carcase would not weigh only 12 lb quarter that is what we call the Franch Marina [French Marino breed of sheep] we have all been sick in the measles this spring. I hope this will find you all well as it leaves us at present

Give my kind love to Mrs. [Elizabeth Coleman] Jennings and little Lesey (?) not forgetting yourself

From your ever affectionate nephew of V Pipe

P.S. if you would be so kind as to write an answer when you have an opportunity and tell us all the news and say how Tom and Mary [Jemima Maria Shire Wyatt] Stickland gets along

I have just received a letter saying the death of dear Tom [Stickland] hoping by the blessing of God he is gone to a happy home. I should like for you to return an answer how things are going, where he died and where he was buried and whether there is any family.

June 24th / 53
John [Valentine] Pipe
Cataract House
Greece Centre
Monrow County
State New York
North America

Elizabeth Stickland Pipe continues

Dear Mrs. Jennings

I now take my pen to write a few lines hoping you will forgive me for not answering your kind and affectionate letter which was so long ago. Mr Salter said you would not think the reason why we did not. John did intend going to see his mother for some time past which he has now done, and I would not write until we knew how they were getting along. John thinks they are doing first rate they are now buying some land. Mary Ann [Pipe] gets from 1 to 2 dollars per week, that is 6/- and 8/ shilling of English money and Tom I suppose in the course of a few months will take himself a wife which is a first rate industrious good girl. She is English, she came over a week before we did. John [Valentine Pipe] saw Joel Knight and his wife and fine son, they are getting on first rate, he has bought 40 acres of land for [blank] and he has not but 100 dollars more to pay on it, he has a cow 2 heifer yearling sow and pigs and runabout ones and all paid excepting the 100 dollars on the land he has ten years to pay that on. Robert Knight lives about ½ mile from us [in Monroe County, New York], they are quite well all of them, but I supposed in the course of a few weeks there will be some increase in the family. We saw Richard Dolling [Dalling] and Wilbram Dunn last Sunday which I suppose will go west [to Wis] cousin in the fall to buy some land Eli Dunn is married about 6 weeks or 2 months ago to a girl that has some money by what I have heard. I have not seen him since was married but he enjoys good health excepting the fits which I suppose he will never be free from them. John [Valentine Pipe] likes Wisconsin first rate which I suppose we shall go in September as our year will be up where are now living but we took it for 3 years. They will not grant licence in this town [Greece Center, Monroe County, New York] which are 18 taverns and we are going to give it up in September. We cannot sell liquor, we sell lemonade, small beer and cigars and keep a store which I attend to that and John [Valentine Pipe] is now shearing sheep, he gets 4 and 5 cents a head. Sutter [Salter] and his wife are now quite well but she has been a little sick since she has been here, now married folks are generally complaining for some little time, but I will leave you to judge what has been the matter with her. My children are quite well excepting the baby [Tom Pipe] and he is cutting teeth, he is now 16 months old. I suppose Mary Ann [Jennings] is a fine child by this time grown up to do you a little good by this time. If you see my brother Tom [Stickland] please to tell him I shall write to him in a week or two, hoping he and his wife [Jemima Maria Shire Wyatt] are both enjoying good health. If you see mother [Elizabeth Wall Stickland Pipe] give my love to her Jack [Bartlett] and Tom [Stickland] goes to school. The weather in this country is now incessantly hot almost hot enough to kill one. Things are looking very prosperous at the present, peaches, grapes, wheat, corn, and potatoes which are now selling at 10 cents to 25 per bushel, that is 5 pence to 1/- English money and as good as anyone wants to eat every one, now we are looking out for the 4 of July which is a holiday throughout the states of America, kept similarly to the 5th November [Guy Fawkes Day], fireworks, everyone goes some-where where are others, that day as it is holiday. I must now conclude, hoping you and Mr. [William] Jennings and Maryann all well. Give my love all enquiring friends not forgetting Mr. Jennings and yourself, thanking Mr. Jennings for his kindness to us which I will own was my duty to write and answer the letter in which we received the money, we have had so much to attend to, we have not wrote a letter since we received yours, hoping you will forgive us this time from

Yours ever affectionately J [John Valentine] & E [Elizabeth] Pipe

John [Valentine] Pipe

Cataract house
Greece
Monroe County
State New York
North America

Dear Uncle   From Nephew John U. Pipe

I must beg to be
forgiven this time for being so neglectful
about writing I hope it will not hinder
you for the trouble you have taken
for me I must return the Compliment
if ever I get achance, I have not Bought
any Farm yet I have Been to Wisconsin
this Spring to see the Cuntry which
I have know made up my mind that
is the best place for aheresay to go with
alittle Property for Land is geting neerly
as high here as in England it is raised
five pounds to the acre since we came
here there is about as much Diference
between this and the West as there is
in England and here every thing dear
to be geting up all through the
sheep that we use to buy for one
Dollar now sells for two and most every
thing else in perpotion 7 of September
Last I hired this Tavern for three years
and sold out the Butchering Buy-
-ness to George Litter we have done
avery good Buisness ever since till
now they or g living so very Comforti
ive this Cuntry and now they have
taken the Lishous away so we Sarvas at
theyear end Elizabeth Lend to the Tavern and
I have Bean sheep shearing this Last three
weeks and now I am Going on buying Cattle
again so we manage to do agood Bisness
one and the other I found Mother and I Pipe

and all the ... and ... we I thought
to have seen ... to Colwan I ... I was within
50 miles of him but the ... was so very
... there was no getting about ... account
of ... so much wet weather I suppose
... ... if ... ...
is worth two shellings of English money here
but it is finder and fetter in quality
than than yours I shorn one sheep the other
day his flees wayed 13½ lb and his hole Carkes
would not weigh only 11 lb quarter that
is what we call the Ranch Marina
we have all been sick in the measels
this spring I hope this will find you
all well as it leaves us at present
Give my kind love to Mrs ...
and little Jesey not forgetten your
self   From your ever affecinat
Nephew J V Pipe

P.S.

... you would be so kind as to write
... answer when you have an opportunity
... tell us all the news and say how Tom
& harry gets along ...

June 24th /53

John Pipe
Cataract House
Bruce Centra
Monroe County
State New York
North America

I have just received a letter
saying of the death of dear ...
hoping he has ... I ... he is gone
to happy home I shall like for you
to return an answer how soon ...
going ... to ... dide and ... he
and ... and when there is any famel

but we took it for 3 years the will not grant license
in this ---- Town which are 16 Towns and we are
going to give it up in September we cannot sell beer
we sell Lemmonaid small beer and Cigars and
keep a stove which I attend to that and John is
now ---- ---- he gets 4 and 5 cents a ----
Setter and his Wife are now quite well but she
has been illable sick since she has been here new
Married folks are generaly complaining for some
little time but I will leave you to judge what as
been the matter with her my children are quite well
excepting the baby and he is cutting teeth he is now 16
months old I suppose Mary ann is a fine Child by
this time grown up ti do you a little good by this time
If you see my Brother Tom please to tell him
I shall write to him in a week or too hoping he
and is Wife are both ---- ---- good health if you
see ---- give my love to their Jack and Tom goes to
school the weather in this country is now excessifly
hot at most hot enough to kill any one things are
---- very prosperous at ---- ---- ----, ----, ----
and potatoes which is now selling at 10 cents to 25 pr ----
that is 5 pence to 1 of English money and as good as any one
wants to eat every one now are looking out for the 4 of
July which is a hollyday through out the states of America
kept ---- to the 5 of November fireworks every one
goes some where or other that day as it is Holliday
I must now conclude hoping you and Mrs Jennings and Mary
all well I give my love all inquireing friends not forget
Mrs Jennings and yourself thanking the Jennings for
his kindness to us which I shall ever my wife and
make answer the letter in which we received the money we
have had so much to attend to we have not ---- ----
we received yours before you will for give us this ---- from

Cataract House   Yours ---- affectionaly
Niagara ---- County State New York North America   E P ----

Letter Number 8

Date: 13 July 1853
Writer: Elizabeth Coleman Jennings
Recipient: Elizabeth Stickland Pipe
Sent from: Northay Farm, Whitestaunton, Chard
                Somerset County, England
Sent to: Greece Center, Monroe County, New York, USA

Key Ideas

- Elizabeth Coleman and William Jennings learn that Elizabeth Stickland Pipe had not known about her brother Tom Stickland's death in May. Neither her mother, Elizabeth Wall Stickland Bartlett, nor sister, Mary Stickland, had written to her.
- Tom Stickland had a sale in early April under the auspices of Mr. Stone of the New Inn. Elizabeth Coleman Jennings had heard that Tom Stickland had been in bed ill at the time.
- After the sale, brother Tom had stayed with Mr. Wyatt at Pithayne Farm for a week. He then moved to Blindmoor to Mr. Wyatt's cottage. Tom got worse in the middle of May and died. He was buried in St. John the Baptist Churchyard in Yarcombe, Devon.
- Elizabeth Stickland Pipe's mother, Elizabeth Wall Stickland Bartlett, and sister, Mary Stickland, were with Tom before he died. Mary Stickland stayed until a few days after the funeral but then needed to leave.
- Brother Tom Stickland died without children. As a result, Elizabeth Stickland Pipe inherits her Uncle John Stickland's property except for Podgers Farm in Yarcombe, Devon, which goes to sister Mary Stickland. Elizabeth Stickland's property is described in John Stickland's will:
  - Much Hill Farm in the parish of Yarcombe aforesaid occupied by Joel King.
  - Combe's Pithayne and the allotment of Mannings Commons in Yarcombe aforesaid now in my own [John Stickland] occupation

- o Whithorns otherwise Bardscombe situate in Membury aforesaid and now in my own [John Stickland] occupation and also Peacross in Membury aforesaid occupied by John Dening with annual sum of £30 to my nephew John Stickland during his life. (See Appendix D.)
- Mr. Ben Hurford, a butcher, leased Pithayne Farm after Tom Stickland had left Pithayne Farm.
- Elizabeth Coleman Jennings supposes that Elizabeth Stickland Pipe will return to England to live at Pithayne Farm. She describes it a "nice, sweet, desirable home."
- Elizabeth Coleman Jennings mentions that she had heard that John Valentine Pipe was "on the water" on his way home.
- Uncle Edwin (Jennings) is living at Martock, Somerset. Miss Hallet left the farm in good condition.
- Mr. Dommett is thinking of leaving Tilbury (likely Tilbury Farm, Somerset).
- Elizabeth Coleman Jennings reports that her 11-week-old son John died on 8 June 1853. He was ill for only two days with the croup.
- Mr. George Bunt's first child is a son. He was married two years last May and is living at Maycraft near Axminister, Devon.
- Mr. Every is married to Mrs. Gill who has a son.
- William Gill is living in one of the Birch cottages and works for Mr. Penny. He married Mary Sprankland of Yarcombe, Devon.
- Cousin Tom Jennings has left for Australia in the early part of May with his uncle Robert Chaffey. Mr. Guppy and family left last fall. Mr. Lang of Donyatt, Somerset, has gone with his family. They are going to the gold diggings.
- Farming and prices are presently good.
- Elizabeth Coleman Jennings' brother Richard and his wife, Susan Coleman, send regards.
- Martha Coles is living with Mrs. Edwards of Wambrook, Somerset.
- John Jennings of Birch Oak Farm received a letter from Charlotte Jennings Pipe Pillar in May.

[crosshatched]

- M.A. (Mary Ann) Pipe is not yet married. She is tall like her aunt, Charlotte Jennings Pipe Pillar.
- Mary Ann Jennings has grown up to be a fine girl, nearly eight years old. She will be going to school in Chard, Somerset, with Mrs. Curtis. Currently, she is staying at Birch Oak Farm, Yarcombe, Devon.
- Tom Stickland's wife has gone to Bristol and is staying with her sister who is married to Livy Doble of Buckland St. Mary, Somerset. Her father married Miss Ann Shire.
- Mary Stickland still lives in London. She is looking terribly ill.
- Elizabeth Coleman Jennings sends regards to Miss Sellen with the request to tell her Miss Carnish is expecting. Her sister Rhodes intends to visit England this summer.
- Elizabeth Coleman Jennings sends her love to John Valentine Pipe and their children with the hope that Elizabeth Stickland Pipe will be returning home to England.

Northay July 13th, 1853

My dear Mrs. [Elizabeth Stickland] Pipe

We received your welcome letter last evening July 12th, was surprised you had not heard the death of your dear brother [Tom Stickland] before, we expected your mother [Elizabeth Wall Stickland Barrett] or sister [Mary Stickland] would have written you. He had a sale the early part of April under execution by Mr Stone of the New Inn. [We] heard the poor fellow was bed ill at the time [section crossed out, and illegible]. After his sale he stayed with Mr. Wyatt of Pithayne [Farm] a week. Then he removed at Blind Moore [Blindmoore] in a cottage near Mr. Wyatt's where I believed he had a bout the middle part of May. He was buried at Yarcombe [Devon]. Your mother [Elizabeth Wall Stickland Barrett] and sister [Mary Stickland] was with him before he died. Your sister [Mary Stickland] stayed

till after the funeral. We did not see her as she was obliged to return in a few days after he was buried. As he has left no child, of course, you know so the property falls to you with the exception of Podgers [Yarcombe, Devon] that comes to your sister. Mr. Ben Hurford entered in Pithayne [Farm] when your brother left. I believe he is a butcher. I suppose there is a chance of seeing you home again. Such a nice home as Pithayne [Farm] is very desirable. Think it a sweet place in fact. I heard last week John [Valentine Pipe] was on the water coming home. Now I must begin another subject. Your Uncle Edwin [Jennings] is living at Martock [Somerset] in a farm. Miss Hallet left it a very nice farm. Mr. Dommett thinks of leaving Tilbury [likely Tilbury Farm, Somerset]. I have not heard he is suited yet. I hope he might better himself.

No doubt you will be surprised to hear I have had a little son. A very fine child he was. He lived eleven weeks never poorly until he was taken for death. Ill only two days. He died of the scroop [croup]. It has been a trial for us, as his name was John. He died the 8th of June. Mr. George Bunt has a fine son. This is the first child, has been married 2 years last May. He is living at Maycraft near Axminster [Somerset], milks about 20 cows. Mr. Every is married to Mrs. Gill, has a son. Wm. Gill is also married living in one of Birch cottages, works for Mr. Penny. He married a girl by the name of Mary Sprankland of Yarcombe, [Devon]. Your cousin Tom Jennings is gone out to Australia, with his uncle Robt. Chaffey the early part of May. No doubt but you have heard Mr. Guppy and family are gone last fall. A number of people are going

out to the diggings. Mr. Lang of Donyatt [Somerset] failed. He is gone with his family. I am glad to tell you farming business is better at present than it has been for some years past. Wheat is worth 7/3 to 7/6 per bushel all other grains are selling well. Cattle is selling high. Sheep are selling very well. We sold 50 ewes 45 shillings per head about a month ago. We are very busy, hay making. The weather has been very unfavourable so far. I hope we shall have it fine for the future. My brother Richard and Susan desires to be kindly remembered to you both. They are both sharing home still. Martha Coles is living with Mrs. Edwards of Wambrook. I suppose there is no chance for the poor girl having ten now. I trust he will get a good wife. Mr. Jennings Birch [Oak Farm] received a letter from Mrs. [Charlotte Jennings Pipe] Pillar in May. [He] has answered it. I should

[other way]

have enclosed a note with him only he wrote about the time my dear baby died. I had no spirit for writing just then. She has written to me a long time ago. I never received her letter. I hope to write the latter part of the summer. Am very glad to hear they are getting on so well. I thought M.A. [Mary Ann Pipe] would have been married before now. Mary Anne [Jennings] is grown into a fine girl, tall but therein very much like Mrs. [Charlotte Jennings Pipe] Pillar. I fancy going to Chard [Somerset]

[other way]

as soon as I have got ready about placing of her at school with Mrs. Curtis. We are very badly situated here for schools. She is staying at Birch [Oak Farm] at present. She is nearly eight years old. Time she was learning.

I forgot to say anything at your brother's [Tom Stickland] wife. I have heard she is gone to Bristol staying with her sister. Her sister is married to Livy Doble of Buckland [St. Mary, Somerset]. He is in some office or other line.

[other way]

I heard she did intend to stay with her until she could get a situation. Her father is married to Miss Ann Shire. Your sister [Mary Stickland] is still living in London. I believe the same place as she has for some time. She was looking very poorly indeed when she was down. She is grown very tall, not very thin. I should very much like to have seen her. I have not seen her since she first went to London. When you see Miss Sellen please give my fond love to her. I suppose she is getting quite grateful. Tell her Mrs. Carnish is expecting an increase soon. Her sister Rhodes to intent coming in this country this summer. I must conclude with kind love to Mr. [John Valentine] Pipe and dear children with yourself. Please to write soon.

From your affectionate
E. [Elizabeth] Jennings
Please do write soon. Tell us if you think of coming home. I should be very glad to see you.

Letter Number 8, Page 1

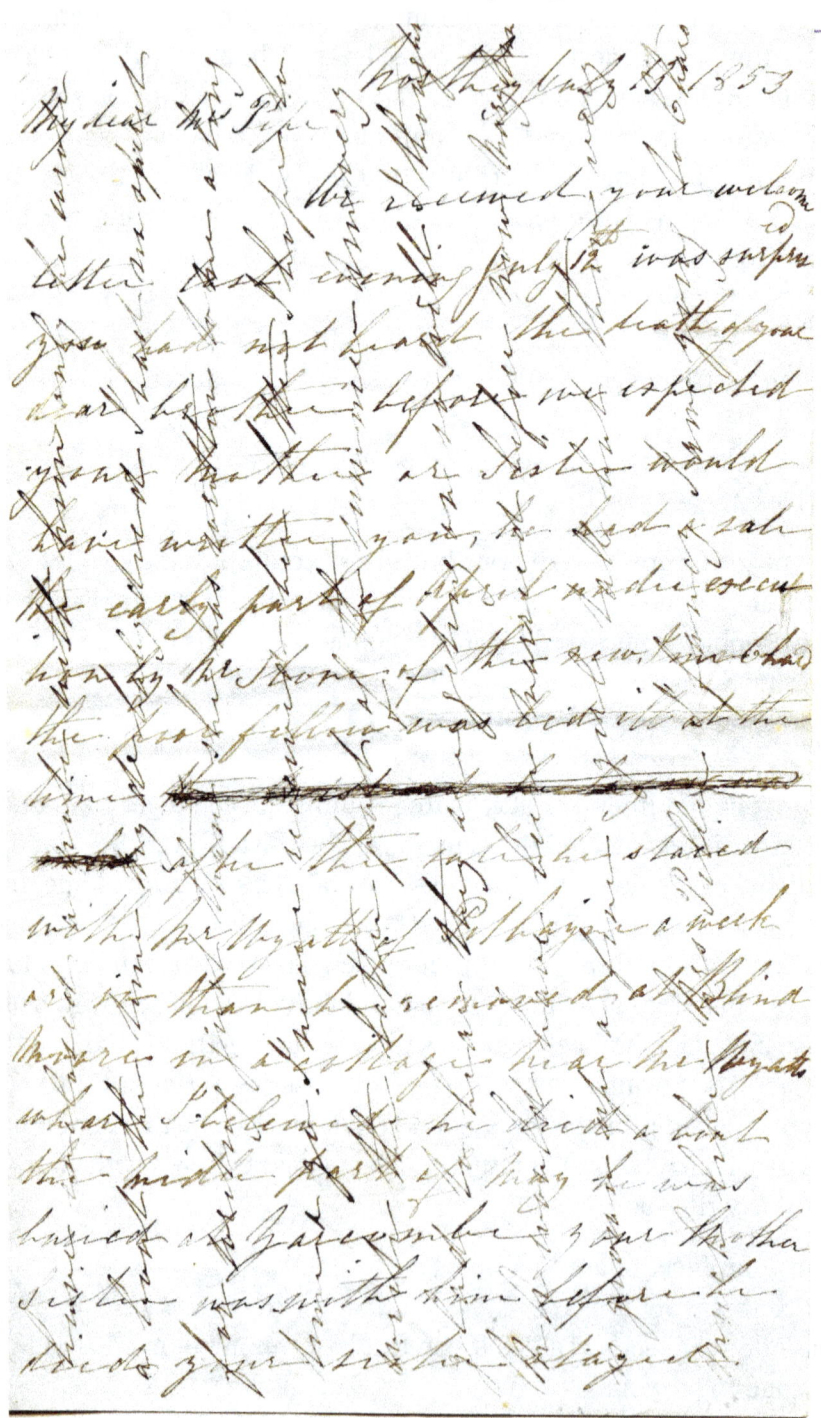

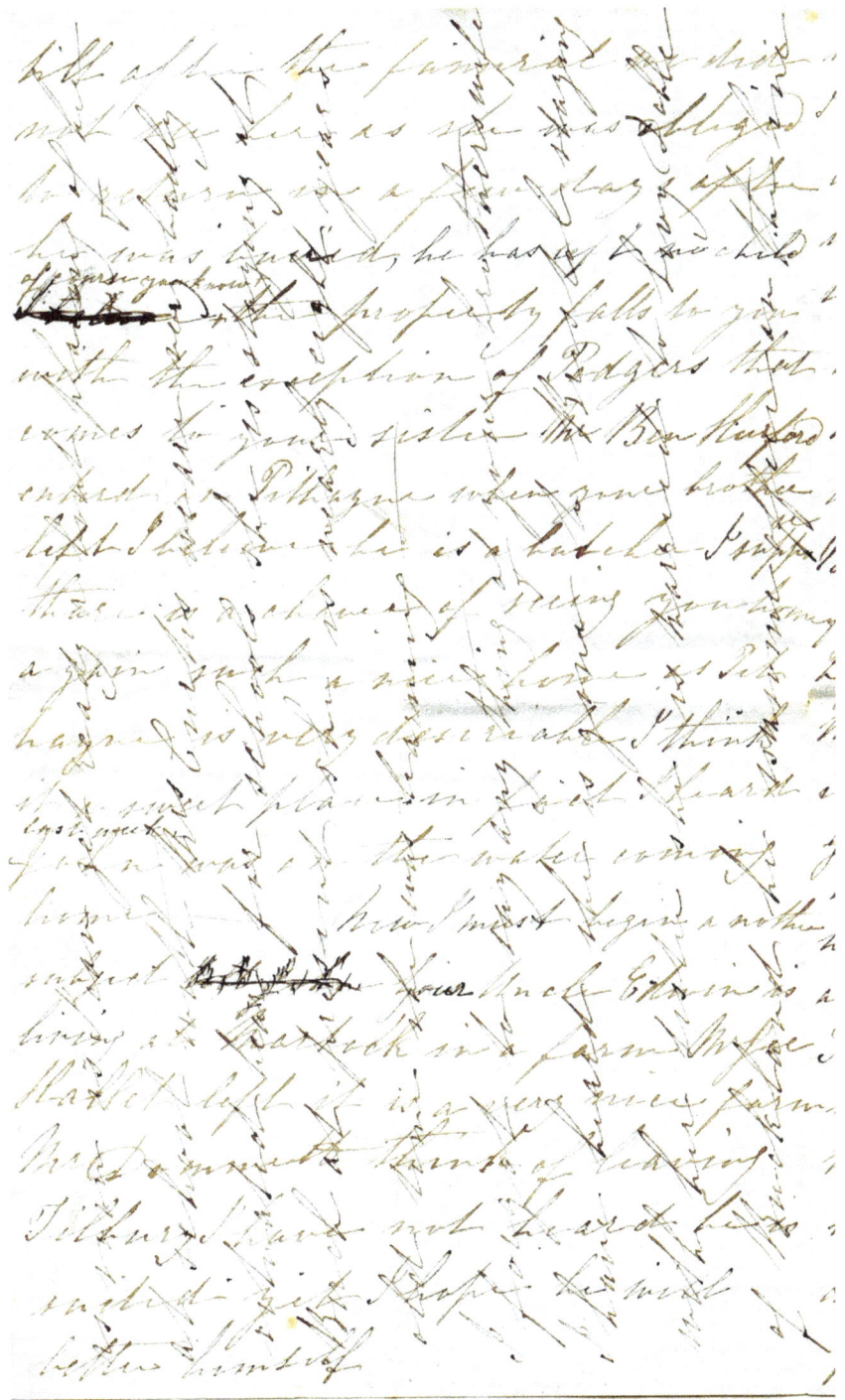

Letter Number 8, Page 3

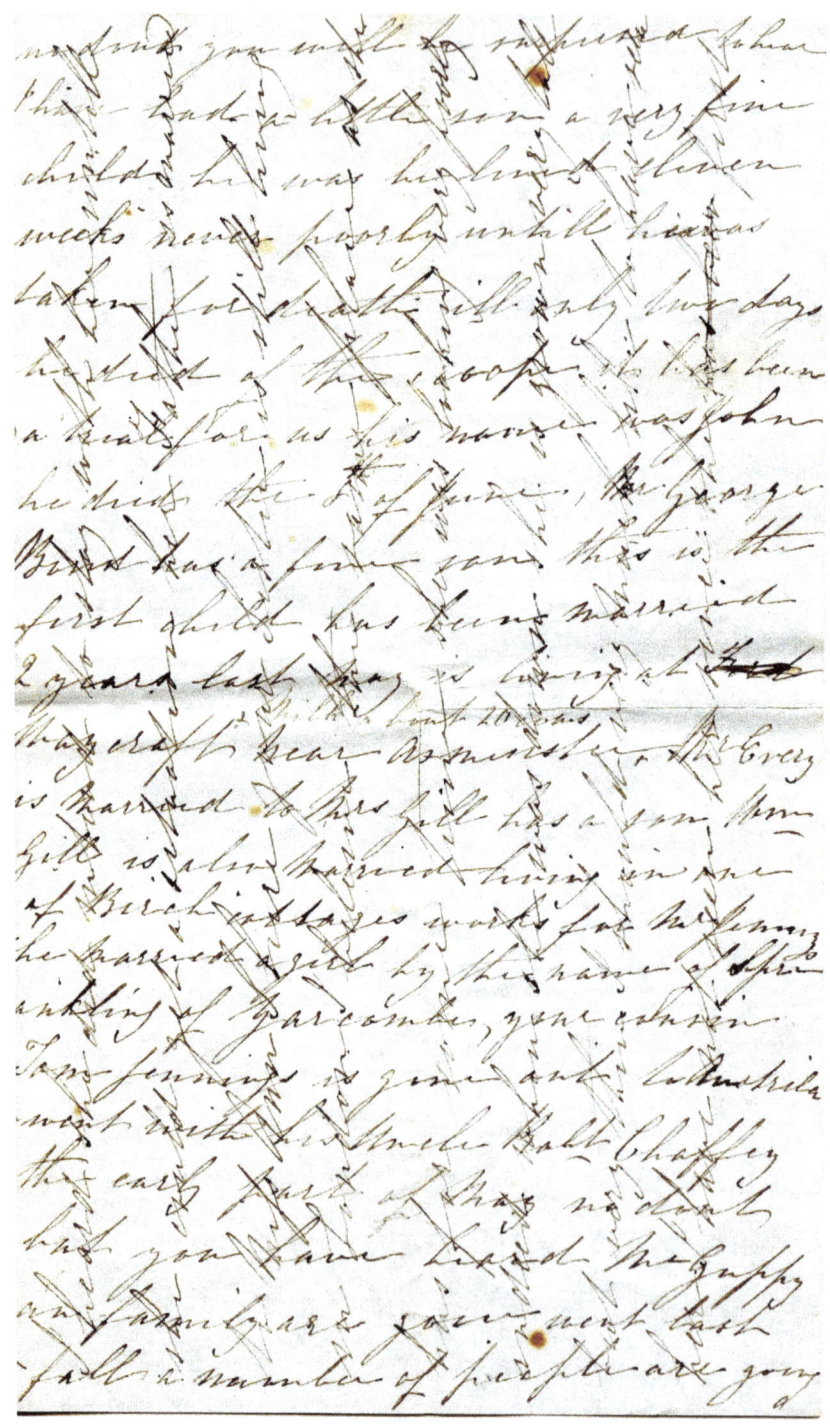

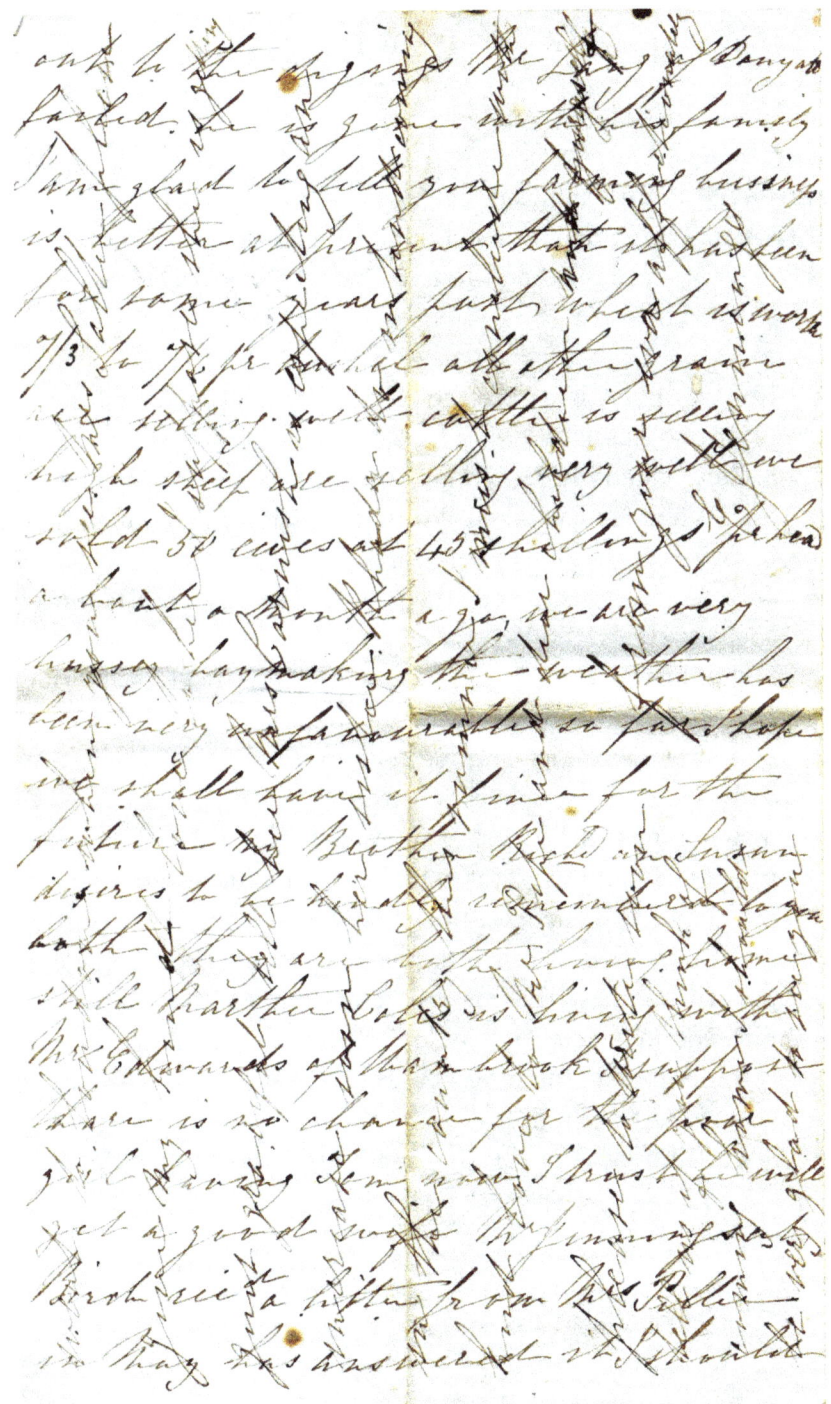

Letter Number 9

Date: 6 August 1853
Writer: Robert Spiller
Recipient: John Valentine Pipe
Sent from: Yarcombe, Devon County, England
Sent to: Greece Center, Monroe County, New York, USA

Key Ideas

- Robert Spiller had received a letter from John Valentine Pipe prior to 6 August 1853.
- Spiller visited Mr. Hutchings from Hill House, Yarcombe, Devon. Hutchings has taken Whitehorn Estate, Yarcombe, Devon, for seven years for £45 per year.
- John Stickland is to keep the property in repair. Hutchings has a lease.
- Spiller has also seen B. Hurford, a butcher, who lives at Pithayne Farm. He had agreed to stay for the rest of the year for about £20 after Tom Stickland left. Hurford will leave at any time if John Valentine Pipe comes back.
- Mr. Dommett asked Mr. Hutchings for John Stickland's annuity. Mr. Hutchings refuses to pay without a receipt from John Stickland. The trustees, Robert Spiller of Pound Farm of Devon and Robert Smith of Dunkeswell of Devon, (See Appendix D) paid two years so there is now more than another due.
- Mr. Dommett told Mr. Spiller, trustee, that Tom Stickland had commissioned Hutchings to rent Whitehorns Estate for seven years at £45 per year.
- John Dinning lives at Peacross Farm, Yarcombe, Devon.

Yarcombe, Devon August 6/[18]53

Dear Sir

I received your letter yesterday and have been to Mr. Hutchings at Hill House and he says he took Whitehorn Estate [Yarcombe, Devon] for seven years from Lady Day [25 March] last for 45 a year. Mr. [John] Stickland to keep it in repair and he has a lease. I have seen Mr. B. Hurford [butcher] also who lives at Pithayne [Farm], and he says he agreed for it a little after Lady Day for about £20 for the remainder of the year when Mr. [Tom] Stickland left and went to

Buckland [St. Mary, Somerset] ill. He says he will leave it any time you wish as he can go back where he came from. He said he thinks he should leave at Michaelmas [29 September].

I suppose Mr. Dommett meant Mr. John Stickland's annuity that he ask Mr. Hutchings for he Mr. H. refusing to pay it without a receipt from Mr. [John] Stickland. We the Trustees paid two years so there is now more than another due.

Mr. Dommett told me that Mr. [Tom] Stickland had commissioned him [Mr. Hutchings] to take it. John Dinning lives at Peacross [Farm, Yarcombe, Devon] still. I hope this will find you all still in good health as it leaves us at present and I remain yours faithfully

Robert Spiller

Letter Number 9, Page 1

Yarcombe Aug.t 6/53

Dear Sir I received your
letter yesterday and have been
to Mr Hutchings at Hill-House
and he says he took Whitehorn
Estate for seven years from
Ladyday last for 45 £ a year
Mr Stickland to keep it in
repair and he has a Lease.
I have seen Mr B Hurford
(Butcher) also who lives at
Pithayne and he says he
agreed for it a little after
Ladyday for about £ 20 for
the remainder of the year
when Mr Stickland leaved

Letter Number 9, Page 2

and went to Buckland
ill. he says he will leave
it any time you wish as he
can go back where he came
from. he said he think
he should leave at Micheal-
onas.

I suppose Mr Dommett meant
Mr John Stickland ~~Annually~~
that he ask Mr Hutchings for
he Mr H refuseing to pay
it without a receipt from
Mr Stickland. we the Trustees
paid two years so there
is now more then another
due.

Mr Dommett told me that

Letter Number 9, Page 3

Mr Stickland had commenissioned him to take it John Dinning lives at Peacross still. I hope this will find you all still in good health as it leaves us at preasent and I remain yours faithfully

Robert Spiller

Letter Number 10

Date: 30 January 1854
Writer: Thomas Pipe
Recipient: John Valentine Pipe
Sent from: Vinland, Winnebago County, Wisconsin, USA
Sent to: Greece Center, Monroe County, New York, USA

Key Ideas

- Thomas Pipe is sorry to hear John Valentine Pipe is having so much trouble with the property in Yarcombe that he has to make a trip to England to settle it.
- William Sinclair has offered to sell his farm to John Valentine Pipe for $4,000 with a $2,000 down payment. The rest can be paid at his leisure for 8 percent interest.
- Thomas Pipe asks his brother to visit Uncle Orlando Pipe when he is home in England. Thomas wants to know if Orlando Pipe found the parchment of Uncle Edward Pipe's will when they exchanged houses. Thomas wants to know if any money was paid for the China War. If so, he requests an overcoat cloth in a drab color.
- Thomas Pipe has visited William and Elizabeth Bradford Coleman.

[*Oshkosh* was written later at the top of the letter.]

Vinland, January 31, 1854

Dear Brother

To my surprise I have just received a letter from Elizabeth [Stickland Pipe] informing me that you had leaved for England. I am sorry to hear of so much trouble concerning the [inherited] property. I hope it will be all put to rights without any further trouble. I had written to you concerning Mr. [William] Sinclair's farm and was just expecting an answer. He seems anxious to sell to you. He offers it to you for $4000 by paying

$2000 down and the remainder to be paid at your own leisure at 8 per cent. Though it is a reasonable price and a good opportunity if you wish to purchase a farm in the west, land is advancing in price very fast and here is everything convenient into house and out of doors. It is now Monday night bedtime and I must leave you.

I will endeavour to finish the scrawl. I have just been to see mother [Charlotte Jennings Pipe Pillar] and have a few lines from her to enclose to you. Give my kind love to uncle and aunt [William and Elizabeth Coleman] Jennings and tell them I hope to make them a visit, but they must not expect to hear anything very interesting from me as you and so many others have been back to tell the wonderments of the country so there can be nothing left for me, but the wild Indian and the Bear and Wolf for an interesting story. I think you leaved about the right time to escape the cold weather, it has been the coldest winter that has been witnessed for many years. I have lost the top of my great toe through being frozen and now I have frozen the top of my nose. I should like to have you call and see uncle Orlando [Pipe] and enquire if he has ever found the parchment of uncle Edward's will as I think he might, he was changing house and also

enquire if there has been any prize money paid for the China war yet. I should like to have you bring me a first rate over coat, cloth I think, a drab would be a good colour.

I have been to see Mrs. W. [William] Coleman, [Elizabeth Bradford]. I found both him and his wife quite well and in every appearance comfortable. I believe they are coming up this way [Vinland, Winnebago County, Wisconsin] to buy some land. I must now leave you by sending my kind love to all my uncles aunts and cousins and all enquirers friends and accept the same yourself from your brother Tom [Thomas Pipe].

P.S. You must excuse this short scrawl as I am so busy that I do not know which way to turn. Write to me as quick as possible

Oshkosh

Finland January 31 1854

Dear Brother

To my seprise I have
just received a Letter from Elizebeth informen
me that you had leaved for England I am
sorry to heare of so mutch truble concernen
the Property. I hope it will be all poot
to wrights without any further truble
I had writen to you concernen Mr Sinclair
Farme and was just expecten an answer
he seems anctious to sell to you he ofersu
it to you for £4,000 by payen $2,000 down
and the remainder to remain to be paid
at your own leasure at 8 per cent I think it a
rasonable price and a good opertunity if you
wish to purtches a Farm in the west
Land is advansen in price very fast
and here is every thing convenient into
House and out of doars) it is now monday
night bead time and I must leave you

Letter Number 10, Page 2

I will now endever to finish this scrawl
I have just been to see mother and have a
few lines from her to enclose to you
give my kind love to Uncle and aunt
Jennings and tell them that I hope to
make them a visit, but they must not
expect to here any thing very interesting
from me as you and so many others has
been back to tell the wonderments of
of the Cuntrey so there can be nothing
left for me but the wild Indian and
the Bear and Should for an interesting Story
I think you leaved about the right time
to escape the cold wether it has been
the coldest winter that has been within
ed for many years, I have lost the top
of my great too through been Frozen
and now I have Frozen the tope of my
nows, I Should like to have you cauls
and see uncle Orlando and inquier if
he has ever found the Parchment of
uncle Edwards well as I think he might
when he was changeing House and also

inquire if thare have ben any Prise
money paid for the Chine wor yet
I should like to have you bring me
a first rate Over Coat Claath & which
a drab would be a good collor

I have ban to see mr A Coleman I found
both him and his wife quit well and in
every apereance Comfortable I belive
they are comen up this way to by some
land) I must now leave you by linden
my kind love to all my uncles annts
and Cusens and all inquireing friends
and exept the same your self from
your ~~stey~~ aff brother Tom

P.S you must excuse this short Scraul
as I am so besy that I do not know
whitch way to turn wright to
me as quick as Posable

Letter Number 11

Date: 5 February 1854
Writer: Charlotte Jennings Pipe Pillar
Recipient: John, Edwin, Thomas, William, and/or Mary Ann [Jennings] Dommett
Sent from: Vinland, Winnebago County, Wisconsin, USA
Sent to: Likely Birch Oak Farm, Membury, Devon County, England. In 1884, land was transferred to Yarcombe, Devon County, England

Key Ideas

- Charlotte Jennings Pipe Pillar reports that Thomas Pipe received a letter from Elizabeth Stickland Pipe saying that John Valentine Pipe left for England.
- She fearfully tells that a steamer, the *San Francisco*, sank on January 4, 1854.
- Charlotte asks John Valentine Pipe to visit Mr. Rogers at the eye infirmary to collect money owed to her by Frederick Boucher and Mr. Welmer.
- The Pillars also loaned money to Jas. Brown of Witheridge in Devon. He had promised to forward the money. Charlotte has written twice, but she has not heard from him.
- (James and Elizabeth Jennings Pipe Pillar were innkeepers at Mt. Pleasant, Nomansland, Devon, before they immigrated to Wisconsin. They are found in the 1851 UK Census.)
- Mathews the smith (blacksmith) also owes money.
- James Pillar left October 5 to cook in the pinery (lumber camps in northern Wisconsin) for a party of twelve men.
- Charlotte Jennings Pipe Pillar states that everything is prosperous in the new country.
- Land is selling fast. James Pillar will go on the Indian land (Chain O' Lakes, Waupaca, Wisconsin) and deed some land this spring.

- Charlotte Jennings Pipe Pillar requests a muff and Victoria if John Valentine Pipe can collect the money. She requests a muff only if there is no money. The muff is not to exceed £1.
- Charlotte Jennings Pipe Pillar says she misses her sister, Mary Ann Jennings Dommett. If it were possible, she would like to visit her.
- Charlotte mentions a letter she had received from John Jennings that expressed his sadness about the loss of baby John, son of William and Elizabeth Coleman Jennings.
- James Pillar will be back in early April. Their son John (James Pillar, Jr.) goes to school. Their daughter Eliz (Elizabeth Pillar) sends her love to her and her mother (Mrs. Coleman) and all the family.
- Charlotte Jennings Pipe Pillar makes inquiries about how her sister Mary Ann Jennings Dommett is doing. She gives best love to her dear friend Mrs. Pynn.
- Charlotte says that because of her husband's hard work, they are happy and comfortable.

[Sideways across the top]

I hope John [torn] has seen his brother W. [William]. I think of him until I am at my wits end. Shall I ever see him again? He may still advance in his station. I have been expecting to hear from him.

Sunday noon. I suppose about 5 in the evening with you.

Vinland Feb 5/ 1854

My dear Brother and Sister

Tom [Thomas Pipe] has just such a letter from Elizabeth [Stickland Pipe] saying my dear John [Valentine Pipe] left her for England and this I say I trust he is arrived same to you [siblings] and that he will settle everything comfortable and [re]turn safe to his dear wife [Elizabeth Stickland Pipe] and children [John Stickland, Tom, and Frank]. I can only comfort him by prayer to an all wise and good God. I have just read of a most awful wreck of San Francisco a fine steamer of eight hundred souls fourteen days of the greatest distress they were a few remaining and rescued on the 4 of January. Should he not have left you when this arrive I should thank him to call on Mr. Rogers eye infirmary as I wrote him a few weeks ago to desire him to Frederick Boucher at Mr. Welmar we gave him an account of [torn] and some money borrowed by Jas. Brown of Witheridge which he promised to forward to us, I have written to him twice on the subject but have received no answer. And also of Mathews the smith [blacksmith] James is not at home so I have not the full account, he left us on 5 of October as cook in the pinery [lumber camps in northern Wisconsin] to a party of twelve men, it is supposed many will make fortunes by it this winter. I am happy to say everything is in a prosperous state in the new county. I suppose James [Pillar] will go on the Indian land and deed some this spring, it is filling up very fast. This will give [?] [William and Sarah] Colemans directions and I hope to write to him, him to me [torn] -row to advise him to come up at once as thinks of coming up [?] matter of [illegible] Thos. have written, he has told you all about his visit there. if John [Valentine Pipe] should be fortunate enough to take some money for me I would like him to bring me home a muff and Victoria but if no money

a muff only and not exceed £1 if John [Valentine Pipe] is not coming up, he sent for it by our Store Keeper and the money, My dear sister [sister-in-law] I shall thank you to look out one for me this is a very cold place the extremes of heat and cold are among the disagreeable but it is a fine county and all who cannot get a comfortable living any means are come to this I am thankful I am here although I think of you all, sometimes till I feel nervous and would fain to be with you if the Lord spares us a few years, I hope to make you a visit, I believe I shall, but thy will be done the more my dear we commit ourselves to God the happier we are, time is short eternity is long, I read a letter from my dear brother John [Jennings] who felt quite sad at your loss of a dear little John Jennings you have now in heaven and so how may we be prepared to meet them and all will ?? I do not expect my dear partner [James Pillar] home till early in April it is a long dreary winter to pass only [torn] my two dear children, John [James, Jr.] goes to school and the weather is extreme

Charlotte Jennings Pipe Pillar and her husband, James Pillar

cold, snow was never known so deep here. My dear sister [sister-in-law] what can be the reason I have never heard from you. I wrote you the very first person June 52 and 54 and no answer. I trust I shall by John [Valentine Pipe] give my love to him and trust the Lord will be with him and guard him home safe. My dear Eliz [daughter Elizabeth Pillar] sends lots of kisses to her dear [aunt] and she is constantly anticipating the time to see her, remember very kindly to your dear mother and all the family is either of you [torn] married, where is dear Mary [either sister Mary Ann Jennings Dommett or daughter Mary Ann Pipe], best love to her not forgetting my dear old friend Mrs Pynn I often wish she was here with me, they said I keep a good table plenty of everything but money is short with us but I do not complain as we brought much here with us, dear J [husband James] has worked very hard and been very careful I can say we are happy you are comfortable. It is more than I would ever say before God bless you my dear and be with you all is the prayer of your absent sister C. [Charlotte Jennings Pipe] Pillar

Letter Number 11, Page 1

Vineland Feby 5/54

My very dear Brother & Sister I am has just recd a letter from Elizabeth saying my dear John left her for Eng'd on the 3 of Jany I trust in God he is Happy arrived safe to you and bless that he will settle every thing comfortable and turn safe to his dear Wife and Children I can only meett him by prayer to an all wise and good god I have just Read of a most awfull wreck of a Sanfrancisco Steamer of Eight Hundred souls fourteen days of the greatest distress they were after remaining and rescued on the 3 of Jany should he not have left you oh this arrive I should thank him to call on Mr Rogers Eye Infirmary as I met him a few weeks ago to desire him to Fredrick Butcher & Mr Belmay we gave him an acct of a ... ... Iab and some money borrowed by Jas Brown of Wetheridge which he promised to forward to us I have written to him twice on the subject but have recd no answer and also of Mothers the Smith James is not at home so I have not the full account he left us on the 3 of ber as Cook in the ... a party of Twelve Men it is supposed many will make fortunes by it this ... I am happy to say every thing is in a prosperous state in this new county I suppose James will go on the Indian Land and deed on this spring it is filling up very fast I has will give me H Columbus directions and I hope to write to him hint how soon to advise him to come up at once as he think of coming up in the fall ... I has have written he has told all about his visit those if John should be fortunate enough to take some money for me I would like him to bring me home a Muff and Victorine but if no money

Letter Number 11, Page 2

a Muff only and not a beech I think if John is not coming by we
send for it by our Store Keeper and the Money My dear Sister
I shall thank you to look out one for me this is a very cold place
the extreams of Heat & Cold ar among the disagreables but it is a fine
Cuntry and all who cannot get a comfortable living my advice is
to come to this I am thankfull I am here although I think
of you all sometimes till I feel nervious and would fain be
with you if the Lord spares us a few years I hope to make you a visit
I believe I shall—but they will be done then more my dear we exert
ourselves to get the happier we ar time is short & Eternety is
long—I received a letter from my dear Brother John who felt very sad
at your loss of a dear little John Jennings you have one in Heaven and
so how I may we be prepaired to meet them and all will have
I do not expect my dear Partner home till early in April it is a long
dreary winter to pass and ⸺ seeing my two dear children go
past to School and the weather is extream cold snow was never
known so deep here My dear Sister what can be the reason that
never hard from you I wrote you the very first person ⸺ Jany 52
now 54 and no answer I trust I shall by John Jenny I love
him and I trust the Lord will be with him and you do him
home safe My dear Liz sends lots of kisses to her dear ⸺ ⸺
and she is constantly antisapating the time to see her remember
very kindly to your dear Mother and all the family is either of you St.
Morrice where is dear Mary best love to her not forgeting my dear
old friend Mrs Byrne I often wish she was here with me they
god I keep a good Table plenty of every thing but Money is short with us
but I do not complain as we may they must ⸺ here with us dear Junker
worked very hard and been very carefull I can say we are happy you
comfortable it is more than we could ever say before god bless you my dear
and be with you all is the prayer of your absent Sister E. Pillar

Letter Number 12

Date: 19 February 1854
Writer: Thos. Kite
Recipient: William Wyatt
Sent from: Stamp Office, Taunton, Somerset County, England
Sent to: Buckland St. Mary, Somerset County, England
                   [Chard on envelope]

Key Idea

- Thos. Kite reminds William Wyatt to send John Valentine Pipe's certificate of baptism so that he can transmit papers.

To Mr. Wm. Wyatt

Buckland St. Mary

Chard

Letter from Stamp Office Taunton

19th Feby 1854

Dear Sir

Don't forget to send me Pipe's certificate of baptism as quickly as possible as I cannot transmit the papers without it.

Yours truly

Thos. Kite

Letter Number 12, Page 1

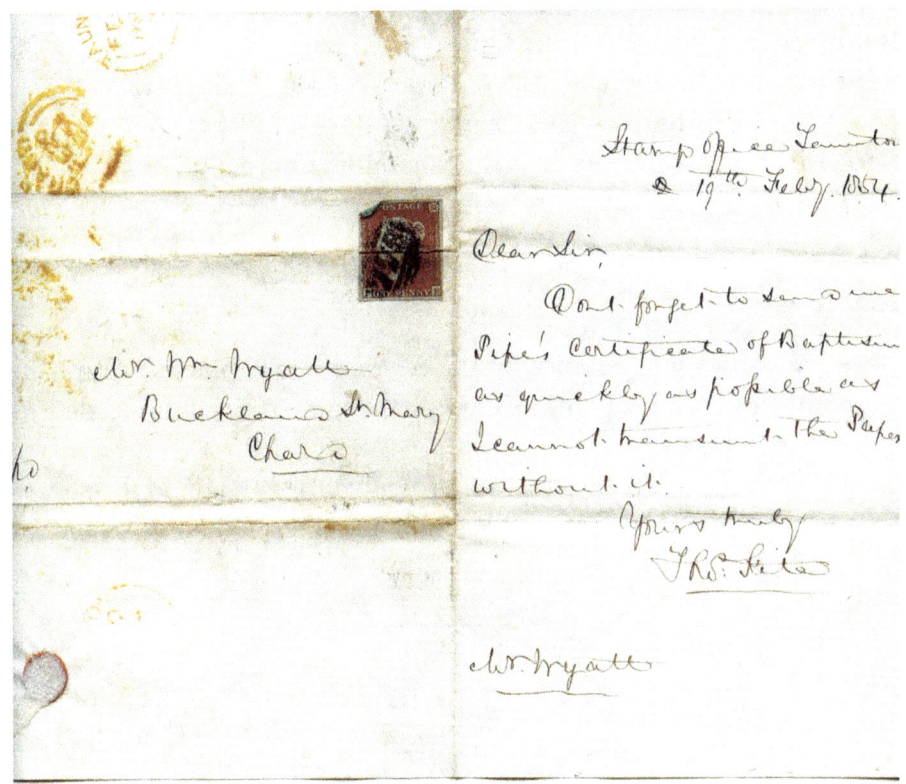

Letter Number 13

Date: 21 February 1854
Writer: William Wyatt
Recipient: John Valentine Pipe
Sent from: Buckland St. Mary, Somerset County, England
[Chard on envelope]
Sent to: Northay Farm, Whitestaunton, Chard,
Somerset County, England

Key Ideas

- W. Miles sent a notice for the certificate of baptisms to William Wyatt. John Valentine Pipe's baptism certificate is needed to settle business.
- William Wyatt says he will have all matters ready in the settlement for the meeting of William Jennings and John Valentine Pipe.

———————

Buckland St. Mary

Feb 21st/[18]54

Dear Sir

Herewith I have enclosed W. Miles notice for the certificate of your baptisms which you will have the kindness to obtain. I shall be glad to see you and W. Jennings so as we may understand about the settlement in the course of this day in order to avoid any delay all will be ready.

Your respectfully

Wm. Wyatt

Beuchland N

Mory Feb.y 21st/54

Dear Sir

herewith I have enclosed
Mr. Niles note for the certificate
of your Baptisens which you will
have the kindness to obtain I should
be glad to see you and Mr.
Jennings So as we may, unless
land about the settlement in the
Course of this day in order to avoid
any delay all will be ready.
yrs Resply

Wm Wyatt

Letter Number 14

Date: 21 May 1854
Writer: Elizabeth Stickland Pipe
Recipient: William & Elizabeth Coleman Jennings
Sent from: North American Hotel (in care of Mr. Chapman),
               State Street, Rochester, Monroe County, New York, USA
Sent to: Northay Farm, Whitestaunton, Chard,
               Somerset County, England

Key Ideas

- Elizabeth Stickland Pipe states that John Valentine Pipe told her the inherited property was not settled any more than when he arrived.
- Elizabeth Stickland Pipe has not heard anything from her husband, John Valentine Pipe, since February 16 when he was at William Jennings' house.
- John Valentine Pipe told his wife that he would be home in New York by March 10. He said he was traveling on the *City of Glasgow*. Miss Jenny Croff was to travel with him.
- Elizabeth Stickland Pipe acquired a list of passengers and saw her husband's name on the list.
- Elizabeth Stickland Pipe supposes that the ship encountered icebergs, was smashed to atoms, and sunk with 373 passengers and 73 officers and crew. Had Elizabeth Stickland Pipe known this would happen, she and the children would have gone with John Valentine Pipe.
- She now feels like everyone thinks. She is a widow with four little children. She was expecting a child and ill when John Valentine Pipe left. On March 14 she was confined to bed. She does not know what to do.
- Elizabeth Stickland Pipe writes to William and Elizabeth Jennings for advice on how to take care of business affairs. She knows nothing about her husband's business. She requests to know about her deceased brother's (Thomas Stickland) prop-

erty. Elizabeth Stickland Pipe specifically asks the number of acres, the amount of rent, and the length of leases on each property.

- The Pipe children all have whooping cough. Baby Mary Elizabeth is only two months old. (Mary Elizabeth was born the beginning of March.)
- Elizabeth Stickland Pipe has now rented a house for $25 a year. The property has berries and grapes in the yard.
- Jenny Croft was traveling with John Valentine Pipe but missed him in Liverpool, Lancashire County. She left March 4 and was three weeks on the water. She died April 14. One of the young Gillingham children brought back the remains.
- Elizabeth Stickland Pipe asks William and Elizabeth Coleman Jennings to look into matters for her. She requests that they send her copies of John Valentine Pipe's will and other pertinent documents her husband left with them.

Greece, May 21st, 1854

Dear Mr. & Mrs. Jennings

As I thought it was time for me to know how Dear John settled his business, I had better write to ask the particulars which I suppose you know as I have not heard from him [John Valentine Pipe] since he wrote to me at your house on 16th February and he said it was not settled any more than it was at the time he went home. He said he was come home on the 1st March by the City Glasgow and Miss Croft with him if he could settle it by that time and when he sailed from Liverpool [Lancashire] he should write me a line to say they had started, having not heard from him I conclude he had not started day after day week after weeks has passed and <u>John</u> is not come. I had a list of the passengers that was on board of the City of Glasgow and I saw his dear name there on the list and the steamer has not arrived which I suppose by the accounts she never will. It is supposed she was encountered ice bergs smashed to atoms and <u>sunk</u> with 373 passengers, 74 officers and crew. Here I am left as everyone thinks a <u>widow</u> with four little children which had but

I known this before we all of us have gone together. When he left I was sick in bed

and had been for a week which I suppose he told you but I expected a child in a short time. And on the 14th of March I was confined on a Tuesday and by the Sunday I thought I should see my <u>dear John</u> but know now never shall more I have had nothing but sickness always ever since he left. He was in partners with a man not knowing how their affairs stood, and he is owed a great deal that I don't know anything of what to do. I don't know now. Write to as your opinion what shall better do. I supposed our John had some writings [documents] which if he had I should take for you to have copies of them and do for me as if it was for yourself as I look to as the only friend I have left. I should like to know what Tom's wife had, how many acres of land it is, how much it is rented for, and for how long a time it is rented. Our dear children have all got the whooping cough and has for the last 6 weeks and the little one has it very bad which I don't think it will live through, as it is now 2 months old last Tuesday. Here I am ?? can't have a stick chopped without pay my hands has been I my pocket ever since he left home and little family to keep. I tell you any one had need to have a good income to keep 4 children and myself house rent to pay, wood to buy. I now moved in 1st May 25 dollars a year a garden cherries and peach trees and 2 grape vines and plenty of currant bushes, everything is very dear now, potatoes 1 dollar a bushel, flour 10 dollars a barrel that weighs 196lbs. That young person [Jenny Croff] that was coming with dear John [Valentine Pipe] did not see him so he went and took her passage on a sailing vessel, she was in Liverpool [Lancashire] by the 1st March as they supposed but did not see each other then and she sailed 4 of March. She lived 3 weeks on the water, died 1st April in the smallpox, we heard the vessel was come at New York and young Gillingham went to meet her at the depot via Rochester but she did not come for several days, the telegraph at New York to know if there was such a person on board of the first thing but did not see any ?? the next day he had a letter from the ship at Staten Island saying she died on 1st April on the banks of Newfoundland of the smallpox and the child was then in the hospital, he went to New York, brough home the child, she lived one week, was buried last Friday week 7 months 1 week old. Dear Mr. & Mrs. Jennings, having so much trouble on my mind I don't know what I am doing half my time. I hope if you will take the trouble for now you will do me a great favour to look into those matters for me. I should like to have the copies if you will send it to me. I should like to hear from you both as quick as possible to hear how matters stand, I now conclude with kind love to you both and hoping Mary Ann is well from

Your ever affectionate niece E. [Elizabeth Stickland] Pipe

Envelope

Please to direct

Mrs. Pipe

In care of Mr. Chapman

North American Hotel

State Street

Rochester

North America NY

Please to write soon

[The following was written later by a descendant.]

Greece Center, NY

May 21st, 1854

Grandma Pipe to Aunt & Uncle

About husband shipwrecked at sea & not heard from

Had names of crew and all on board

373 passengers. 74 officers and crew.

City of Glasgow

Letter Number 14, Page 1

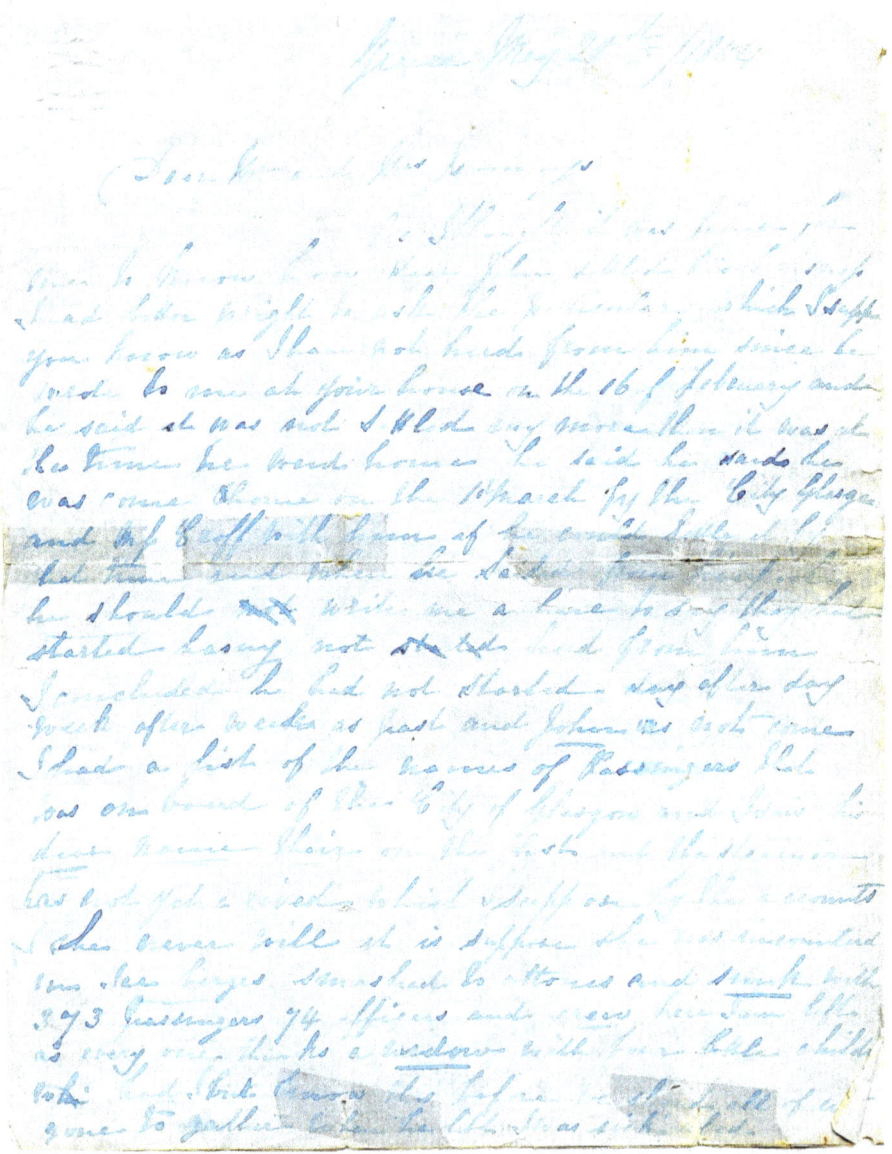

Letter Number 14, Page 2

Letter Number 14, Page 3

Letter Number 14, Page 4

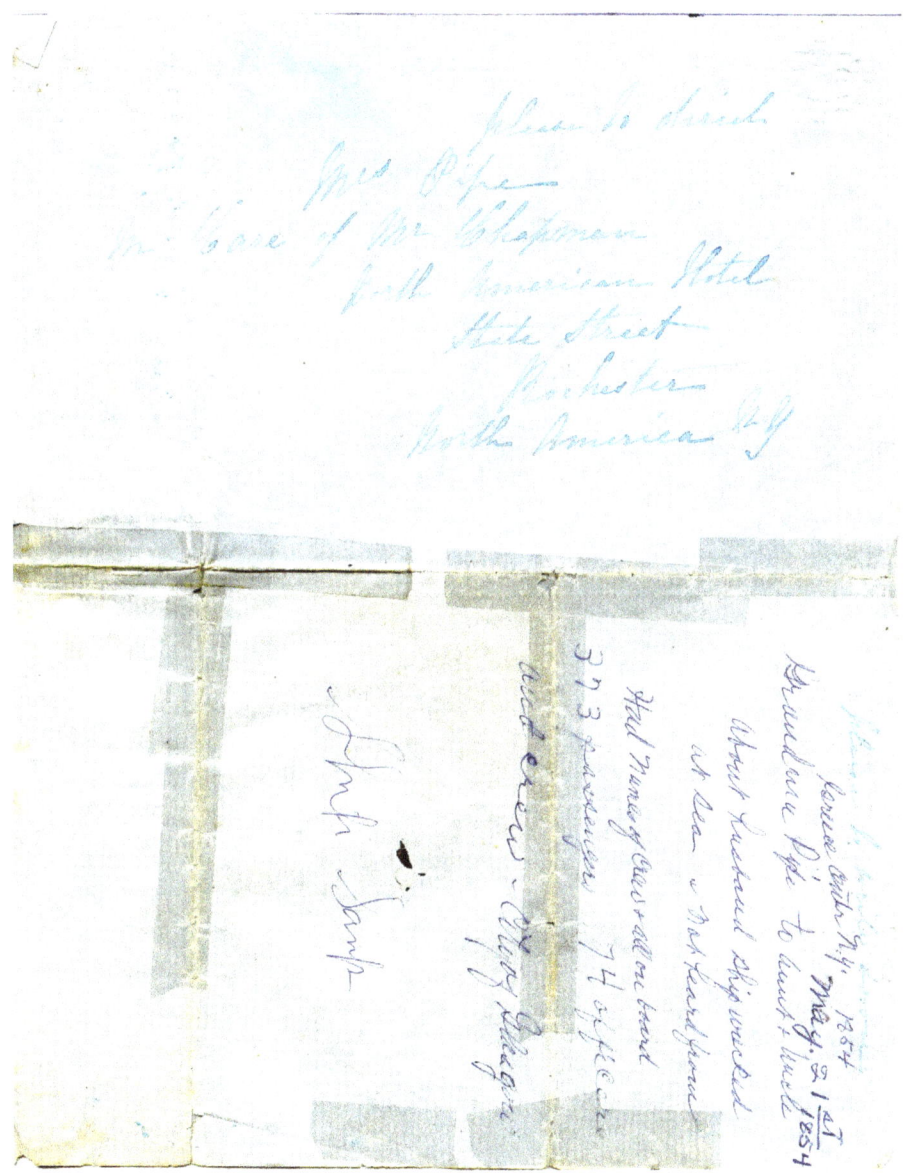

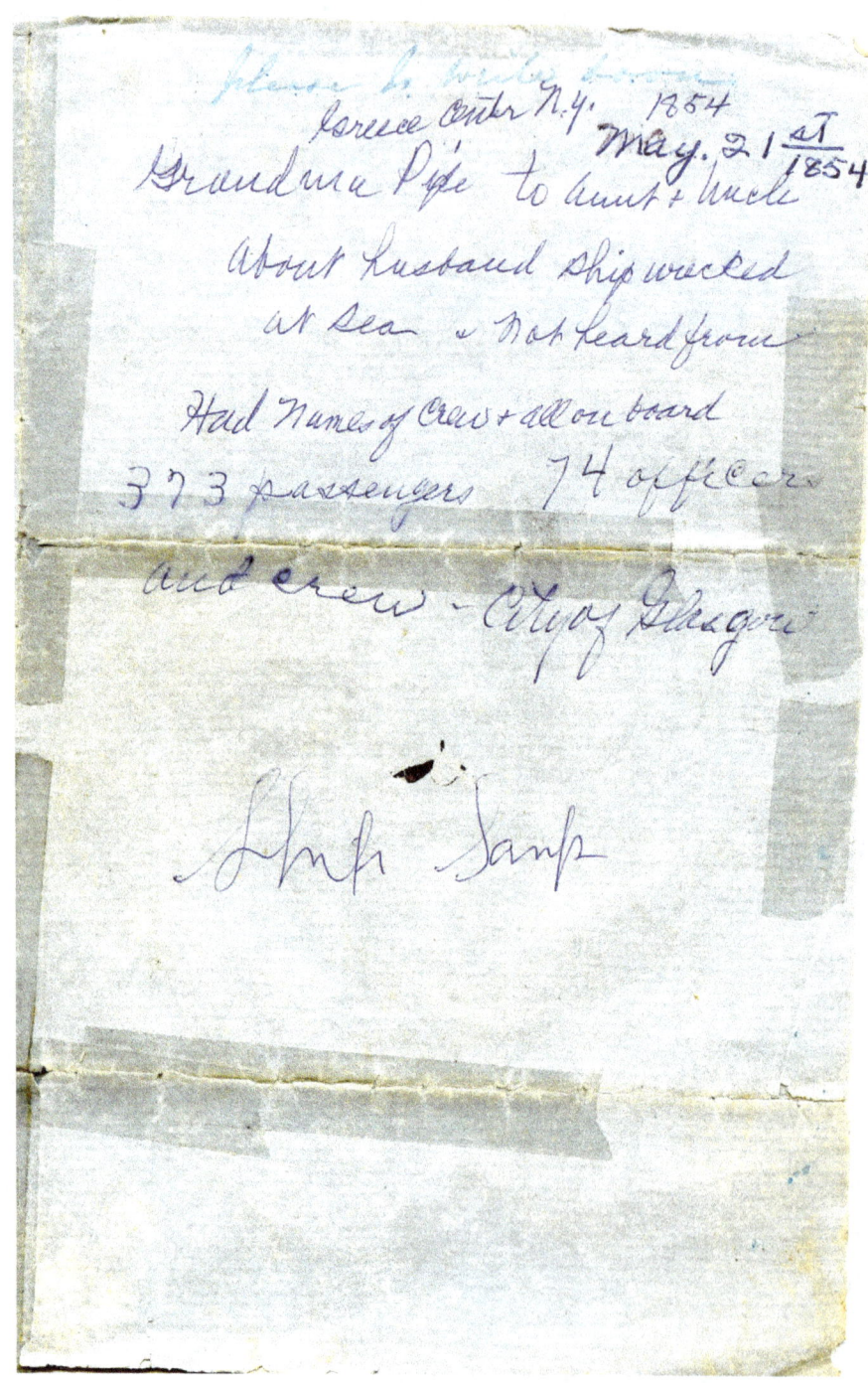

Letter Number 15

Date: 25 May 1854
Writer: John Kenny
Recipient: William Jennings
Sent from: 8 Gloucester Street, West Liverpool, Lancashire County, England [Envelope stamped Liverpool, Lancashire]
Sent to: Northay Farm, Whitestaunton, Chard, Somerset County, England

Key Ideas

- John Kenney reports that he has never received any information about the *City of Glasgow.*
- John Kenny was acquainted with William Jennings Pipe who came with neighbors to inquire about the ship.
- John Kenny reports the *City of Glasgow* was full in steerage. Pipe was offered a second cabin at £15 pounds, 15s. John Valentine Pipe chose the second cabin because he was in a hurry to return home.
- John Kenny claims to have tried to encourage John Valentine Pipe to wait and sail with the others. He was in a hurry and could not be persuaded.

---

8 Gloucester Street, Liverpool

May 25th, 1854

Dear Sir

I am sorry that I have inform you that we never have had any tidings of the "City of Glassgow" which sailed the day you named and I am afraid we never shall. I was thoroughly acquainted with your friend Mr. [William Jennings] Pipe who came here at that time with some of his neighbours. They went in a sailing vessel, the City of Glasgow being full in the steerage the price in the second cabin in her was £15 15s and he chose to go in her as time was precious to him. I said all I could to endeavour to get him to go with the others in a sailing vessel as I never like the screw steamers [steamship powered by propellers] but am very sorry I could not prevail upon him to do so

Yours faithfully

John Kenny

Letter Number 15, Page 1

vessel, the City of Glasgow
being full in the Steerage
the price in the Second
Cabin in her was £15.15:-
and he chose to go in her
as time was precious to him
I said all I could to endeavour
to get him to go with the
others in a Sailing vessel
as I never like a Screw Steamer
but am very sorry I could
not prevail upon him to
do so

Yours faithfully
John Kenny

Letter Number 15, Envelope Front

Letter Number 15, Envelope Back

Letter Number 16

Date: 14 June 1854
Writer: Elizabeth Wall Stickland Bartlett
Recipient: Elizabeth Coleman Jennings
Sent from: Stoford near Yeovil, Somerset County, England
Sent to: Northay Farm, Whitestaunton, Chard,
                 Somerset County, England

Key Ideas

Elizabeth Wall Stickland Bartlett

- Elizabeth Wall Stickland Bartlett has received a letter from her daughter Mary Stickland in London informing her that she has heard from her dear child in America, Elizabeth Stickland Pipe.
- Elizabeth Wall Stickland Bartlett wishes to have William Jennings write to her as soon as possible. She wants to know whether William Jennings has wished her to return immediately, which she feels is the best plan.
- Elizabeth Wall Stickland Bartlett tells of her husband, Mr. Jack Bartlett, dying in her arms. Losing her husband and her son, Tom Stickland in May 1853, is nearly too much for her.
- John Valentine Pipe told Elizabeth Wall Stickland Bartlett that he thought he should insure his life before returning to America.
- She wonders whether John Valentine Pipe had a lot of money with him.
- Elizabeth Wall Stickland Bartlett requests the address of her daughter, Elizabeth Stickland Pipe.

Stoford June 14/[18]54

My d. Madam

I trust you will excuse the liberty I have taken in addressing these few lines to you but the object of my doing so is that I have this day received a letter from my daughter [Mary Stickland] in London informing me that you have heard from my dear child in America Elizabeth Pipe. I should feel particularly obliged to you at your earliest convenience to inform me by letter if Mr. [William] Jennings has wrote to her and if he has wished her to return immediately which I think it the most advisable plan she could adopt, likewise as I do not or are not aware of their circumstances if she has sufficient to bring her to England. I trust dear Mrs. [Elizabeth Coleman] Jennings you will be pleased to excuse this note and imperfections which attend it but believe

me under those severe trials which I am surrounded with I greatly fear it will be a long time ere I shall recover myself. I trust ere this you have also heard of the loss of my dear husband [Mr. Bartlett] who expired in my arms when only a moment before appeared in health and spirits. With those two trials [deaths of son Tom Stickland and husband Jack Bartlett], I can assure you is almost too much for me. I must not forget to tell you that Mr. T. [Tom] Jennings has kindly called on me and likewise sent to me several times and I am also going to inform him of you having heard from dear Elizabeth [Stickland Pipe] as I promised him should I hear of anything particular, I would immediately inform him. I greatly fear the report <u>is too true</u> for us to have the least hope of ever hearing any more particular, but you are aware that John [Valentine] Pipe insured his life which he told me he thought he should do but should

that have been the case I suppose we shall never know however do you think it advisable to write to the agents saying it was his intention to do so when he left his friend. I also trust you are aware of his circumstances as Mr. T. [Tom] Jennings thinks they were doing pretty well, do you also think he [John Valentine Pipe] had much money with him and may I beg dear Mr. [William] Jennings you would inform me all enquiries as I am aware you must enter into my feelings which I assure you under those painful circumstances I cannot describe. Before I conclude what can the poor thing do, should she settle her affairs and come home, such a distance and with children, the thoughts quite make me <u>shudder</u>. Will you be pleased to give me your opinion when you write. Also, may I beg that you would be pleased to forward her [Elizabeth Stickland Pipe] address as I shall on the receipt of your letter, would you be pleased to do so write to her immediately. I beg you to accept my very kind regards and present the same to Mr. [William] Jennings.

I am dear Madam
Yours very truly
Elizabeth [Wall Stickland] Bartlett
Stoford near Yeovil

Letter Number 16, Page 1

Sloford June 14th /54

My Dr Madam +

I trust you will excuse the liberty I
have taken in addressing these few
lines to you but the object of my
doing so is that I have this day received
a letter from my Daughter in London
Informing me that you have heard from
my Dr Child in America Elizabeth
Pipe I should feel perticularly obliged
to you at your earliest convenient
to Inform me by letter if Mr Jennings
has wrote to her and if he has wished
her to return Imidiately which I think
it the most advisiable plan she could
adopt likewise as I do not or are
not aware of their Circumstances
of she has sufficient to bring her to
England I trust Dr Mrs Jennings you
will be pleased to excuse this note and
Imperfections which attend it but believe

me under those severe trygals which
I am surrounded with I greatly fear
it will be a long time ere I shall recover
myself I trust ere this you have
also heard of the Loss of my dr
Husband who expired in my Arms
when only a Moment before appeared
in Health and Spirits, with those
two severe trygals I can ashure you
is allmost to much for me — I must
not forget to tell you that Mr
T. Jennings has kindly called on me
and likewise sent to me several times
and I am going to inform him of
your having heard from dr Elizabeth
as I promised him should I hear of
any thing Perticular I would Imediately
Inform him, I greatly fear the report
is to true for us to have the least
hopes of ever hearing any more perticula
but are you aware that John Pipe
Insured his Life which he told me
he thought he should do but should

that have been the case. I suppose
we shall never know however do you
think it adviseable to write to the
Agents saying it was his Intention to
do so when he left his friend I also
trust you are aware of his circumstances
as Mr. S. Jennings thinks they were
doing pretty well do you also think
he had much Money with him. may
I beg Dr. Mrs. Jennings you would Inform
me all my Inquieries as I am aware
you must enter into my feelings
which I assure you under those
painful Circumstances I cannot
decribe. before I conclude what
can the Poor thing do should she
settle her affairs and come home
such a distance and with 4 Children
the thoughts quite make me Shudder
will you be pleased to give me your.
oppinion when you write also may
I beg that you would be pleased to
forward her address as I shall on the

receipt of you letter would you
be pleased to do so write to her
Imidiately. I beg you to accept my
very kind regards and present the
same to Mr Jennings. I am Dr Madam
yours very truly
Elizabeth Bartlett

Mrs W. Jennings
Northy Farm
Whitestarton
Nr Chard

Stoford Nr Yeovil

Letter Number 16, Envelope Front

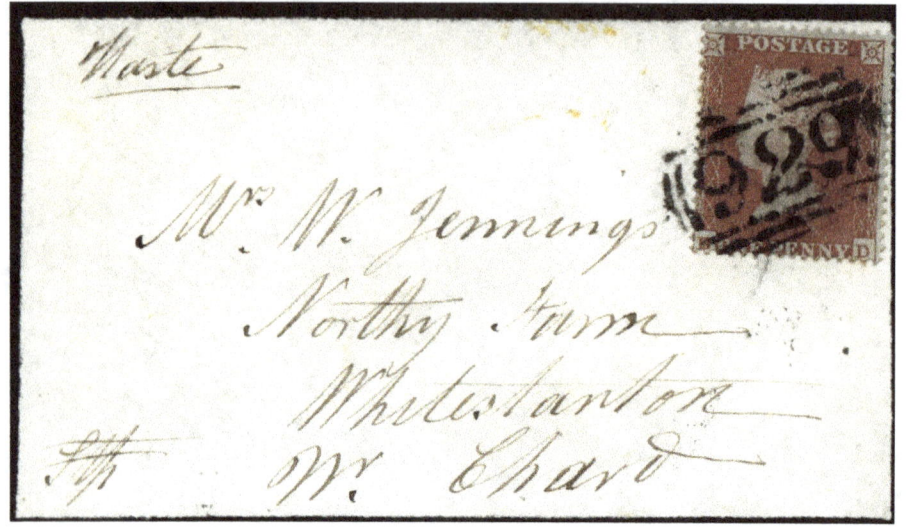

Letter Number 16, Envelope Back

Letter Number 17

Date: 14 June 1854
Writer: William Jennings
Recipient: Elizabeth Stickland Pipe
Sent from: Northay Farm, Whitestaunton, Chard,
               Somerset County, England
Sent to: North American Hotel (in care of Mr. Chapman),
               State Street, Rochester, New York, USA

Key Ideas

- William Jennings wrote to John Kenny in Liverpool, Lancashire, to inquire about John Valentine Pipe's whereabouts. John Kenny told William Jennings that they had not heard anything and fear they never will.
- William Jennings says that he is so glad to have seen John Valentine Pipe. John Valentine enjoyed himself until about a week before he was to leave. He was very eager to return to Elizabeth Stickland Pipe and his children.
- William Jennings explains that he does not know how to advise Elizabeth Stickland Pipe on her business in New York.
- John Valentine Pipe spoke highly of Mr. Chapman. William Jennings thinks that she should contact him for advice. He also recommended Mr. Salter to help her settle matters.
- William Jennings provides an accounting of the properties.

———————

[Written later by a descendant: Grandma (Elizabeth Stickland Pipe) asks help about property in England.]

Northay June 14, 1854

Dear Mrs. Pipe

I received a letter from you saying you had not seen your dear John [Valentine Pipe] since he left, when I first heard of it I wrote to Liverpool [Lancashire] to a Mr. Kinny where the dear fellow stopped and he wrote to me from Liverpool [Lancashire] the morning he sailed and sent me a card as I might know who to wrote and the answer I had was they had not heard any tidings of the vessel and fear they never should. I was quite shocked of such news, I was so glad to see him, and he enjoyed himself till about the last week for he was very anxious to go back to you and the Dear Children. I hope if the Dear heart is gone, he will find the almighty on his side. I hope and trust that the warning was not short. I hardly know what I am about and what much more be to yours you bless you and the Dear Children. Dear Mrs. Pipe I don't know how to persuade you about your business over there only as this I heard Dear John [Valentine Pipe] speak very highly of a Mr Chapman which I hope will do what he can for you to settle things, or Mr Salter. I thought him a nice man, please to look over every paper and account very minutely and I hope they will assist you in putting things straight. Dear Mrs. Pipe I have received from Mr. Hutchings for Whitehorns [Farm] for 18 weeks rent up to Lady Day [25 March] last £15 11s 3d from Mr. Denning

of Peacross [Farm] £3 3s 0d I have got a bill from Dommett at Chard £11 8s 10d and for making the lease £5 0s 0d but the lease is not signed. I don't know what to do about it. I suppose I had better wait till I hear from you. Pithayne [Farm] and Whitehorns [Farm] is let [rented] together to Mr. Phillips at Buckland [St. Mary, Somerset]. Phillips at 80 a year, the lease is 7 years but not sure. Peacross [Farm] is let [rented] to John Dunning at £10 a year. Your brother John [Stickland] has got 30 a year out of the whole, your part is I think 24 a year, and your sisters [Elizabeth Stickland Pipe] 6 a year. There is a year's due to John the 11th of last April, there will be no rent due from the parties till Michaelmas.

Dear John [Valentine Pipe] paid £170 to Mr. Wyatt for giving up all rights that he had and the will and the deed of Pithayne [Farm] once signed by Mr. Stickland except the deeds of Whitehorns [Farm] Mr. Middleton of Chard has got them and won't give them up till he is paid

when has let [rent] go on them that is £26 0s 0d. I don't think you have anything to do when paying your brothers debts. I am told I can get the copy of them £1,000 [?] they ought to be had by right, he said he can get his money, but I don't see how. Dear Mrs. Pipe I lent Dear John [Valentine Pipe] the £170 on a mortgage on Pithayne [Farm] and Whitehorns [Farm] at 4 per cent. I can't tell you how much Mr. Wyatt paid Mrs. T [Tom] Stickland. I don't think your mother [Elizabeth Wall Stickland Bartlett] had anything to do with the property, nor more than I had although she and your sister [Mary Stickland] seem to be put very much out of the way about it. There is one thing I am glad was done, his life is insured in £150. I am going to Taunton [Somerset] concerning it on Monday next. I hope the policy is correct. Dear John [Valentine Pipe] paid for insurance £3 7s 6d and I wish I could hear the dear fellow was home with you. God bless you and the Dear Children

from yours most affectionately

Wm. Jennings

My dear Mrs Pipe please to write soon as we long to hear how you and the dear children are. I don't think your dear John [Valentine Pipe] had any writings [documents] with him of any consequence as he left his will and deeds here [smudged] I do not know whether your brother [John Stickland] might

[other side]

proceeds with it I hope we shan't hear no more about it.

Grandma asks help about property in England

Northey June 14 – 54

Dear Mrs Pipe

I received a letter
from you staying you had not sen
your Dear John since he left,
when I first hard of it I wrote to
Liverpool to a Mr Kinney where
the Dear fellow stoped and he wrote
to me from Liverpool, the morning he sailed, and sent me
a card as I might know to where
to write, and the answer I had
was they had not hard any tidings
of the vessel and fear they never
should, I was quite shock of such
news, I was so glad to see him and
he enjoyed himself till about the
last week for he was very anxious
to go back to you and the Dear Children

I hope if the dear *hart* is gone that he well
find the almighty on his side I hope
and trust that the warning was
not short I harley I now what
I am about and what must mine
be to yours you bless you and the dear
Children. Dear M's Pipe I don't know
how to persuade you about your business
over there only as this I hard dear John
speak very ~~lity~~ of a Mr Chapman ~~which~~
I hope well do what he can for you to
settle things, or Mr Salter I thought
him a nice man, please to look over
every paper very *and amount* minutly and I hope
they well assist you in puting things
straight dear M's Pipe I have
received from Mr Hutchings for
whitehorns for 18 weeks rent up to
ladey day last 15 : 11 : 3 from Mr Denning

of Peacross 3 "3..0 I have got a bill
from Domnett at Church 11 " 8..10 and
for making the Lease 5..6..6 but the
lease is not sined ~~fourth~~ I dont know
what to do about it I suppose I had
better ~~to know of~~ wait till I here from you ~~Sam to may it sined~~ Pithay
and Whitehorse is let together to Mr
Phillips a Buckland Phillips at 80 —
a year the Lease is 7 years but ~~not~~ say
6 acres is let to John Denning at 16
a year your Brother John ~~has~~ got 30
a year all of the whole year I ~~with to~~
I think 24 a year and your Sisters 6 a year
there is a years due to John the 11 of last
april there will be no rent due from
the partys till Michelmas Dear John
paid Mr Wyatt for giving up all rights
that he had and the Will and the Deeds
of Pithayne — and sined by Mr T
Buckland except the Deeds of Whitehorse
Mr Middleton of Church has got them
and wont give them up till he is paid

were he has let go on them that is £te 0 0
I don't think you have any thing to do with
paying your Brothers debts I am told
I can't get the copy of them but they
ought to be had by right he says
he can get the money, but I don't see how
O Dear Mr Pim I task Dear John
the £70 on a Mortgage on Ruthyne and
Whitchurch at 4 ½ Cent I can't tell
you how much Mr Wyatt paid Mr
Strickland I don't think your Mother
had any thing to do with the property
no more than I had, although she
and your Sister seem to be put
very much out of the way about
it, there is one thing I am glad was
done his life is insured in 150 I am
going to Taxation concerning it on
Monday next I hope the Policy is worth
Dear John paid for Insurance 3.. 7.. 6 o d
wish I could have the dear fellow was
home with you god bless you and Dear Children

Letter Number 18

Date: 9 July 1854
Writer: Thomas Pipe
Recipient: William Jennings
Sent from: Greece, Monroe County, New York, USA
Sent to: Northay Farm, Whitestaunton, Chard, Somerset County, England

Key Ideas

- Thomas Pipe writes William Jennings from Greece, Monroe County, New York.
- Thomas Pipe arrived at Elizabeth Stickland Pipe's home the last week of May. He left the Town of Vinland, Wisconsin, as soon as he heard about his brother's death. He reports that Elizabeth and the children are doing as well as can be expected.
- Thomas Pipe and Mr. Chapman have examined all of John Valentine Pipe's papers and account books. They have hired a bookkeeper to enter all records. Account books are not in order. John Valentine Pipe was in partnership with a man with whom he entrusted the books. Thomas mentions considerable notes most of which are John Valentine Pipe's money.
- Thomas Pipe sees it as his duty to straighten out matters.
- Thomas Pipe asks William Jennings to explain his bookkeeping of the properties. Thomas does not understand the reason Mary Stickland is due an annuity. William Jennings stated that Elizabeth is left with five pounds per year, which is a very small amount for her and her family to live on.
- Thomas Pipe states he will do anything to help Elizabeth, but he must return to Wisconsin in the fall. He mentions asking her to go west with him. He says that she could build a house next to his and have a garden. He does not know if Elizabeth would accept his offer. Thomas wants to know about his mother's (Charlotte Jennings Pipe Pillar) legacy left to her by John Bond. (See Appendix E for Will of John Bond of Atherstone, gent., proved 18 May 1854.)

[This note is written later by a descendant: Thomas Pipe. To offer Grandma to live near him. John's brother

Please to direct to me at Greece Monroe County
New York
Greece July 9th, 1854

Dear Uncle

I suppose that you will be surprised to receive a letter from me especially from these regions. I came down here about the last week in May, that was as soon as I heard of the sad misfortune of my brother [John Valentine Pipe], and I think I might say ?? of my sister and her family. Dear Uncle your kind letter of the 14 last [14 June] came to hand on Tuesday last. I am happy to inform you that Elizabeth [Stickland Pipe] and family is as well as might be expected under the same tribe. My self and Mr. Chapman have just commenced examining John's [Valentine Pipe] books and other papers. I fear it will cause a deal of trouble, but that we do not mind if there is nothing lost, which I fear will be the case. It certainly is a great confusion. We have employed a book keeper of the City [Rochester] to intersect the old book, and draw it in a regular form on a new one, so that we might be able

to bring it forward in a regular form which cannot be done at present, the accounts are so much mixed up that it is in a complete fog. It appears that John [Valentine Pipe] put every confidence in the man whom he have been in partnership with, which I fear will turn out anything but an honest man. It is generally supposed that this man holds money of a large amount of John's [Valentine Pipe]. We know that he let him have notes of a considerable amount which became due this spring for the thing sold at the sale. As I consider it my duty I shall spare no trouble in putting the affair as straight as possible and I think Mr. Chapman is a gentleman who will assist me as far as lies in his power. Dear uncle, we do not understand your letter concerning the property at home your statement is that you think Elizabeth's [Stickland Pipe] share is £24 a year, you also stated her sister [Mary Stickland] had a share of £6 a year. I did not understand that Mary Stickland had any share in it whatever, you also stated that the different places was let [rented] at

£90 a year, for a lease of seven years, and taken £30 a year for John [Stickland]

and £6 for Mary [Stickland] leaves £54 a year. I do not know what the expenses will be, but will feel obliged to you to explain the matter in your next as poor Elizabeth [Stickland Pipe] feels quite uneasy about it. She thinks it is but a small portion to maintain her family.

Dear uncle, I feel quite at a loss to know how to advise my poor sister [Elizabeth Stickland Pipe] for the future, under the present circumstances. It is certainly a great trial for her. As for my part I am willing to do anything that lay in my power for her. I shall have to return to the west in the Fall as my business is arranged accordingly. I wish it had so happened that my business was here or otherwise her and her family there so that I might assist her with the boys as I fear they will be a great trouble to her. I think a little of your advice to her might be good. I do not know which would be the best for her, to return to England or stop here. There is one thing I think it would be to the advantage of her family to stop. I suppose it would be useless for me to ask her to go to the west with me. If I thought she would

go, I would a proposition to her. I have land with some improvements on. It is let [rented] at present but please God I am spared until another spring I intend to occupy it myself. If she like to accept she might build a small house by the side of mine, which will not cost but little, there she can keep a cow and have all the land for a garden. She is assured and give the children a good education with any expense. But I think she would not like to go further west. I think I have nothing particular more to say at present but Elizabeth [Stickland Pipe] and children send their kind love to you all and accept the same from your affectionate nephew.

Thos Pipe

P.S. I left the people in Wisconsin all well excepting the trouble which I am sorry to say was great with poor mother.

Please to write as soon as possible. Please to give my kind love to Uncle John [Jennings] and all enquirers and friends, what is the legacy that Mr. [John] Bond left mother [Charlotte Jennings Pipe Pillar].

Letter Number 18, Page 1

Thomas Pipe
Pleas to direct to me at
Johns Brother
at Greece Monro Co
New york

To offer Grand Ma to live
near them

Greece July 9th 1854

Dear Uncle

I sopose that you will soprised to receive a Letter from me, especially from these regions, I came down hear about the last week in may, that was as soon as I herd of the sad misfortuen of my Brother, and I think I might say still moreso of my Sister and her Family, Dear Uncle your kind letter of the 14 Inst came to hand on Tuesday last, I am happy to informe you that Elizebeth and family is as well as might be expected under the sircumstonce, My self and Mr Chapman have just commenced examinen Johns books and other papiers, I fear it will cose a deal of truble, but that we do not mind if there is nothing lost, which I fear will be the case, It sertenly is a great confusen, We have employed a Book keeper of the Citty to enter out the old book, and draw it of in a regular form on a new one, so that we might be able

Letter Number 18, Page 2

to bring it foward in a reagular Forme,
which cannot be don at present, the acounts
as so mutch miest up that it is in a complet foy
It apears that John poot every confidence in the
man whom he have been in partnership with
which I fear will turn out any thing but an
onest man, It is genearly soposed that this man
holds money of a large amount of Johns, We know
that he let him have Nots of a considreable amount which
became due this Spring for the thing sold at the
Sale, As I consider it my duty I shall
spair no trouble in pooter the afair as strait
as posable and I think Mr Chapman is a
Gentleman who will asist me as far as lais in
his pow. Dear Uncle We do not under
stand your Letter concernen the property at
home your statement is that you think Elizebeth
share is 2£ a year you also stated her sister
had a share of 6 a year, I did not underst
and that mary Stickland had any share in
it whatever, you also stated that the difren
places was leet at 90 a year, for a leue of
seven years, and taken 50 a year for John

Letter Number 18, Page 3

and 6 for Mary leaves 5½£ a year, I do not
know what the expences will be, but will feel
obliged to you to explain the mater in your
next as poor Elizebeth feels quit uneasy about
it she thinks it is but a small portion so
maintain her Family,

Dear uncle, I feel quit at loss to know how
to advise my Poor Sister for the future, under
the present surcemstances, It is certenley
a great trial for her, As for my part I am willing
to do anything, that lay in my power for her
I shall have to return to the west in the Faul
as my business is aranged acordenly, I wish it
had so hapned that my business was here or otherwise
her and her family there so that I might
asist her with the Boys as I fear they will be
a great trouble to her, I think a little of your
advice to her migh be good, I don't know which
would be the best for her to return to England
or stop here, there is one thing I think it
would be to the advantage of her family to stop,
I sopose it ould be welsh for me to ask her to go
to the west with me, If I thought she would

Letter Number 18, Page 4

go I would a proparsetion to her, I have Land
with some improvements on, It is let at present
but pleas God I am spard untell a nother
Spring I intend to ocupye it my self,
If she like to accept she might build a Small
House by the side of mine which will not
cost but little, there she can keep a cow
and have all the land for a Garden she is amind
and give the Children a good Education with
any expence, but I think she would not like
to go farther west, I think I have nothing
particular more to say at present but Elizebeth
and Children sends thare kind love to you
all and accept the same from your aff. Nephew

Thos. Pipe

P.S

I left the people in westconsen all
well yesspte the trouble which I am sory to
say was great with poor mother,
Pleas to wright as soon as posable pleas to give
my kind love to uncle Johor and all inquirer
friends, what is the legasy that Mrs. Bond
left mother

Letter Number 19

Date: circa October 1854
Writer: William & Elizabeth Coleman Jennings
Recipient: Elizabeth Stickland Pipe
Sent from: Northay Farm, Whitestaunton, Chard, Somerset County, England
Sent to: Greece, Monroe County, New York, USA

Key Ideas

- William Jennings again requests power of attorney that was sent to Elizabeth Stickland Pipe by Mr. Dommett on January 16, 1854. He is trying to settle the estate.

- William Jennings asks whether Thomas Pipe is with her now. He assures her that Thomas Pipe will do his best for her as he hopes to do.

- Elizabeth Coleman Jennings adds a note asking Elizabeth Stickland Pipe whether she intends to stay in New York, go west with Charlotte Jennings Pipe Pillar and Thomas Pipe, or return to England. Charlotte Jennings Pipe Pillar and Thomas Pipe traveled together from Vinland, Wisconsin, to Monroe County, New York.

- Elizabeth Coleman Jennings says that Elizabeth Stickland Pipe's mother, Elizabeth Wall Stickland Bartlett, is living in London with sister Mary Stickland.

- Elizabeth Coleman Jennings received a letter from Charlotte Jennings Pipe Pillar. They have received three or four letters from William Jennings Pipe who is in military service in Sevastopol Crimea.

- Elizabeth Coleman Jennings recognizes how hard it must be for Charlotte Jennings Pipe Pillar to have lost John Valentine Pipe. Now, she must fear the loss of William Jennings Pipe while he is in the military. Elizabeth Coleman Jennings refers to John Valentine Pipe and William Jennings Pipe as "her two dear boys."

Dear Mrs. Pipe

You have never sent me the power that were sent to you from Mr. Dommett the 16 of January 1854 for which he has charged for on his bill, please do send it as soon as you get this for if Mr. Middleton should proceed he can do as he like, after I have paid Mr. Dommett his bill I shall have £5 in hand up to the 11th October 54, there is a little bill at Mr. Dennings and one at Mr. Hughes that John [Valentine Pipe] promised to pay but they must wait longer.

I hope this will make you sensible how things stand at the estate if it does not I don't know how to tell you more plainer. I should have answered you before but now I can tell you the right of it and how it stands. Is dear Tom [Thomas Pipe] with you now, I should have wrote him a letter, but I thought whether he was gone west if he is with you please give my kind love to him and I hope he will do his best for you as I hope to do. I shall take care of all bills to answer for themselves and to have no more done

than have need for but there must be a great date fetching down. <u>Please don't you delay sending the power of attorney as quick as possible.</u>

My dear Mrs. Pipe

As my dear Wm. [Jennings] had a bit of wastepaper, I thought I would drop a few words to you. I must first ask you if you intend staying where you are, or going west with Mrs. [Charlotte Jennings Pipe] Pillar, or else coming to England, please tell us when you write. I should very much like to see you and the dear children, your mother [Elizabeth Wall Stickland Barrett] is living in London with your sister, they has taken a house. Your sister [Mary Stickland] does a little to her business, her health is very bad, my sister Susan [Coleman] has been to London on a visit, your sister [Mary Stickland] spent a day with her, she looks very ill indeed, she wondered why you did not write to her. Miss Mary Mathews was married about 4 months ago now, she has a fine daughter a month or five weeks old. She married at the summer fair of Stockland [Devon] but she is still living home. I suppose T. [Thomas] Pipe has left you as he said he must go west the falls, I hear Miss M. Coles is living home. I suppose you have received a letter from her. I received a letter from Mrs. [Charlotte Jennings Pipe] Pillar, should have answered before now if her brother John [Jennings] had not written as now I shall delay it a little longer, we have received 3 or 4 letters from Wm. [Jennings] Pipe since he has been abroad, the last he wrote to his Uncle John [Jennings] Sept 1st, he was then in Sebastopo [Sevastopol, Crimea], he wrote in much better spirits than he did last time since he wrote there has been an engagement and many of our men has lost their lives. I hope the poor fellow's life is still spared.

[other way]

him what a trial for dear Mrs. [Charlotte Jennings Pipe] Pillar to think of her two dear boys [John Valentine Pipe and William Jennings Pipe], the thought is dreadful. Have you ever heard any tidings of the ill fate result that Mr. John [Valentine Pipe] sailed. I suppose my old friend you have given up all thoughts of ever seeing him again if you meet not on earth may you both meet in heaven. I must forget to tell you I do expect an increase to my family [Ellen (Nelly) Jennings] between this and Christmas. My little girl [Mary Ann Jennings] has been out to school this last January. I must conclude with kind hope to yourself and your children believe me to remain.

Yours affectionately

E. [Elizabeth] Jennings

Letter Number 19, Page 1

Dear Mrs Pipe

You have never
sent me the power that ware sent
to you from Mr Dommett the 16 of
January 1854 for which he has charged
for on his bill please to send it as
soon as you get this for if Mr
Middleton should proseed he can
do as he like, after I have paid Mr
Dommett his bill I shall have 5
in hand up to the 11th of October 54
there is a little Bill at Mr Dennings
and one at Mr Hugshes that John prom
to pay but they must wait longer

Letter Number 19, Page 2

I hope this will make you sensible
how things stand at the estate
if it dose not I don't know how to
tell you more plainer I should have
answered you before but now I can
tell you the right of it and how it
stands, is Dear Tom with you now
I should have wrote him a letter but
I thought wether he was gone west
if he is with you please give my
kind love to him and I hope he will
do his best for you as I hope to do
I shall take care of all bills to answer
for themselves and to have no more

Letter Number 19, Page 3

done than have need for but there
must be a great deal fatching done
please don't you delay sending the
power of attorney as quick as possible

My dear Mrs Pipe

As my dear Mrs had a bit
of waste paper I thought I would drop
a few words to you I must first ask you
if you intend staying where you are or
going west with Mrs Piller or else coming
to england please tell us when you write
I should very much like to see you on the
dear children, your Mother is living in
london with your Sister they has taken
a house your Sister does a little to her
business her health is very bad, my
Sister Susan has been to london on a visit
your Sister spent a day with her she
looks very ill indeed she wondered

Letter Number 19, Page 4

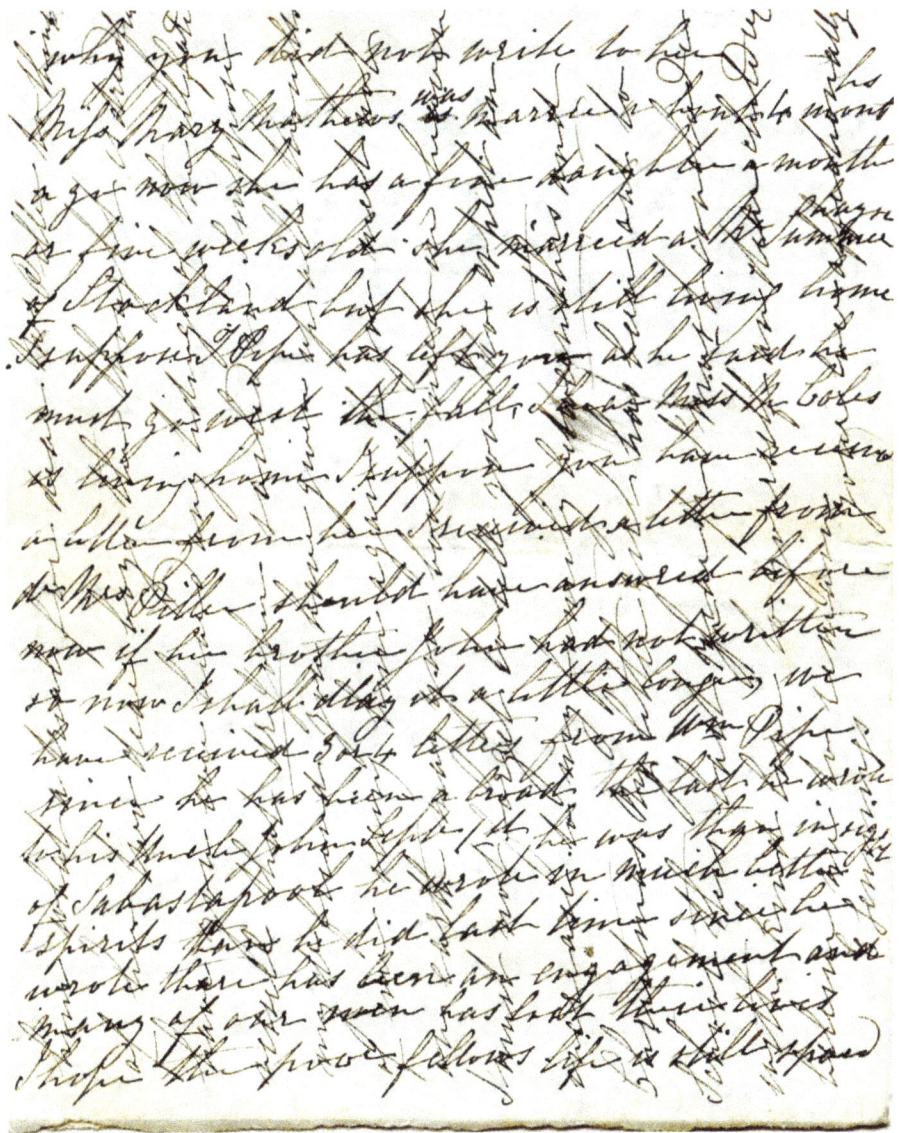

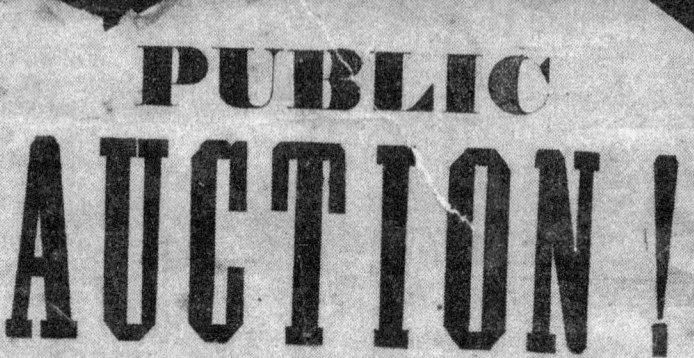

PUBLIC AUCTION!

The Subscriber will sell at her residence in

Greece Center

ON THURSDAY, OCT. 5, 1854,

the undermentioned property:

1 three year old gelding, well broke; 1 top buggy; 1 light buggy, nearly new; 1 one horse wagon; 1 cutter, nearly new; 1 one-horse harness; 2 good milch cows; 1 sow and pigs; 1 large hog; together with HOUSEHOLD FURNITURE, consisting of 3 bedsteads; 1 parlor lounge; 1 kitchen do.; 1 bureau; 3 parlor and kitchen tables; 1 stand; a number of cane-bottomed and kitchen chairs; 2 arm chairs; 1 cook stove, and furniture; 1 parlor stove; 1 large cupboard; 1 sink; 1 churn and butter-bowl; a quantity of tin pans, pails, wash-tubs, measures, and other articles too numerous to mention.

TERMS OF SALE:—All sums of five dollars and under, cash; all over five dollars, three months credit, with good endorsed notes on interest.

☞ Sale to commence at 11 o'clock.

ELIZABETH PIPE.

Greece, Sept. 22, 1854.

ROCHESTER DAILY UNION PRINT.

ONE OF THE TREASURED POSSESSIONS of Raymond Pipe, town of Lanark, is this handbill advertising a public auction more than 100 years ago. The handbill was acquired by Pipe from his grandmother, the late Mrs. Thomas Pipe. It advertises a public auction scheduled for Oct. 5, 1854, at Greece Center, N. Y.

Chapter 3

Vinland, Winnebago County, Wisconsin
1855 - 1857

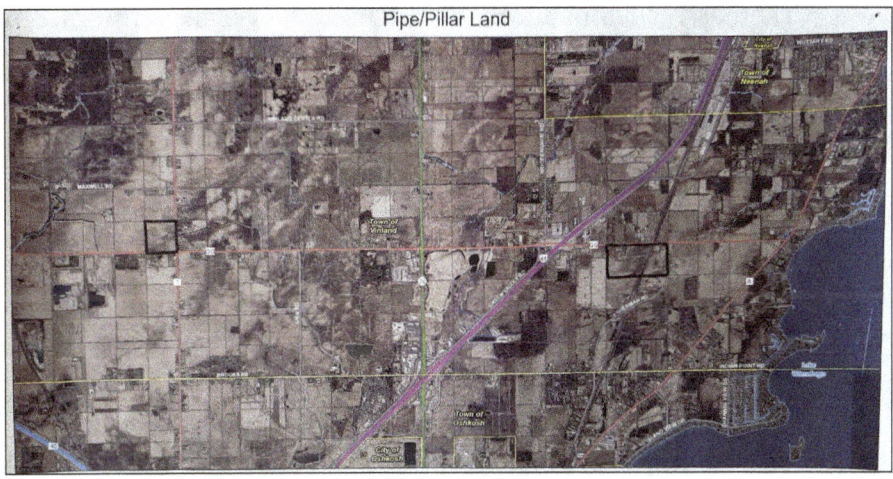
Pipe/Pillar Land

This map of today's town of Vinland, Wisconsin, shows the Pipe land outlined in black in the left-center and the Pillar land outlined due east in the right-center, roughly midway between Neenah to the north and Oshkosh to the south. Lake Winnebago is the blue area to the east.

Chapter 3 includes letters dated 1855 to 1857 while widow Elizabeth Stickland Pipe and her four children with John Valentine Pipe are living with her brother-in-law, Thomas Pipe, in the town of Vinland, Winnebago County, Wisconsin. Elizabeth Stickland Pipe marries Thomas Pipe in 1855 in Vinland. One letter is a descendant's note on an envelope found in the original letter collection box. Six letters are between Thomas and Elizabeth Stickland Pipe and Uncle William and Aunt Elizabeth Coleman Jennings of Somerset, England. One letter is from Thomas Pipe to his Uncle John Jennings of Birch Oak Farm, Membury, Devon.

Letter Number 20

Date: 7 March 1855
Writer: Thomas Pipe
Recipient: John Jennings
Sent from: Vinland, Winnebago County, Wisconsin, USA
Sent to: Birch Oak Farm, Membury, Devon County, England

Key Ideas

- Thomas Pipe announces that he has a housekeeper, Elizabeth Stickland Pipe. They began living together last Christmas.
- Thomas Pipe mentions that he heard that John Jennings got "burnt out at Birch" Oak Farm.
- Thomas Pipe remarks that farming has been good in his area of Vinland, unlike the Eastern states. He understands farming has been good in England.
- Thomas Pipe notes that farming is quite different in America than in England. He suspects John Valentine Pipe told him about farming in the Eastern states, but farming is again different in Vinland.
- Thomas Pipe bought his farm from J. (Joel) Knight. The farm had a log house on it and 13 acres "under the plough." He rented the farm last year (1854) for $40. He gets cedar for his fence from government land.
- Thomas Pipe mentions planting buckwheat which is valuable in Vinland. Buckwheat is used for pancakes.
- Thomas Pipe says he has been unwell the two last summers (1853 and 1854). If he is not better next summer (1855), he thinks he will return to England the following summer (1856).
- Thomas Pipe has received a letter from his brother William Jennings Pipe that was written on December 10, 1854.
- Thomas Pipe reports that James Pillar has been in the pinery, lumber camps in northern Wisconsin, this winter.

Vinland March 7th, 1855

Grandpa Pipe to Uncle [Note was written in pencil by a later generation]

I believe that Elizabeth [Stickland Pipe] intends to enclose a few lines to Uncle William. [Her letter is not here.]

Breaking land buying cedar posts [This note was also added in pencil by a later generation. Thomas Pipe explains in the letter that he has the privilege to cut cedar from government land to make his own rails.]

Dear Uncle [John Jennings]

After the elapse of nearly five years, I am about to take the opportunity of dropping you a few lines. I suppose that by this time you have given up the idea of ever receiving a letter from me. I will assure you that it is not because I had forgotten you, it was only for the want of a resolution to write. You know it is a general failure in the Pipe family.

I suppose that you are aware that I am got to housekeeper and that Elizabeth [Stickland Pipe] is living with me. We commenced keeping house about Christmas last. I understand that you got burnt out at Burch [Birch Oak Farm]. I did not hear whether you was much the loser or not. I understood that your property was insured, but I suppose you did not get its full value. I suppose the farmers have had a pretty good time for a year or two past in England as everything have been fetching a good price, times have been pretty good for a year or two in this country

or rather I should have said in these Western States as I believe the crops failed in a great measure in the Eastern States, especially the wheat which the American farmer has to depend on. Farming is altogether different in this country from what it is in England. I suppose that poor John [Valentine Pipe] gave you some idea how it was in the East, but there is quite as much difference between this and the East as there is in that and England. I suppose you will scarcely credit it when I tell you that a man has to do twice as much work in this county as is generally done in England in order to act alone. I should like to lay the reasons before you as I see them, but that I cannot do as it requires a better penman than what I am to do it, but I can explain it to you in part. In the first place when a man comes here, he gets himself a new farm or rather piece of land and then has to make his own farm which he has to do the greater part himself as labour is so very dear. In the first place he has to make his fence which takes about a thousand rails eleven feet long to build eight rods of fence, which he has to draw from four to twelve miles and most generally do it with oxen on sledges.

I have been myself twelve miles with one yoke of oxen. We find it a little cheaper to go the greater distance as there we have the privilege to cut and make our own rails as it is government land, and it is light timber. It is called cedar. It is not much more than half the weight of oak timber. We generally draw a hundred to a load. I have to make 160 rods of fence this spring. I have 40 acres of land which I bought of[f] J. [Joel] Knight with a log house on it and 13 acres under the plough. I let [rented] it the last year for 40 dollars. It was very cheap at that rent, but I left before the times altered, it was certainly worth one third more as it turned out. I do intend to break 14 acres this summer if it is possible. I do intend to do the whole within myself by change work with my neighbours. It requires 4 or 5 yoke of cattle to break. We use ploughs which cut from 18 to 22 inches to a furrow, and break from 1¾ to 2 acres per day. The ploughing is generally done with one yoke of cattle or pair of light horses and plough 2 acres per day. I do intent to sow 4 acres of spring wheat on my own land and on land which I have taken and 5 acres on my own to Indian corn and the remainder to oats. I intend to sow 2 acres of the breaken to buckwheat a crop which is none but little in England, but thought a great deal of in this country. It is used for making pancake. In the winter it is what we all think we cannot do without in the cold weather. We have had a very severe winter. Elizabeth [Stickland Pipe] says another such would freeze her to death. As for my part I can stand the cold much better than the heat. I have been so unwell the two last summers that I could scarcely get around. I have an idea that I shall be better this summer as I have felt quite different since sickness last time. If I am not, I shall return to England the summer following.

We received a letter from William [Jennings Pipe] about two weeks since it was written the 10th of December. He was well and seemed to be in good spirits. Elizabeth and mother [Charlotte Jennings Pipe Pillar] joins with me in sending our kind love to all uncles and aunts with all enquiring friends not forgotten yourself.

From yours a well-wisher and affectionate nephew

Thos. Pipe

P.S. Should you feel disposed to write me an answer, I should be most happy to receive it. It is more than I can desire as I have been so neglectful myself. [James] Pillar has been in the pinery [lumber camps in northern Wisconsin] this winter.

Letter Number 20, Page 1

(Grandpa Pipe to Uncle)

I beleve that Elizebeth intends to inclose a few lines
to Uncle William

Breaking I said buying Cedar posts
&c   Dear Uncle.

Finland March 4th 1855.

After the elaps of nearly
five years I am about to take the opportunity
of dropen you a few lines. I sopose that by this
time you have given up the idea of ever receiv
a letter from me. I will ashore you that it is
not becose I had forgotten you. it was only for the
want of a resalution to wright. you know it is a
general failer in the pipe family.
I sopose that you ar aware that I am got to house
keepen and that Elizebeth is liven with me. we
comenced keepen hous about Cristmas last I under
stand that you got burnt out at Burch, I did not
hear wether you was mutch the looser or not. I under
stood that your property was inshured, but I sopose
you did not get its fool value, I sopose the Farmers
have had a prety good time for a year ar to past in
England. as every thing have been fetchen a good price
times have been prety good for a year ar too in this
Cuntry

Letter Number 20, Page 2

ar rather I should have said in these western States
as I beleve the crops has failed in a great measure
in the Eastern States. especialy the wheat which the
american farmer has to depend on. Farmering
is all to-gether diferent in this cuntry from what
it is in England, I sopose that poor John gave you
your idea how it was in the East, but there is not
as mutch difrence betwen this and the East as there is
in that and England, I sopose you will scarcely credit
it when I tell you that a man has to do twice as
mutch work in this cuntry as is generaly don
in England in order to get along, I should like to
lay the reasons before you as I see them but that I
cannot do it requires a beter penmen than what
I am to do it, but I can explain it to you in part
in the first place where a man com heare he gets
him self a new farm ar rather peace of land and then
has to make his owne form which he has to do the
greater part himself as laber is so very dear. in
the first place he has to make his fence which
takes about a thousand rails to build eighty rods
of fence. which he has to draw from four to twelve
miels and most generaly do it with oxen on sledges

Letter Number 20, Page 3

I have been my self twelve miels with one yoke of oxen
we find it a little cheaper to go the greater distance
as there we have the priviliedge to cut and make our
owne rails as it is government land, and it is light
timber it is what is cald cedder it is not mutch more
than half the wait of oake timber. we generley draw
a hundred to a lode I have to make 160 rods of
fence this Spring. I have 40 ackers of land which
I bought of J Knight with a log house on it and
13 ackers under the plow. I leet it the last year
for 40 dolars. it was very cheap at that rent but
I leet it before the times altred it was certenly
worth one therd more as it turned out, I doin
tend to break 14 ackers this Summer if it is posable
I do intend to do the hole with in my self by change
work with my neabers. it requires 4 or 5 yoke of cattle
to break we use plows which cut from 18 to 22 inches
to a ferrow. and break from 1½ to 2 ackers per day
the plowing is jineraly don with one yoke of cattle
or span of light horses. and plow 2 ackers per day,
I do intend to sow 4 ackers of wheet Spring on my one land and
8 on land which I have taken and 5 ackers on my one to
indean corn and the remainder to oats. I intend to

Letter Number 20, Page 4

sow a ackers of the breaken to buck wheat a crop which
is nown but little in England. but thought a great
deal of in this buntry it is used for maken pencake
in the winter it is what we all think we cannot do with-
-out in cold wether, we have had a very savear winter
Elizebeth sais a nother sutch ould freas her to death
as for my part I can stand the cold mutch better then
the heat. I have been so unwel the two last summers
that I cold scarsley get round I have an idea that
I shall be better this summer as I have felt quit
difrent since my sickness last faul, if I am not
I shall return to England the summer folowen,
we receved a letter from William about two wicks since
it was writen the 1st of December, he was well and
and seem to be in good sperrits, Elizebeth and mother
joins with me in senden our kind love to all
uncles and aunts with all inquirer friends not
forgeten yourself, From yours a well wisher and
afectionet nephew   Thos Pipe
PS Should you feel disposed to wright me an ans
wer I should be most happy to receive it, it is
more than I can
desire as I have been so neglectful my self,
Pillar has ben in the Tinery this winter

Letter Number 21

Date: 4 May 1855
Writer: Unknown
Recipient: Future Generations
Sent from: NA
Sent to: NA

Key Ideas

- A descendant leaves a note on an envelope in the letter collection box. The note says that Thomas and Elizabeth married on May 4, 1855, in Vinland, Wisconsin.
- Thomas Pipe remarks in Letter Number 25 that he and Elizabeth Stickland Pipe were married on June 24, 1855.

———————

Elizabeth [Stickland Pipe] is keeping house for her brother-in-law [Thomas Pipe] and married him 1855 May 4 [24 June according to Thomas Pipe in Letter Number 25].

Letter Number 22

Date: 8 May 1855
Writer: Elizabeth Coleman Jennings
Recipient: Elizabeth Stickland Pipe
Sent from: Northay Farm, Whitestaunton, Chard,
                Somerset County, England
Sent to: Vinland, Winnebago County, Wisconsin, USA

Key Ideas

- Elizabeth Coleman Jennings tells Elizabeth Stickland Pipe that they received her note included in Thomas Pipe's letter of April 29.
- Elizabeth Stickland Pipe will not receive the money she requested on time because her request took nearly seven weeks to arrive in England.
- William Jennings will put rent money in the savings account at the bank.
- William Jennings is sorry to hear that Thomas Pipe was cheated out of money.
- Little Frank Pipe was on the Indian land (Chain O' Lakes, town of Farmington, Waupaca County, Wisconsin) with Mr. Ames.
- Elizabeth Coleman Jennings sends wishes for better health to Thomas Pipe.
- Brother John Stickland's little girl's health has been delicate this winter.

Envelope addressed to:
Mrs. [Elizabeth] Pipe
Vinland
Winnebago County
State Wisconsin
North America

[crosshatched]

Please to write soon

Northay, May 8th, 1855

My dear Mrs. Pipe

We received a note you enclosed in Thomas's letter the 29th April. William has sent a draft for the £'s you wished him to send. I am sorry you won't get it by the time you said you should want it. Your note was dated nearly seven weeks before we received it.

Mr. Philips nor yet Denning [Peacross Farm, Membury, Devon] has not paid the whole of this last half year's rent. Mr. Philips promised to be here today to settle up but he has not been. He owes to Denning £1. When they have paid it, Wm. will have about ten or twelve pounds in hand. As soon as he can get it together then he will put it in the savings bank for it to bring in a little. If it should be needed it can be drawn at any time. He was very glad to hear you and the children [John Stickland, Tom, Frank, Mary Elizabeth] were well, had been expecting to hear from you for some time. Wm. did not answer Thomas's letter, as he had nothing particular to say at the time, was very sorry to hear you had been cheated out of so much money. It will never do the rogue no good in the end. You said little Frank [Pipe] was on the Indian land [Chain O' Lakes, Farmington, Waupaca, Wisconsin] with Mr. Ames, I suppose that is a long way from you. I suppose Mrs. [Charlotte Jennings Pipe] Pillar has received my letter I wrote her a few days before we heard from you. John Jennings received a letter from Wm. [Jennings] Pipe about fortnight ago. He was very well. He had received the clothes we sent him which he thought was lost. We have heard from him several times this winter

[other way]

Am sorry to hear Thomas's health is so bad. I hope he will be better this summer. Please give my love to him. Tell him I hear Miss Jiffery his old sweetheart is going to Australia.

Miss Mary Mathews is married to one Mr. John Sommers of Stockland [Devon], is living on a farm near Honiton [Devon]. She had a child about 3 or 4 months after she was married. John Mathews has no children. His wife is rather a gay lady. Your brother John's [Stickland] little girl's health has been very delicate this winter. I am happy to say my dear baby is getting on very nicely after her illness. I should like to know what you call your little girl. I hear John Bond is likely to get married shortly to a widow woman, an old sweetheart of his, one of the Miss Jacobs. No doubt, but Mrs. [Charlotte Jennings Pipe] Pillar know her. She has one child. I should like to know how far you live from Mrs. [Charlotte Jennings Pipe] Pillar. Please give our very kind love to her own family. The weather is still very cold and dry. The spring is very backward. Stock in general is very inferior on account of the very severe winter and shortness of help. Wm. would have written to you himself only he is very busy drilling corn. I hope we shall finish today. Wm. joins with me in kind love to you and all friends.

Hoping this will find you all well.

From your affectionate aunt

E. [Elizabeth Coleman] Jenning

Letter Number 22, Envelope

Letter Number 22, Page 1

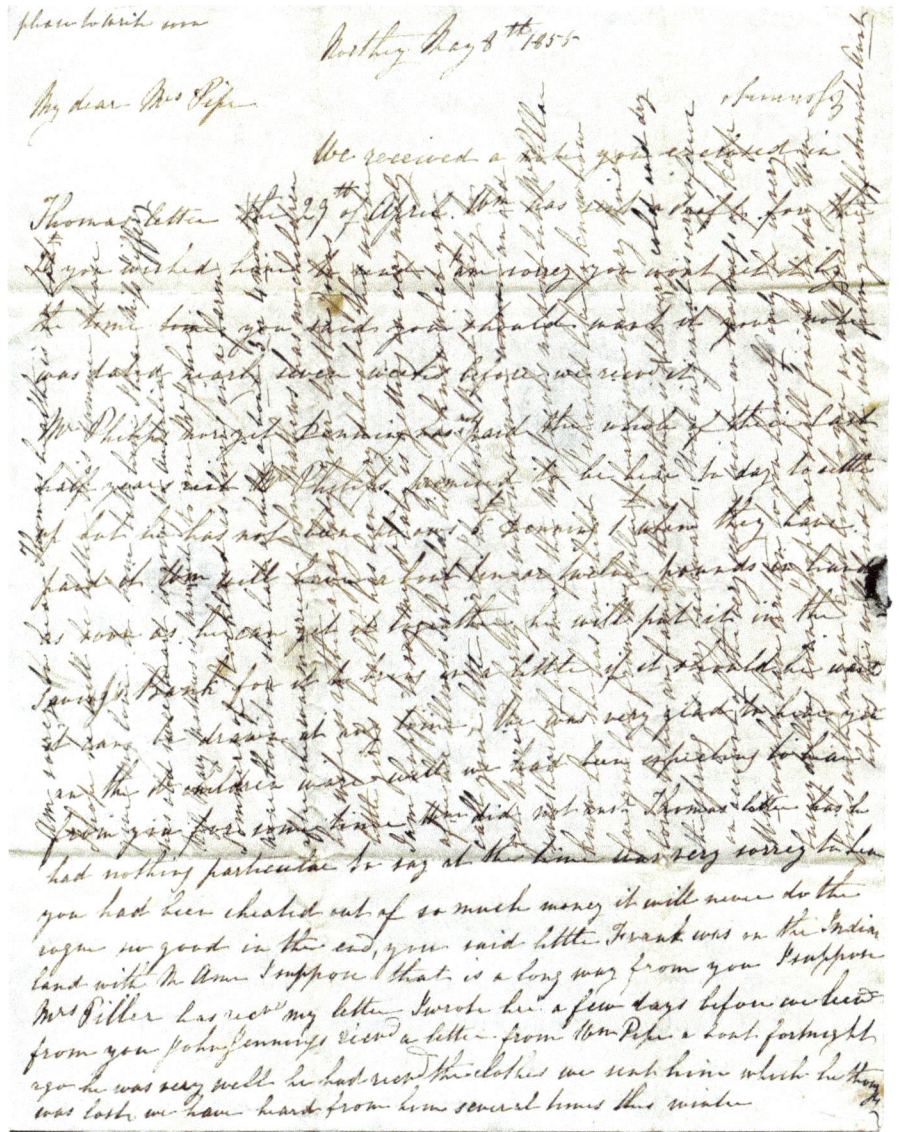

please to write soon

Nothy May 8th 1855

My dear Mrs Pipe

We received a letter you enclosed in Thomas letter the 29th of April...

...had nothing particular to say at the time was very sorry to hear you had been cheated out of so much money it will never do the rogue no good in the end, you said little Frank was on the India land with M Ann I suppose that is a long way from you I suppose Mrs Piller has recd my letter I wrote her a few days before we heard from you John Jennings recd a letter from Wm Pipe about fortnight ago he was very well he had recd the clothes we sent him which he thought was lost we have heard from him several times this winter

Letter Number 23

Date: 21 November 1855
Writer: William & Elizabeth Coleman Jennings
Recipient: Thomas Pipe
Sent from: Northay Farm, Whitestaunton, Chard,
                  Somerset County, England
Sent to: Vinland, Winnebago County, Wisconsin, USA

Key Ideas

- William Jennings received rent of £9 this month. Elizabeth Stickland Pipe had asked earlier about the lease for Pithayne Farm. William Jennings reports that the lease is not signed. He explains to Thomas Pipe that he could not have possession of the property without proper notice.
- Elizabeth Stickland Pipe had asked William Jennings how much capital it would take to stock Pithayne Farm at a profitable advantage. William Jennings suggests at least £500.
- William Jennings warns that taxes are high, and it is hard to be profitable in England. William Jennings reminds Thomas and Elizabeth Stickland Pipe that they are paying an annuity of £24 a year to brother John Stickland. He also states that education is extremely high in England.
- William Jennings recommends that Thomas and Elizabeth Stickland Pipe stay in Vinland since he does not believe the Pipes can be profitable at Pithayne Farm.
- William Jennings was to have money repaid by the deceased John Valentine Pipe as soon as John Valentine Pipe returned home. William Jennings told Thomas Pipe that John Valentine Pipe told him if the money was not repaid, he was to keep the rent. William Jennings tells Thomas Pipe to get life insurance. William Jennings explains that he would not recover the money owed to him by his brother John Valentine Pipe if Thomas Pipe were to die. William Jennings offers to get life insurance for Thomas Pipe at £5 out of the rent.

- William Jennings Pipe has written William Jennings. William Jennings sends his kind love to his sister, Charlotte Jennings Pipe Pillar.
- William Jennings suggests that Thomas Pipe write to his Aunt Coleman who is staying with Mr. Coleman at Whitestaunton, Somerset. She is unwell and may leave him some property when she dies.

[Crosshatched from Elizabeth Jennings]

- Elizabeth Coleman Jennings has sent a local newspaper and has received one from Charlotte Jennings Pipe Pillar.
- Elizabeth Coleman Jennings asks whether Thomas Pipe has seen or heard from her brother, William Coleman, who is carrying on the butcher business.
- Samuel Baker married M.A. (Mary Ann) Borough. They have a son and live at Sea Whan Croft (?).
- Uncle John Jennings has a beautiful house and farm. The house is stylishly carpeted and wallpapered. Elizabeth Coleman Jennings thinks he is making money fast, but he is in a poor state of health.
- Mr. Carrey is also ill.
- Mr. George Bond is living near Axminster, Devon, with two children. Surprisingly, he is living the life of a farmer. Elizabeth Coleman Jennings says, "It is no matter what we do so as we get an honest and respectable living."
- Elizabeth Coleman Jennings has not seen John Bond since he was married. She has heard they live in style much more than when his uncle was living. Most of the family has paid a wedding visit. She does not think they will.
- William Jennings Pipe military service is currently in Sevastopol, Crimea.
- Elizabeth Coleman Jennings asks Thomas Pipe to tell his mother Charlotte Jennings Pipe Pillar that her brother Tom Jennings wife's two children paid a visit, and that son Tom Jennings is doing well in Australia.

Northay Nov 21st, 1855

Dear Thos.

I have delayed writing to you up to the time of receiving the Michael-mas [25 September] rent which I received the 9 of this month. Mrs. [Elizabeth Stickland] Pipe wanted to know if the lease is signed. It is not signed. Of course, you could not have possession without proper notice of times near the turn it would be impossible for him to pay the rent by £15 a year and that the reason he went since the lease it is let [rented] very <u>dear</u> [expensive], but I don't tell him so. Mrs. [Elizabeth Stick-land] Pipe wanted to know how much capital it would take to stock it at a profitable advantage. I think to make a complete thing if it not less than £500. You have a right to use your own mind once that I would do I can only tell you that it won't cost nought for you and your family to have

any profit there are taxes very high and will be higher and are very high and you must consider £24 a year to your [Elizabeth Stickland Pipe's] brother [John Stickland] is cooling very high. I have heard that educa-tion cost a mere nothing where you are and you know that is a fine thing in this country but it's what I am very short of. You have got to go into all those things. You know your circumstances better than I. If you are doing pretty well where you are I should recommend you to stay where you are till you have accumulated something considerable for I am cer-tain you can't do it at Pithayne [Farm]. You asked for my opinion and I have told you but you had need not bide by it. Your estate is very prof-itable hill country place, but there is something more than the produce of that farm wanted for a family.

[crosshatched]

There is one thing I can't tell you better than you know but if you want my opinion you had better to write to any respectable person that you can think of as concerning the money borrowed. I was to have it as soon as dear John [Valentine Pipe] got home and if not paid then I was to keep the rent till it was paid. I suppose you are aware that my money is not safe if you were to drop. The property would come to your family and I have no right to it. Whatever money is worth £5 rent now I will send you the balance on the last and this last half as well if you will pay me 5 for it as [since] I can get it. I know money is great value there and I will do what I can for you but for it to be safe your

[crosshatched]

life ought to be insured when you receive this if you wish to have the money. Please to write and I will send it to you but afterwards I think you had better to pay it as I am not safe in case any thing should happen. Money is a wonderful scarce thing here. They say the war will ruin this country with taxes. We have heard from Wm. [Jennings] Pipe since the Sebastopol [Sevastopol, Crimea]. I hope his dear mother [Charlotte Jennings Pipe Pillar] and Mr. [James] Pillar and family is well. Please to give my kind love to my dear sister [Charlotte Jennings Pipe Pillar] when you see her. Thomas, I think you ought write to your Aunt Coleman. I often see her. She is staying with Mr. Coleman at Whitestaunton. She is very unwell. I am in hopes there is some property for you when she drops.

[other way]

From your affectionate

Uncle Wm. Jennings

[other way]

I sent you a newspaper a week or two ago. I received one from Mrs. [Charlotte Jennings Pipe] Pillar a short time ago. Will send you another soon. I suppose it will be Christmas by the time you get this. I wish you a happy one. Have you seen or heard from my brother [William Coleman] lately. He has changed houses and is carrying on the butchering business. Saml. Baker is married to M.A. Borough. He has been this year and has a fine son lives at Sea Whan Croft [?], used to your uncle John [Jennings] has a beautiful house and farm buildings at Birch [Oak Farm] has his kitchen

[other way]

papered and parlour carpeted they have 4 rooms papered. A flower garden in front of the house. I can assure you it is quite in style. I should think they are making money fast. Your Uncle John [Jennings] enjoys a poor state of health at times. He went to home. Dear Mr. Carrey no doubt but you heard of him before you left that was the later part of the summer. I am happy to say he is better now. Mr. George Bond seems to be getting on very well, is still living near Axminster [Somerset]. He has two children a son and a daughter. He milks about 10 cows. Who should have

[other way]

thought he would be seen about 8 years ago milking of a cow. He often do it now. It is no matter what we do so as we get an honest and respectable living. I have not seen Mr. John Bond since he was married. I hear they live right at style much more so than when his uncle was living. Most of the family has paid the wedding visit. We have not nor neither do I expect we shall directly. Tell your dear mother [Charlette Jennings Pipe Pillar] brother Tom's [Jennings] wife two children

[other way]

paid us a visit a little time ago. They were quite well, desired their kind love to her. Tom [Jennings, Jr.] is doing well in Australia. Wm. thinks I have spoiled his letter, at least made it worse that it was before by scribbling over it. I must conclude with kind love to all. May the Lord send you every blessing is the prayer of your Aunt Elizabeth [Coleman Jennings].

Northey Nov'r 21th 1855.

Dr Thos
I have delayed writing to
you up to the time of receiving the
Michelmas rent which I received the
9 of this month Mr Pipe wanted to
know if the lease is signed it is not
signed of course you could not have
possession way [illegible] proper notice of
[illegible] were to know it would be impossible for him to pay the rent by
15 a year and that the reason he
[illegible] gave the lease it is let very
dear but I dont like him so Mr Pipe
wanted to know how much it capital
it would take to work it at a profit
advantage that is to make a complate thing
of it not less than 500 you have a right
to use your own mind and that I would
do I can only tell you that it wont cost
enough for you and your family to have

Letter Number 23, Page 2

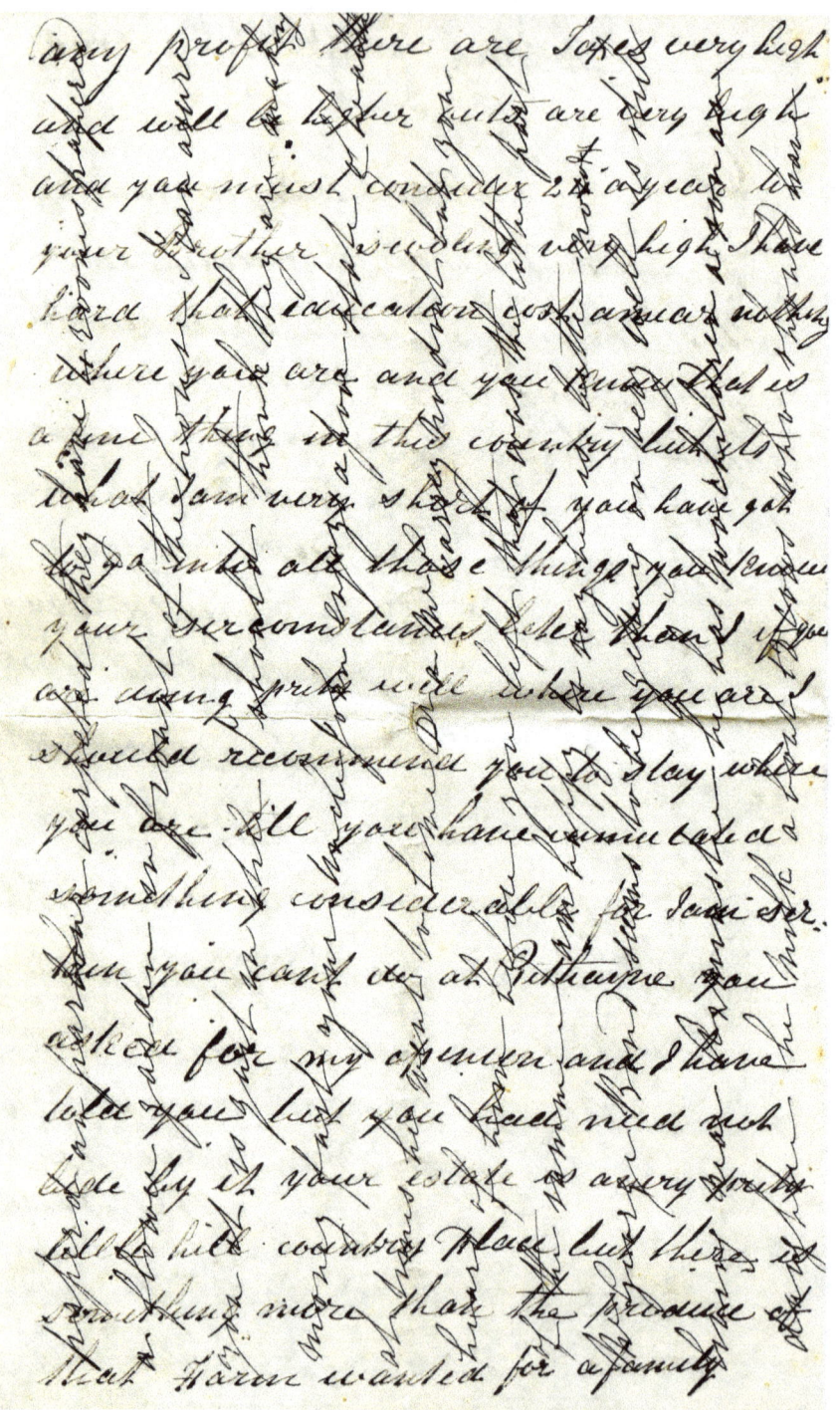

there is one thing I canot tell you better
than you know but if you doubt my
opinion you had better to write to
any respectable person that you can
think of as concerning the money
borrowed I was to hear of as soon
as our John got home and if not paid
there I was to keep the note till it
was paid I suppose you are aware
that my money is not safe if you
was to drop the property would
come to your family and I have no
right to let whatever money is worth
5 p cent now I will send you the balance
due on the note and this last half
as well if you will pay me 5 for it
as I can get it there money is great
value there and I will do what I can
for you but for I to be safe your

life ought to be inshured when
you receive that if you wish to have
the money please to write and I
will send it to you but
afterwards I think you had better
to pay it as I am not safe in
case any thing should happen
money is a wonderful scarce thing
here they say the war will ruin
this country with taxes we have
heard from Pipe since the fall of
sabustapole I hope his & Mother
and Mr Puller and family is well
please to give my kind love to my
Dear Sister when you see her
Thomas I thank you ought write to
your aunt Coleman I ofen see her she
is staying with Mr Coleman at Whitestown
she is very unwell I am in hopes there is some
properly for you when she dies

Letter Number 24

Date: 1854-1855 Accounts
Writer: Elizabeth Coleman Jennings
Recipient: Thomas & Elizabeth Stickland Pipe
Sent from: Northay Farm, Whitestaunton, Chard,
Somerset County, England
Sent to: Vinland, Winnebago County, Wisconsin, USA

Key Ideas

- Elizabeth Coleman Jennings itemizes accounts for 1854-1855.

Accounts 1854-1855

Mr. and Mrs. Pipe I thought you would like to see the accounts, and I have copied it from the book for you to see it

1854 Apr. 3	Received of Mr. Hutchings for 18 weeks rent £15 11s 3d
	From Mr. Denning £3 3s od
	Received of Mr. Philips for ½ year for Caps wood £1 os od
	Received of Mr. Mathews ¼ years rent for Mannings Common £1 15s od
Nov. 1855	received of Mr. Denning ½ years rent £4 os od
1854	What has been paid out
Apr. 3	Letters and stamps 4d
	Ditto for Gray 8d
	Paid Cock's bill 5s 3d

Oct. 16   Paid Mr. Mathews for John Stickland one year and six months annuity £36 0s 0d

Up to Oct 11th, 1854

£2 15s 0d

Disbursements 1s 6d

Grog and stamps 1s 0d

Letter stamps 1s 0d

Nov. 1   Expenses with J. Denning 1s 0d

1855

Apr. 5   Disbursements 8 17s 1 1/2 d

Paid Mr. Mathews annuity £12 0s 0d

One year interest for £170
£6 17s 0d

Paid Mr. Dommett's bill £11 8s 10d

Draft and stamp 2s 0d

Wm. says the disbursements won't be so high another year as it was much out of repair. If you wish to have the money Wm. have in hand, he will send it, I hope your next letter won't be so long coming as the last or yet this so long going to you.

In haste

Unsigned

[squiggle at the bottom which might be a signature.]

Dr Mrs Pipe I thought you would like to see the
as I have copied it from the book for you to
see it

1854			£	s	d
April 3	Recd of Mr Hutchins for				
	18 weeks rent	15	11	3
	from Mr Denny	3	3	0
Oct 10	Recd of Mr Phillips for pigs	40	0	0
	for Caps Wood	1	0	0
	recd of Mr Mathews 1/4 yr			
	rent for Manor Common	4	15	0
Nov 1	recd of Mr Denning 1/2 year	4	0	0
1855					
April 5	Mr Phillips paid in part	35	0	0
	Mr Denning	4	0	0

1854	What has been laid out		£	s	d
April 3	letters and Stamps		0	0	4
	to for Greg				8
	Pd Cooks bill		5		3
Oct 16	Paid Mr Mathews for John Stickland				
	one year an six months annuity	36	0	0
	up to Oct 11th 1854	2	15	0
	disbursments		1		6
	Greg and Stamps		1		0
	letter Sloman		1		0
Nov 1	Expences with J Denning		1		0
1855					
April 5	disbursments		8	17	1½
	one year intrest for 170	6	17	0
	Paid Mr Mathews annuity	12	0	0
	Paid Mr Dommetts bill	11	8	10
	draft & Stamp		2		0

Letter Number 24, Page 2

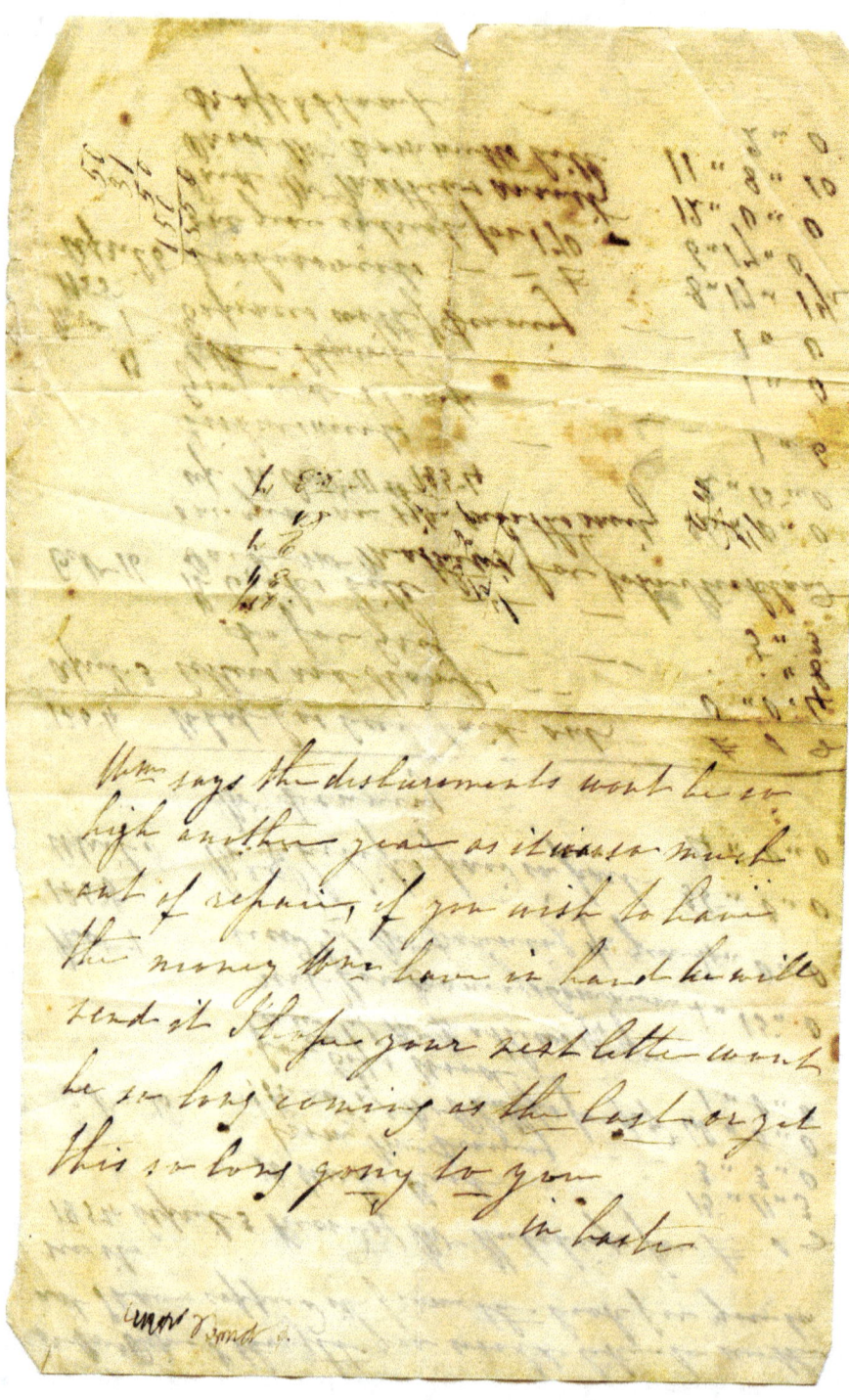

Letter Number 25

Date: Before 24 June 1856
Writer: Thomas Pipe
Recipient: William Jennings
Sent from: Vinland, Winnebago County, Wisconsin, USA
Sent to: Northay Farm, Whitestaunton, Chard,
              Somerset County, England

Key Ideas

- Thomas Pipe writes to William Jennings requesting £120 be sent to him by November so he can expand his farm. The expansion is necessary for him to make a living.
- Thomas Pipe can buy 80 acres, with 40 acres "under the plough" at the back of his farm. He can buy the land for $1,000 with $200 down and the rest in installments.
- Thomas Pipe estimates that he can make $500 to $600 per year with the extra land. The money would allow him to keep a hired hand in the summer. He already has one good horse team which would be able to handle the expansion of land.
- The railroad is expected soon, and Thomas thinks the local economy will improve. He expects the farm, when expanded to 120 acres, will bring him $25 per acre for a total of $3,000.
- William Coleman has moved 16 miles from Thomas Pipe. He is nearly a neighbor because 16 miles is not much of a distance in Wisconsin.
- Thomas Pipe, like many others in the area, came to Vinland with only $200 to $300 but now is worth $6,000 to $10,000. The others bought from 160 to 200 acres of land at $1.50 per acre or $200 for 160 acres. Their property is now worth $25 to $30 per acre.
- Thomas Pipe reflects on Vinland's growth in less than six years. The area has gone from forests and great commons to fine farms fenced with fine fields of wheat and pasture.
- William Coleman thinks the area is one of the most splendorous places ever.

- Thomas Pipe offers to pay William Jennings 5 percent interest and take out a life insurance policy on his or Elizabeth's life.
- Thomas Pipe has found an English insurance company that has a branch in New York. The New York branch has its own branches. One is in Oshkosh, Winnebago County, Wisconsin. Pipe's doctor told him that either he or his wife would qualify for insurance.
- Thomas Pipe mentions that he and Elizabeth will be married one year next June 24.
- Both Thomas and Elizabeth Pipe are nearly worn out from all the hard work farming requires. They need a hired hand and a girl to help with the house. The additional land would produce the income to afford the help.

Married 24 June

Grandpa Thomas Pipe and Elizabeth [Note was written in later by a descendant.]

[Undated]

Dear Uncle [William Jennings]

I suppose that you will be surprised to receive a letter of this description from me so soon, but circumstances oftentimes alter cases, in fact it does with me. The subject which I am about to approach is I want to know if it is possible for me to have one hundred and twenty pounds £(120) sent to me by the early part of November next. As I have the opportunity of making an advantages addition to my little farm, which is very necessary for me to do, as I find it is impossible for me to make a comfortable living of what I have now. The reason I will explain presently. I have the opportunity of buying 80 acres which lies at the back of mine which is worth more to me than any other person. It is offered to me for 1600 dollars by paying of 200 dollars down and the remainder in instalments, so as it can be made off the land. It is under good improvements with 40 acres under the plough. At a low estimate I can make off the land from 500 to 600 dollars per year, with very little extra expense. The principal thing would be to keep a hired hand through the summer. One good horse team would do the whole of the work and that I have to keep now which I find is too much expense without speculation and teaming on the road, which requires considerable extra money

and my attention, and often times when I ought to be at home. I done first rate at it last fall, but I fear the opportunity won't be so good next fall, or in fact the present is not so favourable as everything has taken. I do not expect that land will rise in value a very great deal more or at least not for a while. I think after our railroads get completed it will take another start. It has risen just one half in value in the last two years. The piece which I am talking of getting, by portion that [80 acres] and what I have now have together will increase the value of both wonderfully, even to sell, as it would make a splendid farm, worth at least calculation 25 dollars per acre, which would make 3,000 dollars for the whole. I suppose that you are aware that Mr. W. [William] Coleman is going to be almost a neighbour to us. He is living 16 miles from us which is considered almost nothing in this country. I have been to see him, and both and wife [Elizabeth Bradford] returned the compliments. He likes our neighbourhood first rate. He said he has not but one thing to regret that is that he did not come here when I did. With his little money he might have got him a good farm which would have made him by this time independent. Here is many men in this neighbourhood who came in with 2 or 300 dollars at that time who is now worth from 6000 to 10000 dollars. They bought from 160 to 200 acres of land which cost 1 ½ dollars per acres which would be 200 dollars for 160 acres and is now selling quick at 25 and 30 dollars per acre, count that and the rise in and the breeding of stock which cost not scarce anything and you will find 6000 dollars in a little time.

But that time went by when I like many others in the poor ends had not money, and more than that wild forest and great commons which was there is now fine farms, well fenced with fine fields of wheat and pastures, pool of cattle. It is most surprising to look backward and see the alteration in less than 6 years. Mr. W. C. [William Coleman] says that he had no idea that there could be any such a good farming country, so far back as he had always heard so much against it, but now he is got steel further north and thinks he is in one of the splendid places that can be. It certainly is a nice place and is bound to be quite a large place, but not so much for business as some others. I showed him my opportunity, and he thinks it to be a most good chance and one that he couldn't miss under any consideration. I believe that is now carrying on the butchering business.

Dear Uncle [William Jenning], now if there can be any chance for me to get the sum above mentioned from you or any other person, I will pay 5 per cent and make you secure by insuring my or Elizabeth's [Stickland Pipe] life. I have been making a little enquiries concerning it, and I find there is an insurance company in England which has a capital department in New York and agents through the country. There is one in Oshkosh [Wisconsin], I am not personally acquainted with the agent but I am with the examining physician as he is my doctor. He says this would be no trouble, either for me or my wife. (Wife did I say, yes wife, you understand all about that long ago. I have been informed that the news got to England long before either of us thought of it. We have been married one year come the 24th June next)

I was thinking if you had not the money to part with, you might find some person that have, perhaps without you for out of the family. I think there is no trouble concerning the security. I should not be so anxious to get money sent out here, but I feel it my duty to be doing something whilst I have the opportunity and now is the time whilst the country is new, as I have made up my mind not to go in another new country as it is too much hard work and privation. I find the work which I have to do now is more than I can stand. Both myself and Elizabeth is completely worn out with so much hard work and hot weather. We have both to do our own work. To get any help is impossible to hire the whole season. I cannot afford to of the lands I have and to get a day's work done is quite as much, for there is no one to do it as everyone has something of their own, with the exception of a few young, men who hire for the whole season that they do in order to have a home and constant work. I want to get business enough to pay for a hired hand and keep a girl. If I cannot do that, I must sell out and try something different.

I must bring this scrawl to a close, I shall write to Aunt Coleman in the course of a week or two then I will enclose a line to you with more particulars concerning the insurance. Please to answer this as quick as possible as I might know what to depend on. Elizabeth [Stickland Pipe] joins with me in kind love to Aunt [Elizabeth Coleman Jennings] and all enquiring friends and please to accept the same yourself.

From your affectionate nephew
Thos. Pipe

Letter Number 25, Page 1

and my atention and often times when I ought to be at
home, I don first rate at it last Faul, but I fear the
opertunity wont be so good next Faul, ar infuct the pros
pect is not so faverable as every thing has taken a turn,
I do not effect that Land will raise in value a very great deel more, ar at
least not for a while, I think after our Railroads
get completed it will take another start, It has resen
junst one halfe in value in the last two years,
The pece which I am talken of getten by poohen that and
and what I now have to gether will increace the value of
both wonderfoly, even to sell, as it ould make a splendid
Farm, worth at the least calculation 25 dolars per acher,
which ould make 3000 dolars for the hole, I sopost that
you ar aware that our Mr Coleman is got to be almost
a neiber to us he is liven 16 mills from us which is
considred almost nothing in this cuntry I have been
to see him and both him and wife returned the complinta
he likes our neibredood first rate he sais he has not but
one thing to regret that is that he did not com here
when I did with his little money he might have got
him a good French which ould have made him by this time
independent, here is many men in this neibrehoode
who came in with 2 ar 300 dolars at that time who is
now worth from 6000 to 10000 dolars, they hough from
160 to 200 achers of Land which cost 1¼ dolar per acher
which ould be 200 dolars for 160 achers and is now selling
quick at 25 and 30 dolars per acher, count that and the
rice in and the breaden of Stock which have not cost scarce any thing
and you will fiend 6000 dolars in a little time

Letter Number 25, Page 3

but that time went by when I like many other sutch
poor ends had no money, and now thea that wild Forest
and great comons which was thea is now fine Farms well
Fenced with fine fields of Wheat and Pasters fool of
cattle, It is most sopresen to look back and and see the
alteration in less than 6 years, Mr Wᵐ C sais that he
had no idea that there cold be any satch a good Farming
cuntrey so far back as he had always herd so mutch against
it but now he is got steel farther North and think he is
in one of the Splendes places that can be, it sertenly is
a nice place and is bound to be quet a larg place, but not
so mutch for busnifs as som others, I showed him my oper
tunety, and he thinks it to be a most grend chence and one that
he ouldent mis under any consideration I beleve that he
is now carien on the Butcherin Business,

Dear Uncle now if there can be any chance for me to get the
sum above mentioned from you or aney ather person I
will x5 Per cent and make you sadure by Insuren my or Elzt
Life I have been maken a little inquires concerning it and
I fiend there is a Insurence company in England which has a Capital
deparsted in New York and agents through the Cuntrey there
is one in Oshkosh I am not personly aquainted with the Agtin
but I am with the examiner Phasetion as he is my Doctor
he sais there ould be no truble either for me or my Whife
(Whife did I say - yes Whife you understand all about
that long ago, I have ben informed that the nuse got
to England long before either of us thought of it, we
have ben maried one year come the 21ˢᵗ June nest)

Letter Number 25, Page 4

I was thinken if you had not the money to part with
that you might fiend some person that have, perhaps
with out your for out of the my Familey. I think there
is no trouble concerning the Sacurity, I should not
be so anctios to get money sent out hear, but I feel it
my duty to be doin something whieldst I have the
appertunity and now is the time whilst the contry
is new, as I have made up my miend not to go in a nother
new countrey as it is to mutch hard work and priveation
I fiend the work which I have to do now is more than I
can stand, Both my self and Eliz is compleltey wore
out with so mutch hard work and hot wether we have
both to do our own work, to get any help is imposible.
to hire the hole season I cannat aford to of the land I have
and to get a days work don is quit as mutch so, for thare
is no one to do it as every one hase something of there
owne, with the eptseptsion a few young me ho hers for
the hole season that they do in order to have a home
and curstant work, I want to get busniss a nuagh to
pay for a hierd hend and keep a girl, if I cannat do that
I must sell out and try something diprent,
I must bring this scrawl to a close, I shall wright
to aunt Coleman in the corse of a wek or to then I
will inclose a line to you with more poiticulors conca
ning the Insurence, Pleas to answer this as quick as
posable as I might know what to depend on)
Eliz join with me in kind love to Aunt and all inquiren
friends and pleas to asespt the same your self)
From Your Afet Nephew Thos Pipe

Letter Number 26

Date: circa 1857
Writer: Elizabeth Coleman Jennings
Recipient: Thomas & Elizabeth Stickland Pipe
Sent from: Northay Farm, Whitestaunton, Chard,
                Somerset County, England
Sent to: Vinland, Winnebago County, Wisconsin, USA

Key Ideas

- Elizabeth Coleman Jennings describes her youngest Ellen (Nellie) as just beginning to stand. She has delicate health.
- Richard Coleman, Elizabeth Coleman Jennings' brother, and his wife are expecting a child in February.
- James Coleman, Elizabeth Coleman Jennings' brother, lives ten miles south of Tiverton, Devon, in Oakford Parish on a 200-acre farm.
- Susan Coleman, Elizabeth Coleman Jennings' sister, lives at home and is not married.
- Elizabeth Coleman Jennings does not know Mary Stickland's address. She is doing well in Yeovil, Somerset.
- Uncle John Jennings sent William Jennings Pipe a pair of boots for the winter.
- Dalling's father has not heard from his sons in the United States. She asks whether the Pipes know anything about their well-being.
- Prices are very high. Elizabeth Coleman Jennings says, "if they don't have us in the meat they will in the soup."

[crosshatched] undated

My dear Friends

I thought I must say a word or two just to let you know I am still in the land of the living. How are the children getting on. I often look and admire their dear round little faces. My own little baby [Ellen (Nelly)] is grown nicely. She can stand by things which is more than I thought she would be able to do by this time as her health was so very delicate. My brother R's [Richard] wife is expecting an increase in February. They are very happy together both has been baptised. James [Coleman] lives about ten miles below Tiverton [Devon] in the parish of Oakford in a farm about 200 acres. He has two sons, I think they live very happy. Susan [Coleman] lives home. we tell her she will be an old maid. She desires to be remembered to you both. When you see Mrs. [Charlotte Jennings Pipe] Pillar, please give my kind love to her, also to Mary Ann [Pipe].

[other way]

Accept the same yourselves from your loving aunt

E. [Elizabeth] Jennings

I don't know Miss Stricklands [Mary Stickland] address, no doubt but you have heard from her and know. I have heard she was doing very well at Yeovil [Somerset]. Mr. Mathews heard from your brother John [Stickland] a short time ago. They were well. He was afeared he should be called out in a [cut off] your uncle John [Jennings] has sent Wm. [Jennings] Pipe a pair of boots for the winter.

[Accounts]

Balance on the Cash	£11 19S 6 ½ d
Mr. Phillips ½ year's rent	£40 6s 6d
Mr. Dennings	<u>£4 10s 0d</u>
	£56 9s 6 ½ d
Draft stamps and letter	3s 0d
Mr. Charles Bell carpenters	£1 4s 0d
Mr. Boyland's blacksmith bill	5s 6d
Expenses for receiving the rent	3s 0d
John Stickland's annuity	£12 0s 0d
Half year's interest	<u>£4 5s 0d</u>
	£18 0s 6d
Rent	£56 9s 5d
Gisburnes	<u>£18 0s 6d</u>
Balance in hand	£38 9s 0d

I saw the Dallings Father on Monday. He can't think the reason he has not heard from neither of his sons [in America]. If you can tell me anything of them on your next the old man would be glad to hear, Landlords are rising their rents and outs are so very high so we are sure to be there if they don't have us in the meat, they will in the soup. Tell me how you are getting on. I hope well. I should like to come over but I should dread the journey. If I come by rail I would soon be there.

Letter Number 26, Page 1

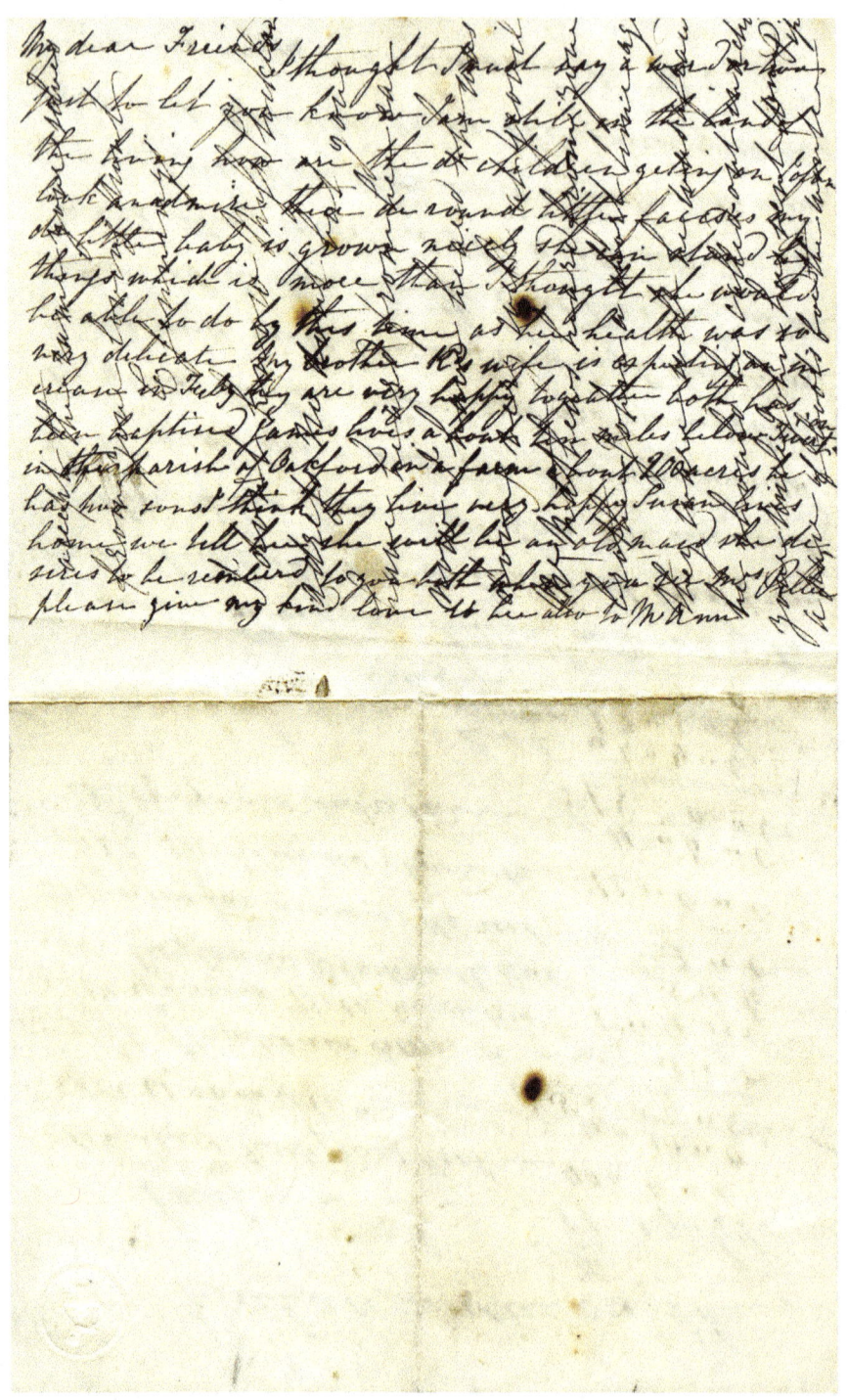

Balance due on the

	£	s	d
last	11	19	6½
Mr Phillips ½ years Rent	40	6	6
Mr Dennys Do	4	10	0
	56	9	6½
Draft Stamps and letter	3	0	
Mr Clarkes Bill Carpenters	1	4	0
Mr Boylands Blacksmith Bill	5	6	
Expences for receiving the rent	3	0	
John Stricklands Annuity	12	0	0
Half years Intrest	4	5	0
	18	0	6

Rent	56	9	6
Disbursments	18	0	6
Balance in hand	38	9	0

I saw the Dallings father on Monday he
cant think the reason he has not hard from
neither of his Sons if you can tell me any thing
of them on your next the old man would
be glad to here landlords are reasing there
rents and outs are so very high so we are
shure to be there if the cant have us in the
meal they will in the sook tell me how
you are geting on shope well I should like to come
over but I should dread the journey if I could
come by rale I would soon be there

Letter Number 27

Date: 5 February 1857
Writer: William & Elizabeth Coleman Jennings
Recipient: Thomas Pipe
Sent from: Northay Farm, Whitestaunton, Chard,
                Somerset County, England
Sent to: Vinland, Winnebago County, Wisconsin, USA
Key Ideas

- William Jennings received rent on December 31, 1856. Mr. Phillips complains that it is too much. Wheat has come back in price.
- William Jennings charges interest on anything over £100. £100 brings £2 10s 0d.
- Mary Stickland came for Christmas. She asked William Jennings to insure Pithayne Farm and Whitehorns Farm in case of fire. Pithayne is insured for £200 and Whitehorns for £100.
- Little Ellen Jennings does not enjoy good health.
- Mary Ann Jennings has not been in school this half year.
- The wife of Uncle John Jennings fell and hurt her knee.
- William Jennings Pipe is described as a nicely behaved, young man.
- William Jennings states that rates and taxes are extremely high in England.

[crosshatched]

- William Jennings requests buffalo skins from America.
- William Jennings makes inquiries about Thomas Pipe's children.
- William Jennings includes accounts and notes on the reverse side regarding needed work on the properties.
- Mr. Mathews sends John Stickland his annuity.
- William Jennings says that Uncle John Jennings does not enjoy good health.
- William Jennings sent money and wants to know when Thomas Pipe receives it.

1857
Northay, Feb 5th

Dear Thos.

I suppose you are thinking I am very neglectful as I have not written to you before, but I did not receive the rent till the 31st of December. Mr. Phillips complains very much that the rent is too much. Wheat is come back. The best is worth 7s per bushel down to 5s you can see by my last account

balance in hand	£36 7s 8d
Mr. Phillips rent	£37 10s 0d
Mr. Dinning	<u>£4 10s 0d</u>
	£78 7s 6d
Disbursements as below	£6 11s 9½d
Balance in hand	£1 15s 8½d

I hope you will take particular care of all the accounts as I have. Mr. Mathews sends the particulars every time.

For Mr. [John] Stickland	£12 0s 0d
½ years interest	£4 5s 0d
Mr. Phillis Bell Reed	4s 9d
Thatcher's bill	<u>2s 0d</u>
	£16 11s 9 ½ d

Now I have received out of the £170, £16 15s 8 ½ d the next payment. I don't charge interest for only £100 which will be £2 10s 0d. I think that will be something like right between both.

Miss [Mary] Stickland was here about Christmas. She asks me if the property that is the premises is insured. I said it was not. She wish me to have it done immediately as there has been so many fires round that part lately so I have had it done as follows: Pithayne house and premises in the sum of £200 Whitethorns in £100 and the barley in the field £50 in all together £350 the amount to be paid every Christmas for insurance is £1 15s 6d which I hope you will approve of it being done. I would not miss if it were my property not for £5 a year. There is a couple days work for a mason in the house to repair the plastering and Whitehorns the same. Dear Thos, I hope you and your wife and family's health is better than when I last heard from you. We are all mending except my dear little

[crosshatched]

Ellen my youngest. She does not enjoy good health. I hope and trust she will soon be better. She is a dour little girl. Mary Ann has not been to school this half. She is a young lady now. I hope your Uncle John [Jennings] is a little better, but his wife fell and hurt her knee and has been crippled a long time and is still crippled. I don't know but all the rest are quite well. I was quite proud to see what a nice behaved young man your brother William [Jennings Pipe] were when he was down to see us. He has improved in his learning very much. I hope your dear mother's husband [James Pillar] and family [James, Jr. and Elizabeth] are quite well and doing well for I can assure you there is a turnabout in this country rates and taxes are so very high. Please to write me soon.

From you affectionate Uncle Wm. Jennings

[other way]

When you come home, plan to take some buffalo skins with you. They are very beautiful things. Mine is very much admired. When you write next to tell me a little about your dear little children. I have three of their little faces. Their aunt wishes to have them too. I pray it too highly to part with it to anyone.

[Accounts 1857]

1857

28 July Received of Mr. Phillips

½ year rent due Lady Day [25 March] last	£37 10s 0d
Mr. Denning	<u>£4 10s 0d</u>
	<u>£42 0s 0d</u>
	<u>£14 11s 0d</u>
Disbursements	<u>£27 9s 0d</u>
Stamps	1s 0d
Mr. Mathews annuity	£12 0s 0d
½ years interest	£2 11s 0d
	<u>£14 11s 0d</u>
Balance in hand	£89 4s 8½d

Nov. 27th received of Mr. Phillips

½ years rent due Michaelmas [29 September] last	£37 10s 0d
Mr. Denning	£4 10s 0d
	£42 0s 0d
	£16 9s 4d
	£15 10s 4d
Mr. Mathews [for John Stickland] Annuity	£12 0s 0d
½ years interest	£2 16s 0s
Insurance	£1 15s 0d
Church rate	<u>4s 4d</u>
	<u>£16 9s 4d</u>

What I have got in hand up to Michaelmas [29 September] last £114 15s 4 ½ d

[Notes on reverse of accounts]

There is a little want doing the inside of the house and a linhay [farm buildings] want thatching at Whitehorns. I think it would be best if it were tiled.

I will do the best I can.

We are all middling.

Your uncle John [Jennings] don't enjoy very good health.

From your affectionate

Uncle Wm. Jennings

Please answer this as your

uncle will be anxious to know

whether you got the money all right.

Northay House at Northay Farm, Whitestaunton, Chard, Somerset County, England, was the home of William and Elizabeth Coleman Jennings. The Jennings left Northay on March 25, 1870, according to Letter Number 63.

Letter Number 27, Page 1

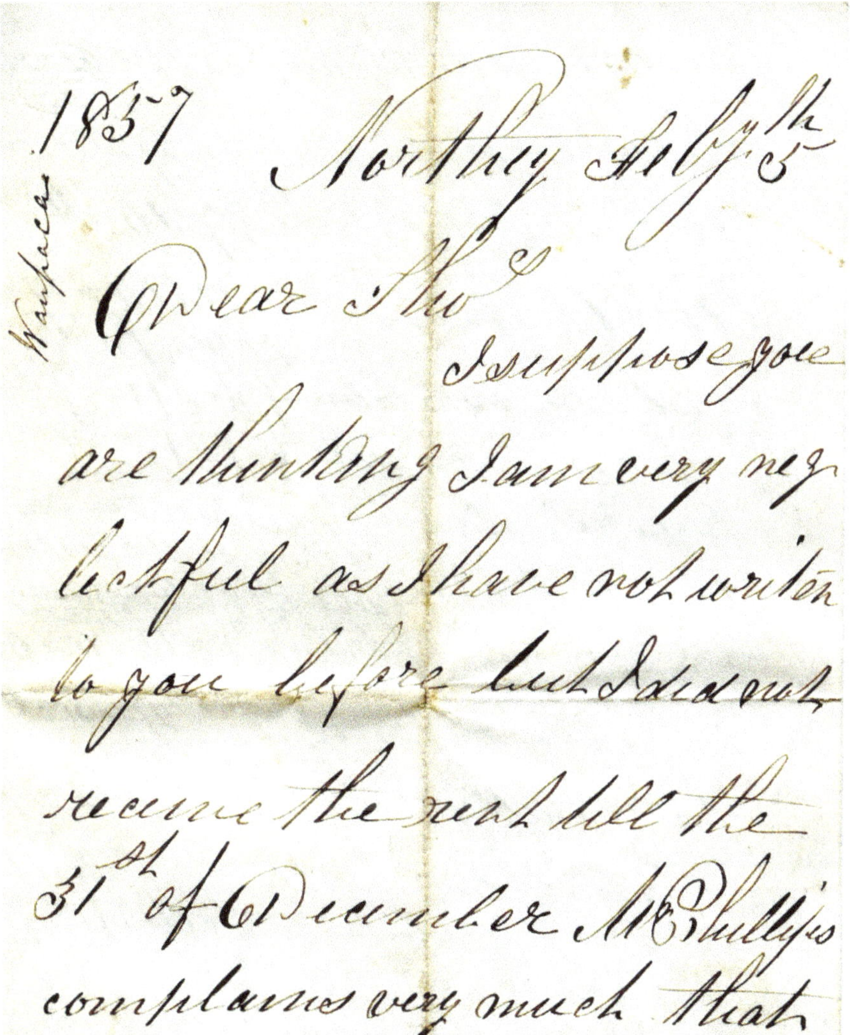

1857 Waupaca

Northey Feby 5th

Dear Thos

I suppose you
are thinking I am very neg
lectful as I have not writen
to you before but I did not
receive the rent till the
31st of December Mr Phillips
complains very much that
the rent is too much Wheat
is come back the best is
worth 7/6 pr Bushel down to 5/

you can see by my last account

Ballance in hand 36..7..6

Mr Chullets rent 37..10..0

Mr Demmey — 4..10..

78..7..6

Disbursments as below — 6..11..9¼

Ballance in hand £ 61..15..8½

I hope you will take particular care
of all the accounts as I have
Mr Mathews sent the particulars every time

for Mr Stickland 12..0..0

½ years Intrest --- 4..5..0

Mr Phillips Bill Recd — 4..9

Thatchers Bill —— ..0

£16..11..9½

Now I have received out of the 770
£61..15..8½ the next payment I dont
charge Intrest for only 100 which will
be £100 I think that will be some-
=thing like right between both

Miss Strickland was here about
Christmas she ask me if the property
that is the premises Insured I said
it was not she wish me to have it
done emeadtly as there has been so
many fires round that part latly so
I have had it done as follows
Prethayne house & premises in the sum
of £200 Whitehorns in £100 and the turkey
in the field in £50 all together £350
the amount to be paid every Christmas
for Insurance is 1:15:6 Which I hope you
will prove of its £ been done I would
not miss if it ware my property not for
£5 av year there is a couple days work
for a mason in the house to repare
the plaistering and whitewash the
the same Dear Sh I hope you and
your Wife and familys helth is better
than when I last hard from you
we are all middling except my deare litt

Ellen my youngest she doth enjoy good
health I hope and trust she will soon
be better she is a dear little girl Mary
Ann has not been to school this half
she is going to day again I hope your Uncle
John is a little better but his Wife
fell and hurted her knee and has been
crippled a long time and is still crippled
poorly however but all the rest are
quite well I was quite proud to see
what a nice behaved young man
your Brother William aware when
he was down to see us he has
improved in his learning very much
I hope your dear Mother Husband & Fam
=ily are quite well and doing well for
I can ashure you there is a turn a
bout in this country rates and
taxes are so very high please to
write me soon from your affectionate
Uncle John Jennings

1857

July 28 Rec'd of Mr Phillips

½ years rent due Lady day last   37 " 10 " 0

Mr Denning — 4 " 10 " 0

42 " 0 " 0

14 " 11 " 0

(Desbursments — 27 " 9

Stamp — 1 " 0

Mr Mathews Annuity — 12 " 0 " 0

½ years Intrest — 2 " 16 " 0

14 " 0 " 11

Balance in hand — 89 " 4 " 8½

Nov 27 Rec'd of Mr Phillips

½ years rent due Michelmas last   37 " 10 " 0

Mr Denning — 4 " 10 " 0

42 " 0 " 0

£   16 " 9 " 4

25 " 10 " 4

Mr Mathews Annuity — 12 " 0 " 0

½ years Intrest — 2 " 16 " 0

Insurance — 1 " 15 " 0

Church rate — 4 " 4

£   16 " 9 " 4

What I have got in hand up to
Michelmas last is £   s   114 " 15 " 4½

there is a little want doing
the inside of the house
and a linehay want fatching
at Whitehorns I think it wants
be best if it ware tiled
I will do the best I can
we are all midling
your uncle John dont enjoy
very good helth
from your affectionate
Uncle Wm Jennings

Plean answer this as your
uncle will be anxious to know
whither you got the money all
right

Letter Number 27, Envelope Front

Letter Number 27, Envelope Back

Chapter 4

Farmington, Waupaca County, Wisconsin
1858 - April 1860

Chapter 4 includes letters dated 1858 to April 1860 while Thomas and Elizabeth Stickland Pipe and their eight children (including four from her previous marriage) are living at what later would become known as Calkins' Place in the town of Farmington, Waupaca County, Wisconsin. Eventually, Thomas Pipe's farmland extends to the shores of Sunset, Rainbow, Otter, Nessling, McCrossen, and Round lakes on today's Chain O' Lakes in Farmington. The Pipes and the Jennings exchange nine letters.

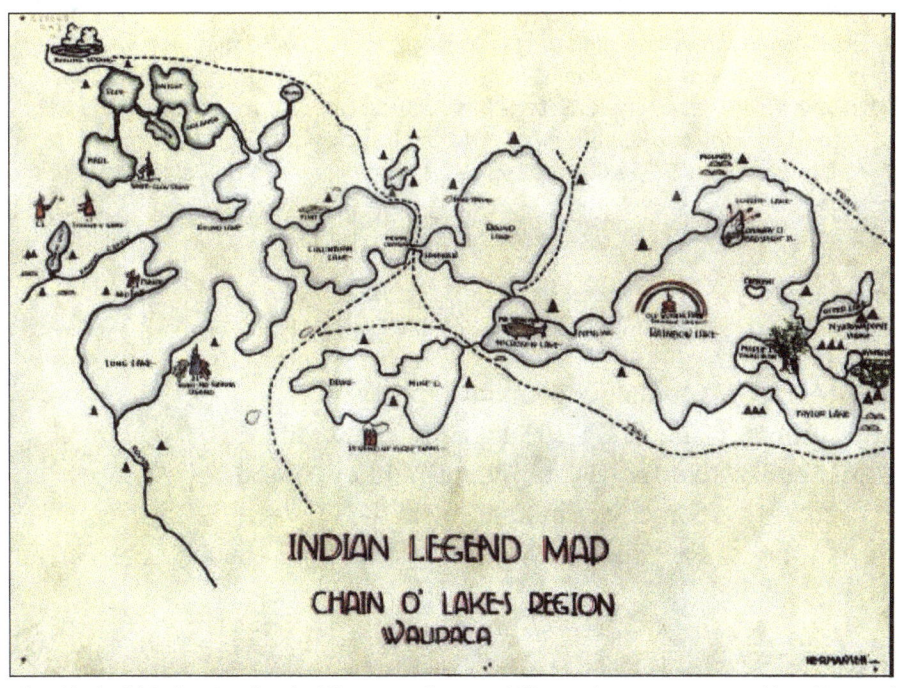

The Chain O' Lakes Region in Waupaca County, Wisconsin, was surveyed in 1851 and became available for purchase in 1852. This map was created in 1941 from the recollection of Patricia Hermansen.

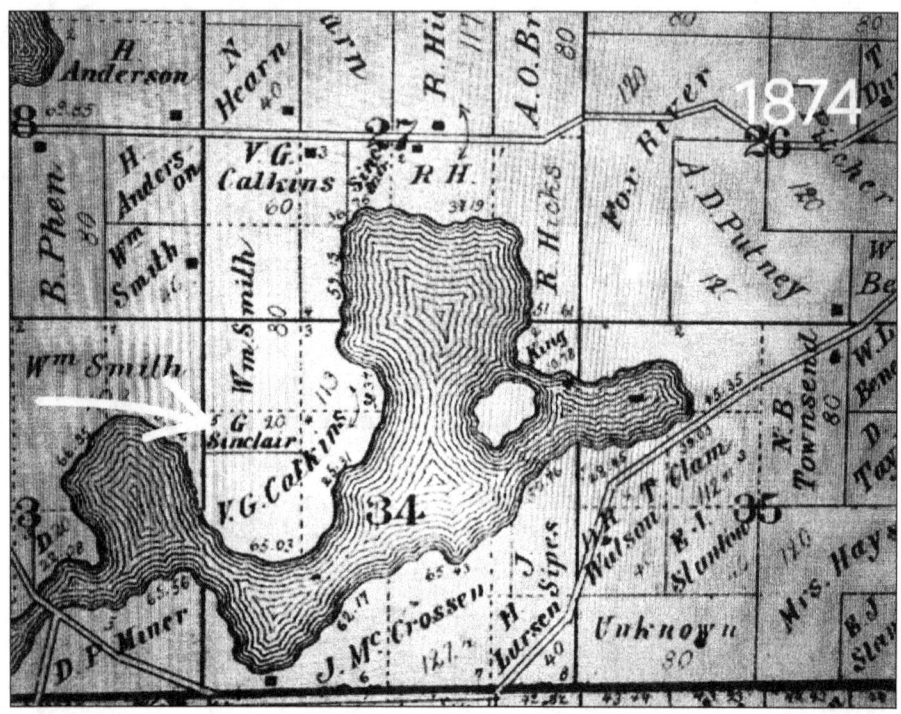

This 1874 map shows the location of the Pipe family land in Farmington which Thomas eventually sold to V.G. Calkins. The white arrow points to George Washington and Mary Ann Pipe Sinclair's land. (George is William Sinclair's son and Mary Ann is Thomas' sister.) Thomas also bought all of William Sinclair's land from his estate in 1859. The Pipes likely lived in the house designated by the number 3 on Calkins' land to the north.

Letter Number 28

Date:	13 January 1858
Writer:	Elizabeth Coleman Jennings
Recipient:	Thomas & Elizabeth Stickland Pipe
Sent from:	Northay Farm, Whitestaunton, Chard, Somerset County, England
Sent to:	Farmington, Waupaca County, Wisconsin, USA

Key Ideas

- Phillips left Pithayne Farm at Christmas without giving any notice. He has taken Rule Farm near Otterford, Somerset.

- Pithayne Farm is now rented to George Bonfield, the elder Bonfield's son, for £80 per year. Bonfield married Miss White at Yarcombe Inn.
- Bonfield of Pithayne Farm wants a seven-year lease.
- William Jennings promised him a five-year lease, but Bonfield did not think that was long enough.
- William Jennings told Bonfield he would need to talk with Thomas Pipe.
- William Jennings says he would like to see the Pipes return to England and enjoy Pithayne Farm.
- William sent Thomas Pipe £25.
- Elizabeth Coleman Jennings saw Elizabeth Stickland Pipe's mother, Elizabeth Wall Stickland Bartlett, and sister, Mary Stickland, at Birch Oak Farm last week. Mary Stickland left Yeovil, Somerset, just before Christmas to travel to Manchester, Lancashire, where she bought a business.
- Mrs. Brazenton and friends live near Manchester, Lancashire County. Elizabeth's mother, Elizabeth Wall Stickland Bartlett, had ague (malaria-like illness with fever and chills). She came to visit friends before going to Manchester, Lancashire County. Then, she traveled to London.
- Elizabeth Stickland Pipe's mother, Elizabeth Wall Stickland Bartlett, and sister, Mary Stickland, wish for her to write. Elizabeth Wall Stickland Bartlett had heard that Elizabeth Stickland Pipe had consumption (tuberculosis) and is worried. Elizabeth Coleman Jennings tells her to write to Yeovil, Somerset, and the letter will be forwarded.
- Mr. A. has been at Bradworthy, Devon.

[crosshatched]

- Polly Dommett has been visiting the last few weeks. William Jennings and Elizabeth Coleman Jennings brought her home with them.
- William Jennings won a silver cup at Crewkerne, Somerset, cattle show for best dairy cow and calf. He also won a prize for his heifers. Mrs. Coate is still living with them.

- John Jennings is looking better. His sheep last year got cothed (diseased).
- Elizabeth Coleman Jennings heard in May from her brother, William Coleman, who lives in America. He is doing well. Her brother mentions that his brother-in-law, John Bradford, is coming home to England. Elizabeth Coleman Jennings says they must be close to each other in America.
- Elizabeth Coleman Jennings' brother, Richard Coleman, and his wife have two children and are expecting a third.
- Richard Coleman's wife's sister, Mary, has three children. Mrs. Matthews has one. Her husband's drinking sometimes causes trouble.

Whitestaunton Jany. 13th,[18]58

Dear Thos.

It is a long time since I wrote to you now I have some news to tell you. Phillips has left Pithayne [Farm] and has taken a farm at Otterford [Somerset] called Rule Farm where old Mr. Smith use to live, he has left this Christmas without giving or receiving any notice. I could make him keep it for another year but that would be bad judgement in so doing for he could injure the farm a great deal in that time, there were a lease made but I could never get him to sign it after he had possession.

I have let [rented] the farm again to George Bonfield, old Bonfield's son, he has been renting a dairy, he married Miss White at the Yarcombe Inn. I think a very active man. I have let [rented] it at £80 per annum. I must make him some amends. I do intend to give him five pounds worth of lime a

[page 2]

1 year then I shall be sure the land has got it. I told him I would, so something to make up the five pounds if he farmed well, so I shall take the whole rent and pay for the lime, then I shall be sure he has had it and get the bill for the same, then there can be no mistake. Mr. Bonfield wants a lease or agreement for 7 years which I think would be the best

way. I promised him five years. He thought that not long enough to bring it in good condition and get paid back for his outlay. I shall bind him not to sell any hay reed straw or stubble. I told him I would not grant him so long as seven years till I have heard from you, but I should strongly recommend you to stop where you are for some years to come if you can lay up but little I would persuade you for the best as I have told you before which I hope you are judge enough yourself, you know the land, if I wanted such a

[page 3]

farm I should not give more than £55 per annum at the present time of selling wheat, It is not worth more than the best than six and sixpence a bushel, that is had paying rent, I should like to see you and your wife and family when you come to your native country to be able to enjoy your little farm without any difficulties whatever, please to mind [pay close attention to] what I say. You must have something beforehand to be able to do so, now I have said what I have. You have got your minds to use, I have sent you the £25 as you requested me. I will do anything that lays in my power for you, but I hope I shall not be nothing baser [lesser?] as I have no showings for this if you should want twenty or the same sum after a while if you can reap a good profit by it I will send it to you. I know money is a fine thing in America and I can tell you, so it is here. The most money the best man.

[crosshatched]

My dear Mrs. Pipe

I thought I would say a few words to you as there is a line or two to spare. I saw your mother [Elizabeth Wall Stickland Bartlett] at Birch [Oak Farm] last week, she was quite well, your sister [Mary Stickland] has left Yeovil just before Christmas, gone to Manchester [Lancashire], took of a business is likely to have a good run. Miss Brazenton and friends lives near Manchester [Lancashire] they heard if it was off in very short time. Your mother [Elizabeth Wall Stickland Bartlett] was left with the whole to be recovered, pay all so she says she has had a very great ague [malaria-like illness with fever and chills] lately. She came down to see her friends before she goes to Manchester. I believe she is in London now, was seeing some friends. She has me to tell you she feels it very much as you don't answer hers or Mary's [Stickland] letters. They have written different times, do write to her. I was sorry to see her feel it so much she had heard you was in a consumption [tuberculosis] that made her feel very anxious about you, you write address at Yeovil it will be forwarded to them. Mr. A. has been at Broadworthy [Bradworthy, Devon].

[other way]

This last week we have Polly Dommett here with us. Miss Dommett has drove home with Mr. [William] Jennings and myself do intend going back with him for a day or two. He has won a silver cup at Crewkerne [Somerset] cattle show for the best dairy cow and calf and one prize besides for heifers, he keeps very good stock indeed. Mrs. Coate is still living with them. John Jennings is looking better than he has for a long time but still he is very delicate. He was very unfortunate with his sheep this last year, got them cothed [diseased], we heard from my brother [William Coleman] in May. He seems to be going very well. He said his brother-in-law [John Bradford] was coming home, but he is not arrived yet. He was coming to fetch his wife. They must be very near in America to come so far. My brother Richard's [Coleman] wife has 2 children and another on the way. Her sister Mary has 3, Mrs. Matthews has 1 child. She is a very dressy woman. He drinks a great deal. He causes her a great deal of trouble sometimes, please give my very kind love to Mrs. [Charlotte Jennings Pipe] Pillar. I certainly will try to write her soon, hope this will find you all well as I am thankful to say we are at present.

From your affectionate aunt E. [Elizabeth] Jennings

1858

Whitestaunton Jany 13th ~58

Dear Thos

It is a long time
since I wrote to you now I have some
news to tell you, C Phillips has left
C Thayne and has taken a Farm at
Otterford called Rule Farm where old
Mr Smith use to live he has left now
this to Xmas without giving or recieving
any notice I could make him keep it
for another year but that would be bad
judgement in so doing for he could
injer the farm a great dale in that time
there ware a lease made but I could never
get him to sine it after he had posasion
I have let the Farm again to George
Bonfield old Mr Bonfields son he has been
renting a dairy he maried Miss White
at the Yarcomb Inn I think a very active
man I have let it at £ per annum I must
make him some amians I do intend to
give him five pounds worth of lime a

1 year then I shall be shure the land has got it, I told him I would do something to make up the five pounds if he farmed well so I shall take the whole rent and pay for the lime then I shall be shure he has had it and get the bill for the same then there can be no misstake Mr Bonfield want a lease or a greement for 7 years which I think would be the best way I promised him five years he thought that not long enough to bring it in good condition and get paid for his out lay I shall bind him not to sell any Hay Reed Straw or stuble I told him I would not grant him so long as seven years till I have hard from you but I should strongly recommend you to stop where you are for some years to come if you can lay up but little I would persuade you for the best as I have told you before which I hope you are judge enough yourself you know the land if I wanted such a

Letter Number 28, Page 3

farm as I should not like to give more
than 55 per annum at the present time
of selling wheat it is not worth more
the best than six and sixpence a bushel
that is bad paying rent I should like to
see you and your wife and family when
you come to your native country to be
able to enjoy your little farm & any thing
any difficultys what ever please to mind
what I say you must have something
before hand to be able to do so now I have
said what I have you have get your
minds to use I have sent you the 25 as
you requested me I will do any thing that
lay in power for you but I hope I shall not
be nothing losser as I have no showings
for this if you should want twenty
or the same sume after a while if you
can reep a good profit by it I will
send it to you I know money is a
fine thing in America and I can tell
you so it is here the most money
the best man

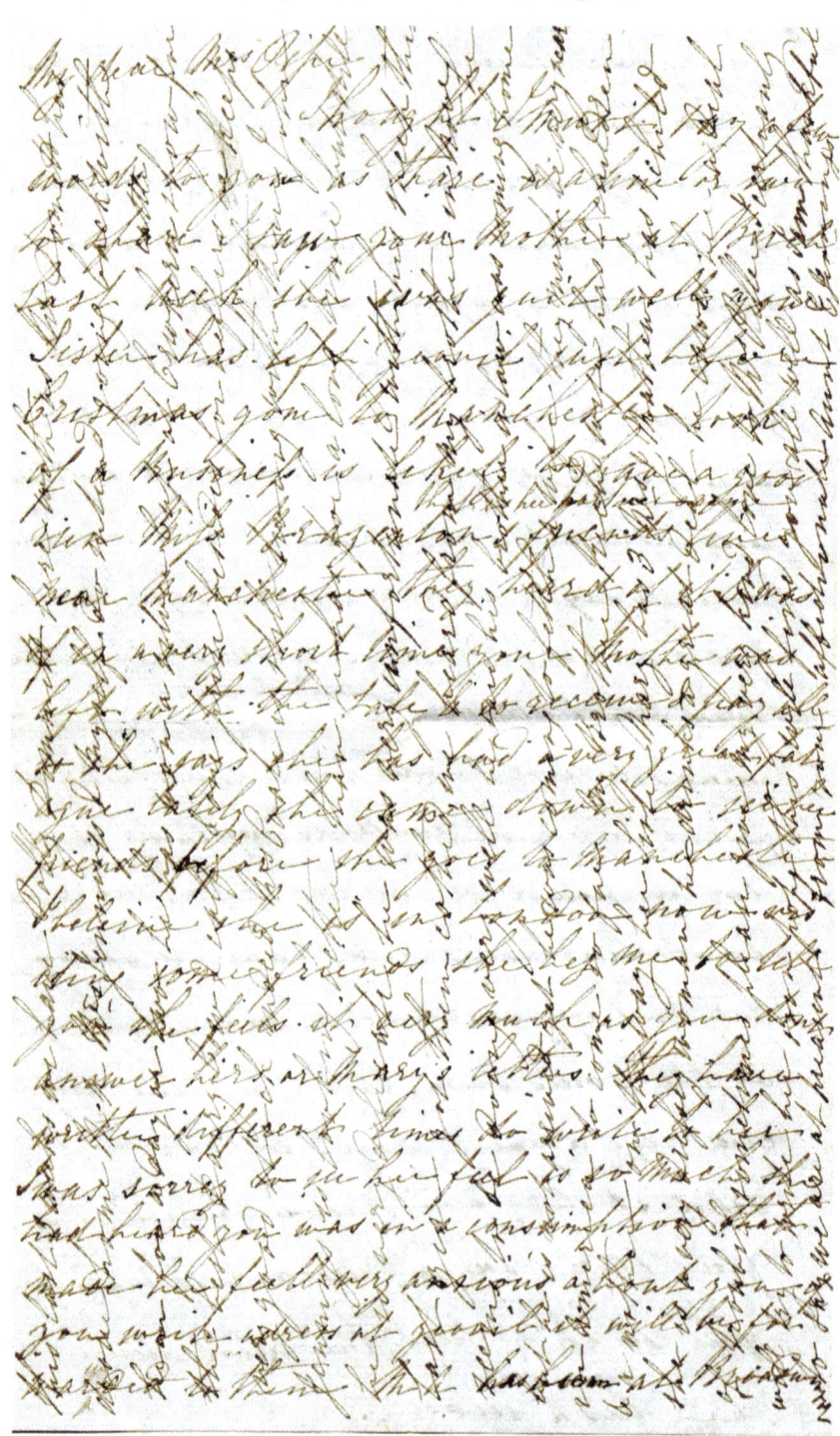

Letter Number 28, Envelope Front

Letter Number 28, Envelope Back

Letter Number 29

Date: circa 8 February 1858 Accounts
Writer: Elizabeth Coleman Jennings
Recipient: Thomas & Elizabeth Stickland Pipe
Sent from: Northay Farm, Whitestaunton, Chard,
Somerset County, England
Sent to: Farmington, Waupaca County, Wisconsin, USA

Key Ideas

- William Jennings does whitewashing on February 8 and pays himself.
- (Pitten Hill may be Pithayne Hill.)

[Accounts] 1858

Mr. G. Bonfield

To Trott

From work done at Pitten Hill	£ 0 0
Feb. 8	
To myself 2 ½ days whitewashing	6s 3d
To a man to do 6 days	12s 6d
To a labourer to do 4 days	4s
Too half a bushel of hay	<u>6d</u>
Received the above G. Bonfield	£1 3s 3d

Letter Number 29, Page 1

1858 Mr S. Banfield

To J Trott

For work done at
pitten Hill

		£	s	d
Feb 5	To my self 2½ days ?	0	6	3
	With working &c.			
	To a Man to do 5 days	0	12	6
	To a Labrer to do 4 days	0	4	0
	To half Bushel of Flare	0	0	6
	Received the above Jch S Banfield	1 - 3 - 3		

Letter Number 30

Date: 5 March 1858
Writer: Thomas Pipe
Recipient: William Jennings
Sent from: [Calkins' Place written in later] Farmington,
                  Waupaca County, Wisconsin, USA
Sent to: Northay Farm, Whitestaunton, Chard,
                  Somerset County, England

Key Ideas

- Thomas Pipe trades 40 acres for another 40 acres which joined it on the Waupaca Chain O' Lakes shore.
- Thomas Pipe bought another 20 acres which laid between it and his house. Now his farm is joined together.
- Thomas Pipe intends to sell 70 acres which lie off in the point between the two lakes. He will be left with a farm of 160 acres.
- Thomas Pipe will add a barn which will bring his farm value to $4,000. He has all materials for the barn except the nails and door trimmings.
- Thomas Pipe tells William Jennings to tile the shed if he thinks it is best to keep the shed in good repair.
- Elizabeth Stickland Pipe does not like the idea of a seven-year lease. She may not want to return to England: her mother, Elizabeth Wall Stickland Bartlett, might be dead, or she may not be able to make the trip home. Thomas Pipe says he will not return until his finances are better and his family is comfortable. He states that it is not his intention to depend upon that place, Pithayne Farm, for support.
- Thomas Pipe thinks if George Bonfield will take a five-year lease, that would be fine. Otherwise, William Jennings is instructed by Thomas to give him a seven-year lease.
- Thomas Pipe says, "Should I feel able and disposed to return before the seven years is up, I can be doing something else, as I am considerable yankeised (likely yankee-ized or Americanized). I am not particular what business or calling I am in so I can make an honest living."

———————

Calkins Place [Written in pen later.]

Farmington March 5th, [18]58

Dear Uncle [William Jennings]

Your kind letter with the Draft came to hand on or about the 15th of last month. I have been very much engaged ever since, or I should have written to you before. I will now say that your kindness is fully appreciated in forwarding me the money. You might rest assured that you shall not be the loser of a fraction by the operation. I will also inform you that it comes just in time to do me great service. I have been in the land speculation again. I have traded forty acres for another forty which joined it on the lake shore [Chain O' Lakes, Farmington, Waupaca County, Wisconsin] and bought twenty acres which laid between it and my house, so now my farm is all joined together. I now intend to sell about 70 acres which lies off in the point between the two lakes. That will leave me a splendid farm of 160 acres. I fear I shall not be able to sell for a year to come as money is so very scarce, but it will pay well to keeping

as it is good timbered land, and that is a scarce article in these parts, I think my farm after selling off that piece and putting a barn on it will be worth at the least four thousand dollars. I have my materials all on the ground and paid for with the exception of nails and door trimmings, but I shall not build this spring now I have bought this land. I must wait and see a change in the air see my way clear for another year.

Now in relation to the business in your hands. I could say as I have always said do the best according to your own judgement if you think it the best to tile the shed do so. I want it to be kept decent, as to the lease I hardly know what to say. Elizabeth [Stickland Pipe] do not like the idea of the seven year lease. She fancy it to be a long while to look forward to, she says that in seven years she might not have any object to return, for her mother might be dead and her own health impaired, so as there will be no comfort in return, but there is one thing certain that I shall not be prepared to return for a few years as I shall have to wait for time to take its own course to bring things round. I was laid out to about four years, but it is impossible to say when time must take its own course, there is one thing certain I shall not be willing to return until I can make myself and family comfortable. It is not my intention to be depending on that place [Pithayne Farm] for a support. I could say that if Mr. Bonfield will take a lease for five years do so and if not give the seven. Should I feel able and disposed to return before the seven years is up, I can be doing something else, as I am considerable yankeised [likely yankee-ized or Americanized]. I am not particular what business or calling I am in so I can make an honest living. I am very sorry to hear of Uncle John's [Jennings] bad luck in relation to his sheep. There is one thing to be thankful for, he have not got me to blame for it this time. I should suppose that he have not got all those old drains opened yet the lower side of the house. I think if he had there would be more trouble. I hope his loss will not be so severe this time as the last. Please to give my kind love to him.

I hope I shall hear from your flock the next time you write, as I have not heard from it for a very long time. I suppose your sheep are good as usual.

I have made a commencement on sheep. I bought 30 ewes. I think there is about half of them in lamb. They won't lamb until next month. I hope another winter to raise to 100. I wish I had a good south down buck or a Devon, I want to run into a good cross between those that I have are a very fine wool, but small mutton. I hope when I write to you again, I shall be able to tell you of an improvement in the times. I wrote to Mary [Stickland] and Mrs. Stickland [Elizabeth Wall Stickland Bartlett] the week after I wrote to you, but I have had no answer yet. I cannot see the reason. Please to my respects to all enquiries in friends and tell them I am pretty well both in health and spirits. I wish to be remembered to Aunt Elizabeth Coleman. I would write to her if I was there. She was at Ilminster [Somerset]. I must bring this to a close by sending you all my kind love and respects, not forgotten Mary Ann [Jennings]. From your dearest nephew

T. [Thomas] Pipe

Letter Number 30, Page 1

Farmington March 5th 5[?]

Dear Uncle

Your kind letter with the Draft came to hand on or about the 15th of last month. I have been very mutch ingaged ever since or I should have writen to you before, I will now ad that your kindneß is fooly apreciated in fowarden me the money, you might rest ashured that you shall not be the looser of a Fraction by the oppration, I will also informe you that it com just in time to do me geat service, I have been in the Land Speculation again, I have Traded a forty ackers for a nother forty which joined it on the Lake Shore, and bought twenty ackers which laid between it and my House, so now my Farm is all joined to gather, I now intend to sell about Seventy ackers which lais of in the point between the two Lakes, that will leave me a Splended Farm of 160 ackers I fear I shall not be able to sell for a year to com as money is so very searce, but will hay well for a keepen

Letter Number 30, Page 2

as it is good Timbered Land. and that is a scarce
article in these parts. I think my Farm after
selling of that piece and posten a Barn on it
will be worth at the least four thousand dollars
I have my materials all on the ground and paid
for with the exeption of nails and door trimens
but I shall not build this Spring now I have
bought this Land, I must wait and see a change in the
or see my way clear for a nother year
Now in relation to the business in youre hands
I ould say as I have always said do the best
accrdein to youre one judgement if you think it
the Best to stile the Shead do so, I want it
to be kept decent, as to the leace I hardly
know what to say, Elizebeth do not like the idea of
the seven year leace she fancy it to be a long
while to look foward to, she sais that in seven
years she might not have any object to return
for her mother might be dead and her one health
impaired so as there will be no comfort in return
but there is one thing sertin that I shall not
be prepared to return for a few years

Letter Number 30, Page 3

as I shall have to wait for time to take its
one coue to bring things round, I was lain
out to about fore years, but it is imposable
to say when time must take its one corse, there
is one thing sertin I shall not be willing to
to retutn untel I can make my sellf and
Family comfortabell, It is not my intention
to be dependent on that place for a Soport.
I ould say that if Mrs Bonfield will take
a leace for five years do so and if not give the
Seven, Should I feel able and disposed to retun
before the Seven years is up I can be dorin
Somthing else, as I am considrable yankeised
I am not particular what Business or callin
I am in so as I can make an onist liven
I am sorey to hear of Uncle Johns bad luck
in relation to his Sheep, there one thing to be
thankful for he have not goot me to blame for it
this time, I should sopose that he have not goot
all those old dreains oppned yet the lore side
of the House, I think if he had there ould be more
more trouble, I hope this loos will not be so sever this
time as the last, pleas to give my kind love to him

Letter Number 30, Page 4

I hope I shall hear from your flock the next time you
wright, as I have not hord from it for a very long
time I hope your sheep is good as usual,
I have made a commencement on sheep I bought 30 Ews
I think there is about halfe of them in lamb they
wont lamb untell the next month, I hope ither winter
to raise to 100, I wish I had a good South down Buck
or a Devon I want to run in to a good Cross betwin
the two, those that I have is a very fine wool
but small brutes, I hope when I wright to you
again I shall be able to tell you of an improvement
in the times, I wrote to Mary and Mrs Stickeland
the weke after I wrote to you, but I have had no
answer yet I cunot see the reason, Pleas to give
my respects to all inquiren Friends and tell them
I am prsty well both in health and Sperits,
I wish to be remembered to Aunt Coleman
I ould wright to her if I was shoure she was at
Ilminster, I must now bring this to a close by
sendeng you all my kind love and respects, not forgeten Mary Ann, From your Aft. Shepherd
J. Pope

Letter Number 31

Date: December 1858 [Charles Crabb died 2 October 1858]
Writer: Elizabeth Coleman Jennings
Recipient: Thomas & Elizabeth Stickland Pipe
Sent from: Northay Farm, Whitestaunton, Chard,
Somerset County, England
Sent to: Farmington, Waupaca County, Wisconsin, USA

Key Ideas

- John Matthews still lives at Hay Farm, Yarcombe.
- Richard Coleman lives at Marsh Farm, Membury. The farm was in Membury Parish, Devon, until 1884, when it was transferred to Yarcombe, Devon.
- Charles Crabb died on October 2, 1858. His life was insured.
- Mr. Willey from America has been staying with Richard Coleman. Mr. Willey is picking up his mother and taking her with him.
- Daniel Long is home from America to settle property of his recently deceased wife.

[Letter undated, start not included]

Old Mr. Coles of Hares died the latter part of the summer. The youngest daughter lives in the place. She married one Seaward of Stockland [Devon]. Mrs. John Matthews has 2 children. They still live at Hay [Farm]. She is a very dressy woman. I have met her a few times at my Brother Richard's [Coleman] at Marsh [Farm]. Do you remember Charles Crabb of Yarcombe? He died about 2 months since with a very short illness, left a wife and 4 little children. It is a good thing for them his life was insured in £500. Do you remember

[crosshatched]

 Miss Spillar of Dancing? She is married to one Cheek [Henry Chick]. He was a servant, lived with her brother Robert [Spiller], they are living at Dancing. Old Mrs. Spillar is dead. The old gentleman lives with his daughter Mrs Pring. We are expecting the pleasure of seeing a young man from America. It is Mr. Willey. He has been with my brother [William Coleman]. He is coming to fetch his mother. We heard a few days ago that George Salter had failed to [sell?] the carriage and pair

[other way]

though his wife said she kept [hopes?] it sold. Daniel Long is home from America, but I have not seen him. His wife is dead, so he came home for a little property she left. I must conclude wishing you a happy and prosperous year.

From your affectionate

Aunt E. [Elizabeth Coleman] Jennings

Letter Number 31, Page 1

Old Mr Coles of Hares died the latter part
of the summer the youngest daughter lives
in the place she married one Seaward
of Stockland, Mrs John Mathews has 2 chil
dren they still live at Hay she is a very
dressy woman I have meet her a few times
at My Brothers Riords at Marsh, do you
remember Charles Crabb of Yarcombe he
died about 2 months since with a very
short illness left a wife & 4 little children
it is a good thing for them his life was
insured in 500£ do you remember

Letter Number 31, Page 2

Letter Number 32

Date: 3 December 1858
Writer: Thomas Pipe
Recipient: William Jennings
Sent from: Farmington, Waupaca County, Wisconsin, USA
Sent to: Northay Farm, Whitestaunton, Chard,
                Somerset County, England

Key Ideas

- Thomas Pipe reports that the economy is so bad that it will take three years to recover. He compares prices of 1858 to 1856.
- Thomas Pipe cannot sell anything. He trades and barters for what he needs.
- Thomas Pipe sees suffering, especially some of his own country's people who did not have a shoe all summer. He tries to help them, but he cannot get "swamped" himself.
- Thomas Pipe speculates that one half of the county will be "sold for takes" this winter. He can feed his family from his farm.
- Thomas Pipe asks William Jennings to forward £25 or £30 as soon as possible. Then, he will not need to sell his grain at a low price. Money loaned in America is 4% and 5% per month. If not paid, there is no mercy.

———————

Farmington, Dec 3rd, 1858

Dear Uncle

I have delayed writing to you for some time past as I was in hope to have better sense to tell or rather be able to speak of better times this winter as the prospect is very poor at present. I am sorry to inform you that this part of the country has met with so great a stagnation as to require at least three years to recover, and I think you will not dispute me when I give you the present prices and amount of crops raised this year, and compare it with the prices two years ago. In the first place I will give you the amount raised. I believe to take the county through the wheat crop will not average seven bushels per acre, and the oats not over 18 per acre. The Indian corn is pretty good and also the potato crop, barley very light. It won't give over 12 bushels per acre. The prices are as follows in English currency. Wheat 2s 3d per bushel, barley 2s 3d, oats 10d per bushel, potatoes 9d per bushel, corn 1s per bushel, butter 9d per pound, cheese 4d. In May 1856 the prices were as follows, wheat 6s 6d per bushel, oats 4s 6d per bushel, barley 5s per bushel, corn 5s per bushel, potatoes 3s per bushel, butter 1s 6d per pound, cheese 9d per pound. You will perceive by these figures the difference is so great that the farming community has to suffer immensely.

As to horses and cattle there is no sale for them for money. It is all trade and barter. I have a lot of stock which I want to sell but the only chance I have is to trade. I have cattle which I had to take back which I sold nearly a year ago. I had to take them or nothing. I am now trading them for lumber and such things as I can lay by and not cost anything to winter and will bring the cash at some time.

I often think I never saw as much suffering in England as I see here now, and the greatest suffering is with those who has property. I know lots of men who have from 80 to 120 acres of land and haven't had a shoe to their foot the whole summer. I might speak of some of our old neighbours in that way. Perhaps I had better call no names, but it is some of our own country people what is putting one back as much as anything, by trying to help them out of the mire, I was like to get swamped myself. Now I find it is as much as I can stand to attend to my own family. I do not know what will become of lots of families this winter, for the want of clothing to keep them warm. I am happy to say that I have a plenty to eat such as a farmer can raise. I have a plenty of beef, pork, potatoes and wheat, and I think we shall not freeze this winter, as to money I can scarcely find a dollar. I think one half of the county will be sold for takes this winter. I have been informed that times are quite decent in England. I hope it is so, I have no means of knowing for the truth.

Dear Uncle, if it is possible I want you to forward me £25 or £30 at the earliest opportunity. I was in hopes to have swung clear of debt before I could ask you again, but the times are so very hard that I shall have to sacrifice a great deal by selling my produce before the next summer, and you was so kind as to offer me that amount. If you could send it, it was really needed, and I am sure it could never be more beneficial than at the present time. I flatter myself that by getting a little money so as to keep along and keep my grain and other stuff a few months longer that I shall save myself pretty well. But I will assure that there is lots of people that was well off a year ago that are ruined now. There is no money loaned now only at 4 and 5 per cent per month, and if not paid at the time there is no mercy shown, but the payment forced, the people in this country are noted for being cut throats at all such times as these. They lay all kind of traps to insure, I hope this will find you all well and comfortable. Please to remember me to all enquiring friends and tell that our health is pretty good at present and are anxiously waiting for better times. Elizabeth joins with me in sending her kindest respects to Aunt and family and not forgetting yourself. From your affectionate nephew and well-wisher.

Thos. Pipe

[More modern hand] Farmington 1858 Grandpa Thomas Pipe

Letter Number 32, Page 1

Farmington Dec 5 1858

Dear Uncle,

I have delaid wrighton to you for sumtime
past as I was in hopes to have better chense to tell
or rather be able to speke of better times, but I
feel we shell have no beter times this winter, as
the prospect is very poor at present, I am sorry
to informe you that this part of the Cuntrey has
met with so great a stagnation as to require at
least three years to recover, and I think you
will not disput me when I give you the present
priceses and amount of Crops raised this year,
and compare it with the prices two years ago
in the first place I will give you the amount
raised, I beleve to take County through the Wheat
Crop will not averidge seven Bushels per acre, and the
Oats not over 18 bu per acre the Indean Corn is pretty
good and also the Patato Crop Barley very light it
went go over twelve bu per acre, the prices is as
folows Wheat 2..5 Per bu Barly 2..3 Oats 10 Per bu
Patatos 9 Per bu Corn 1 Per bu Buter 8 Per lb Chees
in May 1856 the prices ware as folows Wheat 6..6
Per bu Oats 4..6 Per bu Barly 5 Per bu Corn 5 Per bu
Patato 3 Per bu Buter 1..6 Per lb Chese 9 Per lb,
you will preceve by these figurs the diffrince is so great
that the Farming cominurty has to suffer eminely

Letter Number 32, Page 2

as to Horses and Cattle there is no sale for them for
money it is all trade and Barter, I have a lot of
Stock which I went to sell but the only chance I have
is to trade, I have Cattle which I had to take back
which I Sold nearly a year ago, I had to take them
or nothing; I am now traden them for Lumber
and sutch things as I can lay by and not cost any thing
to winter and will bring the Cash at som time)
I often think I never saw so mutch Suffren in England
as I see here now, and the greatest Suferen is with
tho hes propertys, I know of lots of men who has from
80 to 120 acres of land and havent had a Shoue to there
Foot the holl Summer, I might Speak of som of our
Old Neibors in that way Perhaps I had better tell no names
but it is som of our one Cuntry people that is puton
me back as mutch as any thing, by tryen to help them
out of the shire I was like to get Swampt my self
Now I fiend it is as mutch as I can atend to to atend
to my One Family, I do not know what will becom
of lots of Familys this winter for the went of Clothing
to keep them warme, I am happy to say that I
have a plenty to eat sutch as a Farmer can raise I
have a plenty of Beef Pork Potatos and Wheat, and I
think we shall not freese this winter, as to Money
I can scarcley fiend a dollar I think one half of the
bought will be sold for taxes this winter, I have been
informed that times are quit deacent in England
I hope it is so, I have no means of nown for the truth
of it

Letter Number 32, Page 3

Dear Uncle, if it is posible I want you to forward me 25 or 50 £ at the earliest opertunity, I was in hopes to have swong clear of debt before I cold on you again, but the times are so very hard that I shall have to sacrafice a great deal by selling My Produce before the next Summer, and you was so kind as to offer me that amount in your last if it was reely needed, and I am shure it cold never be more benyyefical then at the present time, I flatter my self that by geten a little money to askheep along and keep my brain and other Stuf afew months longer that I shall save my self prety well, but I will assure that there is lots of people that was well of a year ago that ar ruined now, there is no money loned now onley at 4 and 5 Per cent Per month and if not paid at the time there" no Mercy Shewn but the peyment posceed, the people in this Country ar noted for been cut throats at all satch times as these, they lay all kien of traps to insnare, I hope this will fiend you all well and Comfortable, pleas to remember me to all inquiren friends, and tell them that our health is prety at present and ar anctiously waiten for beter times Elizebeth joins with me in senden her kindest respects to Aunt and family, and not forgoten your Self. From yours aff Nephew and well wisr

Thos Pope

Letter Number 32, Page 4

Letter Number 32, Envelope Front

Letter Number 32, Envelope Back

Letter Number 33

Date: December 1858 [Ellen (Nelly) is 4 years old.]
Writer: William & Elizabeth Coleman Jennings
Recipient: Thomas Pipe & Elizabeth Stickland Pipe
Sent from: Northay Farm, Whitestaunton, Chard,
Somerset County, England
Sent to: Farmington, Waupaca County, Wisconsin, USA

Key Ideas

- William Jennings tells Thomas Pipe that he does not intend to charge Thomas with any more interest.
- William Jennings sends his love to Thomas Pipe's mother, Charlotte Jennings Pipe Pillar.

[Crosshatched]

- Elizabeth Coleman Jennings asks whether Elizabeth Stickland Pipe's two older boys, John Stickland and Tom, are getting useful and whether she has had any more children.
- She says that William Jennings Pipe is looking ill: his ankles swell and his knees are weak. He is staying at Birch Oak Farm. Uncle John Jennings asked him for advice about his mare. William Jennings Pipe is taller than his brother, Thomas Pipe.
- Elizabeth Coleman Jennings has heard from Elizabeth Stickland Pipe's sister, Mary Stickland. Mother, Elizabeth Wall Stickland Bartlett, is doing well.
- Mary Ann Jennings is growing tall and is home from school. Elizabeth states that Ellen (Nelly) is now four years old this month. (Ellen was born in December 1854.)
- John Stickland went further up the country in Australia. His wife, Elizabeth Matthews who is expecting a baby (Anna), did not go with him. Anna Stickland was born in Fremantle, western Australia in 1859. Anna Stickland writes Letter Number 80 in Chapter 8.

———

Dear Thomas

I am glad to tell you there is but £31 14s 1½ d more to pay me when I shall be made happy to send you the whole. I don't intend charging you any more interest. I shall look to the draining often for that is a permanent improvement. With kind love to all and your dear mother [Charlotte Jennings Pipe Pillar] when you see her, trusting this will find you all well from

Your affectionate

Uncle
Wm. Jennings

[crosshatched]

My dear Mrs. Pipe

I thought I must just write a line to enquire of the dear children, I suppose the two eldest boys [John Stickland and Tom] are getting useful, have you any further increase to your family, I can assure you poor Wm. [Jennings] Pipe looks very ill. His ankles swell very much towards night if he takes much exercise. He is very weak in his knees. It makes him walk quite halt. He has been at Birch [Oak Farm] house a week. He came here Monday, went to Birch [Oak Farm] again Tuesday to meet the mare as his uncle John [Jennings] wish him to have his advice. Hope he will soon get better. I think him a very nice young man. If he was stout, he would be a remarkable fine man as he is so very tall, if any he is taller than your husband [Thomas Pipe]. I heard from your sister [Mary Stickland] about fortnight since,

[other way]

she said she had just received a letter from you herself. Your mother [Elizabeth Wall Stickland Bartlett] was quite well, how is dear Mrs. [Charlotte Jennings Pipe] Pillar and family. Please give my love to her, hope she will write to me soon. My two children are growing up nicely. M.A. [Mary Ann Jennings] is as tall as myself. She has been home from school this last year. I have to send her again at Christmas. Our little Nelly [Ellen] was four years old the first of this month, so you see I have not a son yet. Mrs. Matthews received a letter from her daughter [Elizabeth Matthews Stickland] and your brother John [Stickland] was gone further up the county [Australia]. She poor thing could not go with him as she was expecting [Anna] to be confined. Her little girl [Elizabeth] she left with her father is at boarding school at Kilmington [Devon].

Accounts 1858

I have sent you the account of the two lasts payments

Aug. 16 received of Mr. Phillips for rent due Lady Day [25 March] last

£37 10s

Mr. Denning	<u>£4 10s</u>	
Total	£42 0s	
What I have paid		
Jan. 13	Mr. [Thomas] Pipe	£25 0s 0d
	Mr. [John] Stickland	£12 0s 0d
	Fire insurance	£1 15s 0d
	½ year's interest	£2 10s 0d
	2 Lime shaling [flaky texture]	5s 6d
	Order and stamp	<u>2s 0d</u>
	Total	£41 12s 6d

£42 0s 0d

<u>£41 12s 6d</u>

£1 7s 6d

<u>£114 15s 4 ¼ d</u>

In hand £115 2s 10 ¼ d

Up to lady Day [25 March] last

Dr. Joan Naomi Steiner

[Accounts] 1858

Oct. In receipt of Mr. Bonfield

Half yearly rent due

Michaelmas [29 September] last	£40 0s 0d
Mr. Denning	<u>£4 10s 0d</u>
	£44 10s 0d

What I have paid out

Mr. [John] Stickland	£12 0s 0d
Mr. Bonfield's 1 ¼ carts reed	£2 10s 0d
Mr. Dommett half lease	£2 10s 0d
Mason's bill	£1 3s 3d
Thatcher's bill	£1 2s 9d
½ years interest	£2 0s 0d
Letter stamp	<u>1s 0d</u>
	£21 7s 0d
	£44 10s 0d
	<u>£21 7s 0d</u>
	£23 3s 0d
	<u>£115 2s 10 ½ d</u>

£138 5s 10 ½ d in hand up to Michaelmas [29 September] last

Dear Thomas

I am glad to
to tell you there is but
£31..14..1½ more to pay me
when I shall be most happy
to send you the whole I don't
intend charging you any more
intrest I shall look to the
draining offen for that is
a permanent improvement
with kind love to all and
your Dear Mother when you
see her trusting this will
find you all well from
Your affectionate
Uncle H Jennings

1858

I have sent you the
account of the two last payments
Aug 16 Rec of Mr Phillips
for Rent due Lady day last 37"10

Mr Deming 4"10

£42"11 "

What I have paid

Jany 13 Mr Pipe 25"0"0
Mr Shuttland 12"0"0
Fire Insurance 1"15"0
½ Years Intrest 2"10"0
2 Htd Lime & haling " 5"0
Order & Stamps 2"0

41"12"0

£
42" 6"
41"12"0
" " 7"
114"15"4½y
In hand 15 " 2 " 10 ½ up to Lady day last

1858

Oct 11 Rec⁽ᵈ⁾ of Mr Bonfield

half years rent due

Michelmas last ———— £ 1 8

Mr Deming ———— 4 " 16 " 0

44 " 10 " 0

What I have paid out

Mr Shotbland ———— 12 " 0 " 0

Mr Bonfield 1 1/4 Recd ———— 2 " 10 " 0

Mr Domniett half Sewn — 2 " 16 " 0

Masons Bell ———— 1 " 3 " 3

Thatchers Bell ———— 1 " 2 " 9

1/2 Years Intrest ———— 2 " 0 " 0

Letter Stamp ———— " 1 " 0

£ 5

21 " 7 " 0

44 " 10 " 0

21 " 7 " 0

23 " 3 " 0

115 " 2 " 10 1/2

intrest 3 8 " 5 " 10 1/2 up to Michelmas last

Letter Number 34

Date: 17 January 1859
Writer: William Jennings
Recipient: Thomas Pipe
Sent from: Northay Farm, Whitestaunton, Chard,
Somerset County, England
Sent to: Farmington, Waupaca County, Wisconsin, USA

Key Ideas

- William Jennings says he is sorry to hear things are so bad in "Merica" (America). He has sent £30.
- William Jennings remarks that Mr. Willey from America is visiting England. He has been living with William Coleman. He is accompanied by William Bradford.
- William Jennings tells Thomas Pipe that his brother (William Jennings Pipe) is better and will be returning to his regiment on Monday. He is well behaved and too often invited out to parties.

1859   Northay, Jan. 17th

Dear Thos.

According to your request I have sent you thirty pounds which I hope you will receive safe. I was sorry to hear times is so bad in Merica [America] and very bad here, best wheat less share £1 a sack. I am glad to say that I have heard since I received yours from a Mr. Willey that has been living with William Coleman that you are doing very well, that Mr. Willey is come to England with Mr. William Bradford. Your brother Wm. [Jennings Pipe] is still among us. He is rather better. He is going to return to his regiment on Monday.

Nephew, he desires to be kindly remembered to you all particularly to his dear mother. I can assure you that he is a well-behaved young man and too often invited out to parties while his health is not good.

With our kind love to your wife and family from your

Affectionate uncle

Wm. Jennings

When you receive this please to write as I may know you have received it.

[Accounts] 1858

Mr. Jennings to G. Bonfield

¼ cwt [hundredweight] of reed   £2 1s 4d

Settled Oct 29. G. Bonfield

[Account]

Mr. Wm. Jennings

1 April for Mr. & Mrs. Pipe

And Mr. George Bonfield

To Dommett Canning

1858 October Instructions for drawing and engrossing lease by Pithayne [Farm] and Whitehorns [Farm] for seven years at £80 per annum and attending obtaining you and Mrs. White's execution thereof

Paid Stamp and parchment

£5 –

1858 Nov. 15

By Cash £5, Dommett and Canning

Letter Number 34, Page 1

1859

Northay Jany 17th

Mr Pike

According to your request
I have sent you thirty pounds which I
hope you will receive safe I was sorry to
here times is so bad in America and very bad
here best wheat less than 7 a sack I am glad
to say that I have harde since I wrote yours
from a Mr Willey that has been living
with William Coleman that you are doing
very well this Mr Willey is come to England
with Mr William Bradford your Brother
William is steel among us he is rather better
he is going to return to his regiment on Monday

Letter Number 34, Page 2

meph he desires to be kindly remembered
to you all partiegulary to his dear
brother I can ashoure you that
he is a well behaved young man
and a two often invited out to partys
while his helth is not good
with our kind love to your
wife and family from your
affectunate Uncle

Wm Jennings

when you receive this please to
write as I may know you have
recd it

Letter Number 34, Page 3

1858 Mr. Jennings
to Ly Bonfield
£ s
1/14 pmt of Reed — 2 10 11

Settled Octr 28.
J Bonfield

Letter Number 34, Page 4

Mr Wm Jennings
(April for Mr & Mrs Pipe)
and Mr George Bonfield
to
Domnett Manning
1858 October. Instructions for
drawing & ingrossing
lease of Pikage and
Whitehorns for seven
years, at £80 per
annum, & attending
obtaining your & Mrs.
White's execution thereof.
Paid Stamp & parchment
1858 Nov 15
By Cash
£5
Domnett Manning

£
5—

Letter Number 35

Date: 10 March 1859
Writer: Thomas & Elizabeth Stickland Pipe
Recipient: William & Elizabeth Coleman Jennings
Sent from: Farmington, Waupaca County, Wisconsin, USA
Sent to: Northay Farm, Whitestaunton, Chard,
Somerset County, England

Key Ideas

- Thomas Pipe thanks William Jennings for sending a draft of £30.
- Thomas Pipe thought he would feed a yoke of oxen over the winter and sell the cattle for beef in spring. However, his horses got sick. Now, Thomas does not know how the spring work will get done.
- Grain prices have gone up, but many farmers sold their grain too early for a lower price. These farmers will need to buy grain at a higher price as they need it.
- Thomas Pipe has one consolation. He has plenty to eat for his family and animals.
- Thomas Pipe just returned from visiting his mother, Charlotte Jennings Piller Pipe. She is well but wonders why she has not heard from William Jennings Pipe.
- Thomas Pipe supposes Mr. William Bradford is home for a wife, Susan Coleman. He wishes them happiness if that is the case.

Elizabeth continues

- Elizabeth has received a letter from her sister, Mary Stickland. Elizabeth Stickland Pipe had requested Mary Stickland to send her some items. Elizabeth Stickland Pipe has not yet received them.
- Elizabeth Stickland Pipe reports that Mary Ann Pipe Sinclair is now their neighbor. She lives only one field away. Mary Ann Pipe Sinclair has been quite sick. Her 18-month-old baby girl (Ellen Joan Sinclair) does not enjoy good health. (Ellen Joan

Sinclair married Henry Smillie in Vinland, Winnebago County, on October 20, 1881.)

- Elizabeth Stickland Pipe says her family is well except for herself and William Edwin (Willy). They both have bad colds.

Farmington, March 10th 1859

Dear Uncle [William Jennings]

I am happy to inform you of the reception of your kind letter with the draft for thirty pounds, which came to hand about two weeks since. It came rather unexpected as I thought probably you would not send it until you heard from me again as your first and my letter must have met on the way. I was somewhat in hopes that such would be the case at first, but as it turns out nothing could happen better. In the first place I thought the times would brighten up a little and by feeding a yoke of oxen which I thought I might spare and turn them into beef this spring. I thought I could rule through, and just as I had them fairly on the way my horses commenced gotten sick. I here had four of them down at once. I have one colt which we had to lift up every day for six weeks. My best mare has been sick for one month, and what is most singular, she eats and drinks hearty and yet we cannot get her out of the stable. I have but one three year old colt that is fit to do anything with, out of five horses it just takes one more to attend to them regular by those means I have to take my cattle to work, and then I hardly know how my spring work is going to be done without my horses mend very fast.

I am happy to inform you that the prices on grain has very much improved since I wrote to you last but it will not benefit but few as the greater part have sold their grain, and some has to buy again and by these means I fear it will not benefit the country. I have one consolation that is I have a plenty to eat for family and teams and about 14 barrels of flour to sell and 100 bushels of corn. Flour is worth 8 dollars per barrel. That is about 5s 6d per bushel English currency for wheat. Corn is worth about 3s. Oats about the same. I have just returned from Vinland. I am happy to inform you that I found mother quite well. She is wondering the reason that she do not hear from William [Jennings Pipe]. I hope he will write soon as she frets a great deal. I suppose that

Mr. Bradford is home after a wife in it Miss S[arah] Coleman I wish her much joy if such is the case. I do not know that I have anything more particular to write about. I shall leave the other half sheet for Elizabeth [Stickland Pipe]. Mother [Charlotte Jennings Pipe Pillar] wishes to be kindly remembered to all. Please to give my kind respects to all enquiring friends and accept the same yourself.

From yours a well-wisher and ever affectionate nephew

Thos. Pipe

Dear Aunt [Elizabeth Coleman Jennings)

I was most happy to receive your kind and most interesting letter and likewise to hear that you were all well. I received a letter from my sister Mary [Stickland] about Christmas which she intended to send me a few articles which I expected to receive before this but have given up as I think it could not have been fastened up very secure. I shall write and see if she sent them as she stated that was in a few days after she wrote my letter.

Dear Aunt I have to tell you that Mary Ann Sinclair Pipe [Mary Ann Pipe Sinclair] that was is now our nearest neighbour, lives 1 field from us. She has been quite sick and fevery but she is somewhat better, but her little girl is not, She does not enjoy very good health. She is an 18 months old. She is very often sick. Our family is well with the exceptions of myself and Willey [William Edwin] which we have had bad colds that I can scarcely hold up my head to write this scrawl. Give my love to all enquiring friends not forgetting your brother Richard and wife. I would write a little more but Thomas is going to the [post] office with it which he cannot stay for me to write more. Please to give my kind love to Uncle [William Jennings] and the 2 children [Mary Ann and Ellen (Nelly)], not forgetting yourself and all friends, which I hope once all are enjoying good health from

Your affectionate niece

E [Elizabeth Stickland] Pipe

Letter Number 35, Page 1

Farmington March 10th 1855

Dear Uncle,

I am happy to inform you of the reception of your kind letter with the draft for thirty pounds, which came to hand about two weeks since, It came rather unexpected as I thought probbely you ould not send it untill you heard from me againe as youre first and my letter must have met on the way, I was somewhat in hopes that sutch ould be the case at first, but as it turns out nothing could hapen better In the first place I thought the times ould brighten up a litle and by feeding a yoke of Oxen which I thought I might Spare and turn them in to Beef this Spring I thought I could rub through, and just as I had them fairily on the way My Horses comenced geten sick I have had four of them down at once I have one Colt which we had to lift up every day for six weeks, My best Mare has been sick for one month, and what is most singular she eats and drink harty and yet we canno get her out of Stable, I have but one three year Colt that is fit to do any thing with out of five Horses, it just takes one more to atend to them regulor, by those means I have to take my Cattle to work, and them I hardly know how my Springs work is goin to be don without my horses amends very fast

Letter Number 35, Page 2

I am happy to informe you that the prices on grain has
very mutch improved since I wrote to you last
but it will not bennifet but few, as the greater
part have sold there grains and som has to buy again
and by theade means I fear it will not bennifet
the Bunkrey, I have one consolation that is I
have a plenty to eat for families and teems and
about 14 barls of Flower to sell and 100 bushells of
Corn, Flower is worth eight dollars Per barell
that is about 5 6 Per bushell English Currency for wheat Corn
is worth about 3 Octo about the same, I have just
returned from Bintend, I am happy to informe you
that I found Mother quiet well she is wondrous
the reason that she do not hear from William
I hope he will wright soon as she frets a great deel
I sapose that Mr Bradford is home after a wife
is it Miss I Coleman I wish her mutch joy
if sutch is the case) I do not know that I have
any thing more particular to wright about I shall
leave the other half sheet for Elizebeth
Mother wishes to be kindley rembred to all
Pleas to give my kiend respects to all inquiring
Friends and accept the same your self
From yours a well wisher and ever aff Nephew

Thos Pipe

Letter Number 35, Page 3

Dear Aunt

I was most happy to receive your kind
and most interesting letter and likewise to hear
that you were all well I received a letter from
my sister Mary a bout Christmass which she intended
to sende me a few articles which I expected to receive
before this but have given up as I think it could
not have been fasened up very secure I shall write
and see if she sent them as she stated that
was in a few days after she wrote my letter,
Dear Aunt I have to tell you that Mary Ann
Sinclair Pipe that was is now our nearest neighbour
lives 1 field from us she has been quite sick and feby
but she is some what better but her little girl
is not she does not enjoy very good health she is a
18 months old she is very often sick our family is
well with the exception of myself and Willey which we
have bad colds that I can scarcely hold up my head
to write this scrawl give my love to all inquiring
friends not forgetting your Brother Richard an Wife
I would write a little more but Thomas is going to the
office with it which he cannot stay for me to write more
please to give my kind love to Uncle and the 2 dear
children not forgetting yourself and all friends
which I hope one all are enjoying good health from
              Your affectionate Niece
                S Pipe
   write soon   excuse haste

Letter Number 36

Date: April 1860 [envelope stamped 7 May]
Writer: Charlotte Jennings Pipe Pillar
Recipient: William & Elizabeth Coleman Jennings
Sent from: Vinland, Winnebago County, Wisconsin, USA
Sent to: Northay Farm, Whitestaunton, Chard,
                Somerset County, England

Key Ideas

- Charlotte Jennings Pipe Pillar announces the death of Mary Ann Pipe Sinclair, who died on the 8th of March at the age of 30, according to the *U.S. Federal Mortality Schedule for 1860* and *Yarcombe Parish, Devon, Birth Records*. The letter is not edged in black.
- Mary Ann Pipe Sinclair had recently joined the Episcopal Church. (Likely the church is St. Marks in Waupaca, which was founded in 1856 and was a center of Yankee ethnic life for much of the nineteenth century.)
- (Mary Ann Pipe had married George Washington Sinclair, son of William Sinclair.)
- Charlotte Jennings Pipe Pillar expresses her deep grief.
- Charlotte Jennings Pipe Pillar refers to her son, James Pillar, as John. He is doing well in school and works hard on the farm.
- Elizabeth Pillar is James and Charlotte Jennings Pipe Pillar's daughter. She does not learn as fast as her son, James Pillar, but she sings from morning to night.
- Charlotte Jennings Pipe Pillar hears that Mr. Willey is home to settle the family estate.
- Charlotte Jennings Pipe Pillar asks her sister-in-law to give her dear friend, Mrs. Prynn, her kindest love.
- Charlotte Jennings Pipe Pillar asks whether her brother Tom Jennings or his son Tom Jennings has returned to England from Australia.

———————

Vinland, April

My very dear Brother and Sister [in-law (William and Elizabeth Coleman Jennings)]

With a nearly broken heart I write you the sad tiding of the departure from this world my very dear Mary Ann [Pipe Sinclair]. She died on the 8th [March] quite sudden leaving a dear baby [John Phillip] only eleven days old. She appeared to be quite well having sat at the table with the family at dinner and tea. She rose from her chair to go to the bed and dropped in a fit of apoplexy. This was nearly 5 in the evening and a little before 12 the dear creature breathed her last. She was sensible but could not speak. She clasped the dear children [William Edward, Ellen Joan, and John Phillip] to her cheek and the tears welled down. Oh my dear sister [in-law] if I could rest assured that she was ready with her lamp burning to be received into everlasting glory, I should be somewhat reconciled as I know her cross was full. Her husband [George Washington Sinclair] is a lazy, shapeless fellow and she full of life and ambition, but her heart was broken. She saw all would soon be gone. The dear soul pined in secret sadness. I had not seen her for over a year, which grieves [me] very much. I am happy to say she had recently joined

the Pissable [Episcopal] Church and requested her husband [George Washington Sinclair] to give her dear little girl [Ellen Joan] to an old friend of hers. She is a pretty gentle little thing of 2 years last September and a fine boy [William Edward] of five. All this is a great charge and trial for me, so much that I believe I shall not be long after the dear creature. It has brought on such a weakness at my stomach and palpation of heart. Be steel and know that I am God. Will you be so kind as to let dear William [Jennings Pipe] know of it and desire him to write to me. I cannot think the reason I do not hear from him oftener. I hope he is steady, so my dear sister [in-law] when you write tell me what you think of him and also to Brother John [Jennings]. I never hear from him. Indeed, I think myself almost forgotten, you are the only one that answers my letters promptly. My dear sister [in-law] this world is but a wilderness, but it is passing away. It is through much tribulation we are to enter the kingdom of heaven. I am happy to say I do look forward to a glorious eternity purchased by the Book of Christ, oh let us lay hold of the blessed promises offered in God's holy word. They are great. Amen. I hope dear Brother and Sister [in-law] you are both set at

the Table of the Lord.

We shall perish everlastingly if we do not come to Christ. I often think if all my dear relatives were bending their knees at the bedside when I do before I go to rest what an [occasion?] it would make in heaven. All the riches and honours of the world will afford us no comfort at the last hour. May we all be as dependent on Christ, as an infant is [dependent] on its nurse.

My dear sister [in-law] I am happy to say we are getting along pretty well. Our farm is improving fast, but it is so much hard work James [Pillar, son] grows very fast. He is slender chipping down heavy timber and lifting heavy logs is I fear hurting him. He complains a good deal of his back. I am happy to say he is a good boy. He thinks of nothing else but to the farm to work or at his studies which he loves much if the Lord spares and prospers him. He intends making you a visit before many years. He is very like dear William [Jennings].

I hope to have their likenesses [photos] taken some one of the Grants intend coming home in the fall when I will send them over. My dear Elizabeth [Pillar] is a loving little thing. She is as joyous and gay as the lark.

No wind [or] weather can keep her from school, but she don't learn so fast as her brother, sing from morn to night, always ready to help her father on the farm, and she is built like him, short and stout. She sends her kind love to her dear cousin MA [Mary Ann Jennings] and thanks her kindly for the bookmark. She hopes to send her some little specimen of her work soon. There is nothing in the needle-way is taught at school. Please remember us very kindly to all your family. Tell me when or what part your William [Coleman, brother] is in. I hear Mr. Willey is home after his mother and family property is or I should say landed property is selling very hard and industrious man with 5 [sons?] could now fix himself in a very pretty home.

Kindest love to all my dear brothers and sisters, also to your dear children [Mary Ann and Ellen Jennings], not forgetting my old friend Mrs Prynn. I hope we shall all meet in heaven and spend a long and happy eternity together where trouble cannot enter.

We have had a pleasant winter and a busy full spring, but it is rather cold now. Please tell me if any of the Whites are returned to England or my brother T [Tom Jennings] son Tom, how we are scattered up and down on the earth as fugitives all this [??] to wean us from this wicked world.

God bless and be with you for ever

From your affectionate sister [in-law]

C. [Charlotte Jennings Pipe] Pillar

Letter Number 36, Page 1

Vinland April

My very dear Brother & Sister
With a nearly broken
I write you the sad tidings of the departure fur
~~the this~~ world My very dear Mary ann
She died on the 8th quite sudden leaving a
dear Baby onley Eleven days old she appeard
to be quite well having sott at the Table with
the Family both at Dinner and Tea
She rose from her Chair to go to the Bed
and dropped in a Fitt of Applepexy this
was nearly 5 in the even and a little before
12 the dear creature breathed her last
she was sensible but could not speak she
~~clasped the dear~~ Children to her Cheek and
the Tears rolld down — oh my dear Sister
if I could rest assured that she was ready with
her Lamp burning to be received into everlasting
Glory I should be somewhat reconsiled
~~to her Cup was full~~ her Husband is
a lazy shafless fellow and she full of life
and ambition but her hart was broken
she saw all would soon be gone the dear soul
pined in secrett sadness I had not seen her
for over a year which grieves very much
I am happy to say she had recently joind

Letter Number 36, Page 2

The Pissable Church and requested her Husband to give her dear little Girl to an old friend of hers she is a pretty gentle little thing of 2 y last Sept and a fine Boy of June all this is a great Charge and trial for me so much that I believe I shall not be long after the new Creature it has brought on such a weakness at my Stomack and Palpitation of heart Be steel and know that I am God Will you be so kind as to lett dear William know of it and desire him to write to me I cannot think the reason I do not hear from him oftener I hope he is steady do my dear Sister when you write tell mee what you think of him and also to Brother John I never hear from him Indeed I think my self almost forgotten you are the only one that answers my Letter promptly My dear Sister this world is but a willderness but it is passing away It is through much tribulation we are to enter the Kingdom of Heaven I am happy to say I do lookforward to a glorious Eternity purchased by the Blood of Christ oh lett us lay hold of the blessed promises offered in Gods holy word they are yea & amen I hope my dear Brother & Sister you both lett at

Letter Number 36, Page 3

The Table of the Lord
We shall perish everlastingly if we do not come
to Christ. I often think of all my dear relations
were bending there knees at there Bed sid
when I do before I go to rest what an case it
would make in heaven all the riches
and honours of the world will afford us no comfort
at the last hour — may we all be as dependent
on Christ as an Infant is on its nurse
My dear Sister I have thought of writing you
some time past I am happy to say we are geting
a long pritty well over Learn is improving fast
but it is so much hard work James grows
very fast he is very slender choping down
heavy Timber and lifting heavy logs is
I fear hurting him he complains a good ell
of his back I am happy to say he is a good boy
he thinks of nothing else but on the Learning
to work or at his Studies which he loves much
if the Lord spairs and prosper him
he intend making you a visit before many
years he is very like dear William
I hope to have there Likenesses taken soon
one of the Grants intend coming home
in the fall when I will send them over
My dear Eliz^th is a loving little thing she is as
Joyous and gay as the Lark

No wind or Weather can keep her from
School but she dont learn so fast as her Brother
busy from Morn to Night always ready to help
her Father on the Farm and she is built
like him short and stout She sends
her kind love to her dear Cousin Mary and
thanks her kindly for the Book mark
she hopes to send her some little specimen of her
work soon there is nothing in the Needle way
is taught at Schools Pease remember me very
kindly to all your family tell me where or what
part your Br William is in I here Mr Willey is
home after his Mother and Family Property is
or I should say Landed property is selling very low
and industerous man with with 5 00 could
now fix him self in a very pritty home
kindest love to all my dear brothers and Sisters
also to your dear Children not forgetting my old
friend Mrs Pym I hope we shall meet in
Heaven and spend a long and happy Eternity
together wheare trouble cannot enter
We have had a pleasant winter and a busy fall thing
but it is rather cold now pease tell me if aney
of the Whites are returned to England or my
Brother I Son Tom how we ar scattered up and
down on the earth as fugatives all this isolated
towean is from this wakish world God bless and be
with you for ever from your afflicted sister E Pillar

Letter Number 36, Envelope Front

Letter Number 36, Envelope Back

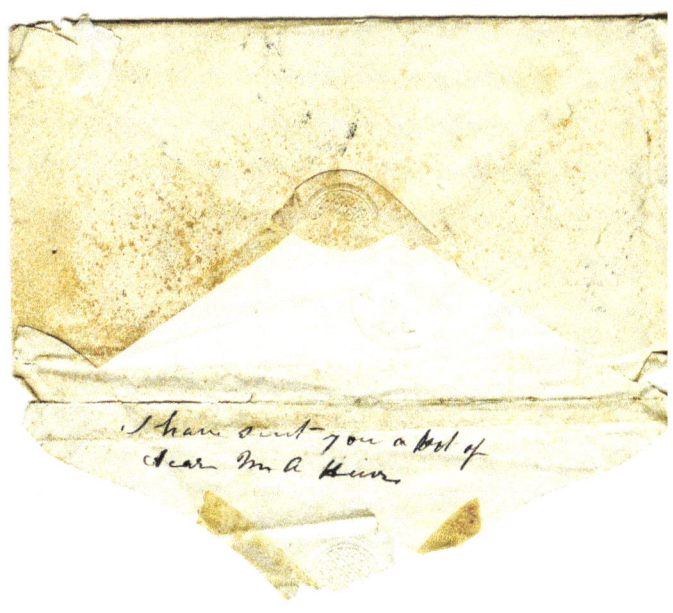

Chapter 5

Village of Waupaca, Waupaca County, Wisconsin
December 1860 - 1863

Chapter 5 includes letters dated 1860 to 1863 while Thomas and Elizabeth Stickland Pipe are living in the Village of Waupaca. The Pipes and the Jennings exchange nine letters. Included is an annuity receipt from John Stickland. Charlotte Jennings Pipe Pillar writes one letter to her brother William Jennings. Two letters are to William Jennings Pipe. Elizabeth Stickland Pipe writes to her brother-in-law William Jennings Pipe with a special request. Charlotte Jennings Pipe Pillar writes one letter to her brother and sister-in-law, William and Elizabeth Coleman Jennings. Charlotte announces the death of her daughter, Mary Ann Pipe Sinclair, in March 1860.

Letter Number 37

Date: 2 December 1860
Writer: Thomas Pipe
Recipient: William Jennings
Sent from: Waupaca, Waupaca County, Wisconsin, USA
Sent to: Northay Farm, Whitestaunton, Chard,
                   Somerset County, England

Key Ideas

- Thomas Pipe reports his family is well except for Elizabeth Stickland Pipe who has a cold. His mother, Charlotte Jennings Pipe Pillar, is also well.
- Thomas Pipe has not farmed much this last summer because he is working in his butcher business. He keeps an open market in Waupaca, Waupaca County, Wisconsin.
- Thomas Pipe has left his farm in Farmington, Waupaca County, Wisconsin. He has rented all but 10 acres which he intends to work himself.
- Thomas Pipe has lost about $700 on his horses. He hopes to get some of his money back. The times are bad. He hopes to regain his loss in about three years.
- Thomas Pipe bought a place to live in the Village of Waupaca at a very good price.
- Thomas Pipe asks William Jennings for an accounting of the money his brother John Valentine Pipe owed him.
- Thomas tells about the railroad extending from Neenah to Waupaca. The line intersects the Chicago and North Western Lines in Neenah, Winnebago County. Thomas predicts that the railroad will improve the economy.
- Thomas Pipe asks William Jennings to ask John Stickland to write. He feels he may have offended the family. Thomas Pipe offers to inform them of his lives and explain anything to them.

[Written later by a descendant: Before railroad was built from Neenah to Waupaca. RR came then in 1871]

Waupaca, Dec 2nd, 1860

Dear Uncle [William Jennings]

After neglecting you so long, I find the opportunity to drop you a few lines, happen they will find you all quite well, as it leaves us all pretty well at present with the exception of slight cold of which Elizabeth [Stickland Pipe] complained yesterday. I heard from mother about two weeks since. They were all quite well then. I am informed that you are having good times in England. There was a rumour that the crops were all spoilt in the summer but I understand on the whole it has turned out favourable. I hope such is the case. The grass in the northwestern states [Wisconsin] are extremely wonderful, where it will all find market is a mystery to be solved yet. Wheat sold pretty well at the early part of the season but it is extremely low at present. The price of wheat at present is about 2s 3d per bushel English money. I have not farmed it much this summer, am in the butchery business. I keep an open market all the while in Waupaca [Waupaca County, Wisconsin]. You might think I have not wanted leisure since the summer after killing two to three cattle per week with other things in proportion and travel to mills every night and morning.

I am now living in Waupaca. I have let [rented] my farm on shares, all but ten acres which I intend to work myself. I hope that we shall have a moment in times shortly as I am anxious to get a little of my lost money back through my bad luck with horses and the hard times. I estimate my loss at 700 dollars. I have a plenty real estate now to make me pretty well off should we have good times again. I think it is on the mend now. I have just bought me a place where I now live and very cheap. I bought it for what it used to cost rent every four years. I think I shall treble [triple] my money in three years. I am sure I shall if the time gets half as good as they were three years ago. I hope that you are made whole by that time on the money you lent [borrowed] poor John [Valentine Pipe]. I should like if it is possible to have it all straight and the balance up to Lady Day [25 March] next sent on so that I might have it by the

15th of May next as I have made calculations to know it at this time, that is if I do not sell sixty acres of lands which I now offer for sale. I think it doubtful if I sell it before the next summer and then the prospect is I shall have to wait for my money two or three years. We are having a railroad built from Nenah [Neenah, Winnebago County] to Waupaca [Waupaca County] which is about 40 miles. It is built by subscription [financed, in part, by individuals and businesses]. It intersects the great Chicago and Northwestern line at Nenah [Neenah]. That is likely to add four times the present line to Waupaca as that

will be the terminus [?] for many years to come that most rail property for ten miles around as much as 50 per cent and three times that in the immediate neighbourhood. All these ideas are with reasonable grounds as we have a splendid fine country, can raise bountiful crops, and all we need is an outlet to get it to market. The loss that we have to sustain in getting of this year's produce is sufficient to fuel the road. I am informed that Mr. John Stickland has returned and that he lives at Yarcombe. If such is the case I should like very much to receive a letter from him as I wish and hope to be on other than good terms with each other as I see no reason to be otherwise with any of the family. We have not heard either Mrs. or Miss Stickland [Elizabeth Wall Stickland Barrett or Mary Stickland] since the great demand [perhaps disagreement over the inherited property]. I presume that they are offended with me, but for what I do not know. I think if the circumstances were reversed they would be no more fair with us than we were with them. I wish you to tell JS [John Stickland] that it would be great pleasure to us to receive a letter from him or either of the family if they want any explanation in anything that I might know. I will give it to the best of my ability. Please to give my best respects to him and his wife and family, also to all enquiring friends, not forgetting yourself and family. May I hear from you shortly

From your affectionate nephew Thos Pipe

R.R. came thru his
1871

*Before railroad was built from
Neenah to Waupaca*

Waupaca Dec 2 60

Dear Uncle,

After neglecten you so long
I fiend the opperitunity of droppen you
a few lines I hoppen they will fiend you all
quit well, as it leaves us all pretty well at
present with the exception of Slight Colds
of which Elizbeth complained yesterday, I herd
from Mother about two wicks Since they were
all quit well then, I am informed that you
ar having good Times in England, there was
a rumer that the Crops were all Spoilt in the
Summer but I understand on the whole it has
Turned out favreabell I hope winter in the tea
The Crops in the North Western Stats ar efficem
By wondurfull, where it will all fiend Market
is a mistery to be Solved yet wheat Sold pre
well at the early part of the Season but it is
extreemly low at present the price of wheat at
present is about £ .3. Per bushell English Money
I have not Formed it Mutch this Summer I
am in the Bootchering Bysiness I keep an
open Market all the while in Waupaca, you
Might think I have not had Mutch leasure
time this Summer after keeling from two to three
Cattle Per wecke with other things in proportion
and traviell i mills every night and Morning

~ 313 ~

Letter Number 37, Page 2

I am now leaven in Waupaca I have let my
Form on Shares, all but ten ackers which I
intend to work my self, I hope that we shall
have a inniement in times Ritter as I am anctiors
to get a little of my lost money back, through
my bad luck with Horses and the hard times
I estimate my loss at 900 Dollars I have a splendid
Real Estate now to make me pretty well off Should
we have good times again, I think it is on the
amend now, I have just bought me a place where
where I now live, and very cheep I bought it
for what me to cost Rent every four years, I think
I shall trible my money in three years I am Shure
I shall if the time gets Left as good as they were
three years ago, I hope that you ar Made whole
by the time on the Money you lent Poe from
I Should Like if it is possabell to have it all
Straight and the Balance up to Dadseler next sent
on So that I might have it by the 15th of May next
as I have Mace Calculations to use it at that time
that is if I do not Sell Sixty ackers of Land which
I now offer for Salt I think it doubtful if I Sell
it before the next Summer and then the prospect is
I shall have to wait for my money two or three years
We ar haven a Rail Rood Built from Menah to
Waupaca which is about 40 Mills it is Built by
Subscription it intersects the Great Chicago and
North Western Line at Menah, that is likely to
ad four times the present Line to Waupaca As that

Letter Number 37, Page 3

will be the Terminess for many years to the
that must raise Traporty for ten Miles around
as Much as 50 Per cent and three times that in
the emediat Neberhood, all these Ideas or with reason
abell Grounds as we have a Splended Fine Country
can raise Bountyful Craps and the need is a outlet
to get it to Market The Crop that we have to
Sastaine in geting of this years Produce is soficent
to build the Road,   I am informed that Old
John Strickland has rechtured and that he lives at
Darcomb if Sutch is the case I Should like
very Much to receive a Letter from him as I
wish and hope to be on no other then good
tarms with each other as I See no reesons to
to be otherwise with any of the Family, we have not
hered either Mr or Mrs Strickland Since the great
demend I jurst nune that they ar ofended with no
but for what I do not know, I think if the Surcom
-stances were reversed they ould be no Spirit fere
with nse than we were with them, I wish you
to tell J. S. that it ould be a great pleasure
to nay to receive a Letter from him or either
of the Family if they want eny explenation on any
thing that I might know, I will give it to
the best of my ability, Pleas to give my best
respects him and his wife and Family also to all
inquiren friends, Not forgetin your Self and
Family, May I hear from you Shortly
  from your Aff Nephew Tho Pipe,

Letter Number 38

Date: November or December 1860
[Florence was born 5 January 1860.]
Writer: Elizabeth Stickland Pipe
Recipient: William Jennings Pipe
Sent from: Waupaca, Waupaca County, Wisconsin, USA
Sent to: London, England

Key Ideas

- Elizabeth Stickland Pipe mentions her surprise that her brother-in-law (William Jennings Pipe) is returning so soon to England.
- Elizabeth Stickland Pipe has heard from her brother, John Stickland, but she has not heard from her mother, Elizabeth Wall Stickland Bartlett, or sister, Mary Stickland, for four years.
- Elizabeth Stickland Pipe says that they have 6 children: John Stickland (Jack), Tom, Frank, Mary Elizabeth, William, and Florence. (Effie was born in 1863. Charlotte was born in 1865.)
- Elizabeth Stickland Pipe mentions Charlotte Jennings Pipe Pillar and remarks that James Pillar is a changed man from when he was in England.
- Elizabeth Stickland Pipe wishes William Jennings Pipe, her brother-in-law, Merry Christmas.
- Elizabeth Stickland Pipe gives a list of items she wants William Jennings Pipe to send to her.
- Thomas Pipe stands 6 feet 1 inch. He has long arms and broad shoulders.

[Stars and stripes flag hand drawn and coloured]

Direct

Thomas Pipe

Waupaca

Waupaca Co.

Wis.

America

Dear Brother [in-law, William Jennings Pipe]

We were rather surprised to think of your returning to England again so soon, but I am thinking you must have some young Lady there that you think a little of to call you to London. When you write, you must tell us the real truth about it whether it is so or not.

We had a letter from my brother [John Stickland], the first we ever had from him since our being in America. As for my sister [Mary Stickland] I have not had any from her or mother [Elizabeth Wall Stickland Bartlett] for four years.

I will tell you the length of our family which are 6 children, and it takes a great deal to bring them up and clothe them as everything is very dear in this country.

I will now give you a list of Articles which we should like for you to buy. I will

give you a price of these articles what they were when we lived in England. I presume the prices has varied, but I must leave that to your own judgment. I also state the prices those articles in this country which are almost double to what they were a year ago.

You might send and get the money of Uncle William [Jennings] and have him to charge the amount to our account. Your mother [Charlotte Jennings Pipe Pillar] was quite well the last account. [James] Pillar is quite an altered man to what he was in England. They are doing as well as their neighbours, likewise built a new house, have a span of colts, sheep, 3 cows, a yoke of cattle, hogs and lacks everything [or nothing?] to live and get along with and very close with his money always say he has no money and yet a plenty. As to the children and ourselves, we are quite well. As to the weather it is very wet and has been for 2 or 3 weeks, nothing but rain and wind. I must now conclude, wish you a merry Christmas. If you live till it comes as we shall not be likely to write until we receive the box. Hope you are in good health as it leaves all of our family.

From your ever

Affectionate sister [-in-law]

E. [Elizabeth] Pipe

[Shopping list]

10 yards of white flannel	18d	28d
3 pair of black worsted stockings	2/-3s	0d
10 yards of small pattern dark prints narrow width 6d		9d
10 yards of purple wide width print 9d		16d
2 print dresses not alike 20 yards 6d		9d
6 common pocket handkerchiefs 6d		12d
3 turkey red pocket handkerchiefs 6d	can't get them	
2 silk neckerchiefs 4/-	not to be found	

2 silk pocket handkerchiefs 3/-	6s 0d
1 printed cashmere dress not very dark	can't get
1 dress Scotch plaid 14 yards 2/-	can't get
7 yards of delaine [wool or worsted fabric] 1/-	1s 6d
3 yards of good bonnet ribbon not very dark	4s 0d
3 pair of cotton sheets 4/-	can't get
10 yards of cotton corduroy 20d	4s 0d

Remember the length inside seam 35, we want sufficient woollen cord to make Thomas a pair of pantaloons, ½ over for mending not to be found

I want sufficient pilot cloth to make an overcoat and the coat already made for. I think a coat that will fit you [William Jennings Pipe]. Thomas is height 6 feet 1 inch. Thomas arm is long and shoulders wide.

Also, cloth for a suit of clothes which will require about 9 yards, as to colour I not particular so that it is something that will not show spots very readily.

Buttons and trimmings for the same ¼ lb. of black sewing silk

Where you buy the goods you had better get them to packet it in a box secure as they can with iron bands as things are thrown about a great deal in crossing.

In haste

Letter Number 38, Page 1

Direct

Thomas Pipe

Waupaca

Waupaca Co

Wis

America

Dear Brother

We were rather suprised
to think of your returning to England again
so soon but I am thinking you must have
some young Lady their that you think
a little off to call you to London, when
you write you must tell us the real truth
about it whether it is so or not,
We had a letter from my Brother the first
we ever had from him since our being in
America, As for my Sister I have not had
any from her or Mother for four years

I will tell you the length of our family
which or 6 children and it takes a great deal
to bring them up and clothe them as every
thing is very dear in this country

I will now give you a list of Articles
which we should like for you to buy I will

Letter Number 38, Page 2

give you a price of these articles what they were
when we lived in England I presume the price's
has varied but I must leave that to your own Judgement
I also state the prices those articles in this country
which or almost double to what they were a
year ago

You migh send and get the money of
Uncle william and have him to charge the
Amount to our account Your mother was quite
well the last account Pillar is quite an altered
man to what he was in England they are doing well
as their neighbours likewise Built a new House
have a span of Coalts sheep 3 Cows Goulk of Cattle
Hogs in Jack every thing to live and jet a long
with and very close with is money always say he
has no money and yet a plenty as to the
Children and ourselfs we are quite well,
As to the weather it is very wet and has been
for 2 or 3 weeks nothing but rain and wind
I must now conclude wish you a merry Christmas
if you live till it comes as we shall not be likely
to write untill we receive the box hope you
are & in good health as it leaves all of our family
From your ever
affectionate sister
E Pipe

Letter Number 38, Page 3

10 yds of White Flannel 18   6 „28

3 pr of Black Worsted Stockings 2/-   3 „ 0

10 yards of small pattern narrow width Dark Print 6   „ 9

10 yard of Purple wide width Print 9   16

2 Print Dreses not a like 20 yds — 6   9

6 Common Pocket Handkerchiefs 6   12

3 Turkey Red „ Do „ Do — 1/-   cant get them

2 Silk Neckherchief ——— 4/-   not to be found

2 Silk Pocket helfs — 3/-   — 6 „ 0

1 Printed Chashmere Dress not very Dark   cant get

1 Dress of Scotch Plaid 14 yds 2/-   cant get

7 yds of Delain ——— 1/-   . 1 „ 6

3 yds of good Bonnett ribbon not very Dark   4 „ 0

3 pair of cotton Sheets 4/-   cant get

10 yds of Cotton Corderoy 20   4 „ 0

rember the length you side I every 35 rodr

want sufficient woolen cord to make Thomas   not to be found

a pair of Panttoons ½ yd over for mending

I want sufficient Pilot Cloth to make a over Coat

or the Coat all ready made for I think a coat that

will fit you will Thomas 6 „ fifty 6 feet 1 inch Thomas arms

is long and shoulders wide.

Also cloth for a suit of clothes which will require

about 9 yards — as to color I am not puticular so that

it is something that will not show spots very readily

Buttons and trimings for all the same ¼ lb of Black Sewing

Silk

Letter Number 38, Page 4

Where you buy the goods you had better
get them to packed it in a box secure
as they can with Iron Bands as thing. or
thrown about a great deal in crosing
the ~~Ocean~~

Letter Number 39

Date: 26 June 1861
Writer: Thomas Pipe
Recipient: William Jennings
Sent from: Waupaca, Waupaca County, Wisconsin, USA
Sent to: Northay Farm, Whitestaunton, Chard
Somerset County, England

Key Ideas

- Thomas Pipe tells William Jennings that he received his letter and the money.
- Thomas Pipe has just returned from a trip to Winnebago County where he saw his mother, Charlette Jennings Pipe Pillar. They are all doing well. Charlotte Jennings Pillar Pipe is worried about the times.
- Thomas Pipe feels for years the country has had the "most rotten government under the sun. I believe it to have been an object of speculation from the President down to the most petty office in the country." He goes on the say "our banks are all failing and smashing up, especially in the western part."
- Thomas reports Milwaukee, Wisconsin, had a great riot because of the banks. Two thousand soldiers were brought in to clear up the mob and to guard the city. See *Bank Riot* of 1861 at https://www.wisconsinhistory.org/Records/Article/CS1963.

- Thomas states the national debt is increasing at a rate of $1 million to $1.5 million per day.

- The letter is missing its last pages.

From Elizabeth Pipe and Thomas [Written later by a descendant]

Waupaca, Jan 26th, 1861

My Dear Uncle [William Jennings]

I am happy to acknowledge the receipt of your letter with the draft for the £45 15s 9d which came to hand about ten days ago. We was most happy to hear that yourself and family was quite well. May this find you the same. We are all enjoying pretty good health at present thank God for it. I am just returned from a trip through Winnebago County [Wisconsin] and a visit to Mother. I found them all well as to health but somewhat troubled in mind on account of the bad times. I am sorry to say that this country is in a very sad condition. I very much doubt if it was ever half as bad since it became an independent government. How it will terminate the lord only knows. I think it beyond the judgment of man to tell. I think it has for the last ten years been the most rotten government under the sun. I believe it to have been an object of speculation from President down to the last petty office in the country.

Our banks are all failing and smashing up especially in this western part. The money that is in circulation is good for nothing. As to gold it seems there is none to be found and silver is almost as bad. If a man goes to a store to trade with a passable bank bill, the only change that he can get is a bit of paste board paper with the amount stamped on it with the storekeeper's name written on under it. I understand that they had a great riot in Milwaukee [Wisconsin] on Monday on account of the banks there, throughout the banks in the country which they had agreed to sustain until next December. That has proven to be nothing more than a promise for their own convenience and speculation. I suppose they had an awful time on Monday. They had to call for 2000 soldiers to clear up the mob and to guard the city that night. I hope these state of things will soon be over, for I think this country cannot stand such grief a great while. I understand the National Debt is running up at the rate of a million to a million and a half per day at the present.

Letter Number 39, Page 1

From Elizabeth Pipe
and Thomas

Waupaca June 26th 1861

My Dear Uncle,

I am happy to acknowledge the receipt of your Letter with the Draft for the £45..15..9 which come to hand about teen days ago. We wes must happy to hear that your Self and Families wes quite well, may this fiend you the same, we ar all enjoyen pretty good Health at present thank God for it, I am just redurned from a trip through Winabago County, and a visit to Mother, I found them all well as to Health but som what troubled in mined, on account of the bad Times, I am Sorey to say that this Country is in a very sad condition, I very mutch doubt if it wes ever half so bad since it becom a Indipendent Govern ment, how it will terminate the Lord only knows, I think it byon the judgement of man to tell, I think it has for the last ten years been the most Rotten Government under the Sun, I believe it to have been an object of Speculation from the Presidan down to the lowest pety ofice in the Country

Letter Number 39, Page 2

Our Banks ar all Failing and Smashing up
Especialy in this Western part, the Money
that is in Circulation is good for nothing
as to Gold it Seems there is none to be
found, and Silver is almost as bad,
If a Man goes to a Store to Trade with
a peacebell Bank Bill the only change that
he can get is a Lot of Post Card paper
with the amount Stampt on it with the
Store Keepers name writen on under it,
I understand that they had a great Riot
in Milwaukee on Monday on acount of the
Banks there throughen out the Banks in
the Countrey which they had agreed to
to Sostaine until next December, that has
proven to be nothing More then a promise
for thare one convenance and Speculation
I Spose they had an Aful time on Monday
they had to call for 2000 Soldgers to draw
up the Mob and to gard the Citty that night.
I hope these State of things will soon
be over, for I think this Countrey
cannot Stand Sutch Grief a Great while
I understand that the National debt
is runen up at the rate of a Melion
to a Melion and half Per day at the Present

Letter Number 40

Date: October 1861
Writer: William & Elizabeth Coleman Jennings
Recipient: Thomas Pipe
Sent from: Northay Farm, Whitestaunton, Chard
                Somerset County, England
Sent to: Waupaca, Waupaca County, Wisconsin, USA

Key Ideas

- Mr. Matthews receives John Stickland's annuity and delivers it to him.

[Accounts 1860 Oct.]

1860 Michaelmas [29 September]

Paid Mr. Matthews Mr. [John] Stickland's annuity	£12 0s 0d
Bill for reeds	£4 10s 0d
Thatcher's bill	£1 15s 6d
Six apple trees	£2 0s 0d
Due to me on the last	<u>£6 4s 6d</u>
	£26 9s 11d
Received in rent	£44 10s 0d
	<u>£26 9s 11d</u>
Due to Mr. [Thomas] Pipe	£18 0s 1d

The Upper Pithayne farmhouse was one of Elizabeth Stickland Pipe's inherited properties that William Jennings managed for 21 years while she lived in America. A tile with the letter 'S' for 'Stickland' is still in the house today.

1861

Paid Mr. Matthews	£12 0s 0d
Fire assurance	£1 15s 6d
Pipe for draining	8s 10d
Allowed for lime	<u>£2 10s 0d</u>
	£16 14s 4d
received for rent	£44 10s 0d
Due to Mr. [Thomas] Pipe on the last half	<u>£18 6s 1d</u>
	£62 10s 1d
	<u>£16 14s 4d</u>
Due to Mr. [Thomas] Pipe	£45 15s 9d

[Back of the receipt is blank except for the words *The Accounts*.]

[Back of the receipt is blank except for the words *The Accounts*.]

1860 Michelmas
Oct.— Paid Mr Mathews Mr Stich
                     £ s d
Land's Annuity ———   12 . 0 . 0
   Bill for Seeds —   4 „ 10 „ 0
   Mathews Bill ——— 1 „ 15 „ 6
   Six Apple Trees   2 „ 0 „ 0
  Due to Me on the last 6 „ 4 „ 6
                       26 „ 9 „ 11

Received in Rent . £ 44 „ 10 „ 0
Due to Mr Pipe — £ 26 „ 9 „ 11
                 £ 18 „ 0 „ 1

1861 Paid Mr Mathews 14 „ 0 „ 0
  Fire Assurance   1 „ 15 „ 6
  Pipe for Draining   8 „ 10
   Allowed for lime — 2 „ 10 „ 0
                   16 „ 14 „ 4

Received for Rent 44 „ 10 „ 0
Due to Mr Pipe on the
last half — — 16 „ 0 „ 1
               £ 2 „ 10 „ 1
               16 „ 14 „ 4
Due to Mr Pipe £ 45 „ 15 „ 9

The Lower Pithayne farm and farmhouse is another inherited property that William Jennings managed for Elizabeth Stickland Pipe in her absence.

Letter Number 40, Page 2

The Account

Letter Number 41

Date: 2 November 1861
Writer: William & Elizabeth Coleman Jennings
Recipient: Thomas & Elizabeth Stickland Pipe
Sent from: Northay Farm, Whitestaunton, Chard
                 Somerset County, England
Sent to: Waupaca, Waupaca County, Wisconsin, USA

Key Ideas

- The Jennings provide an updated list of transactions.

Whitehorns farm and farmhouse, another of Elizabeth Stickland Pipe's inherited properties managed by William Jennings, is an example of a thatched roof that typically needs ongoing maintenance. The receipt in Letter Number 41 lists expenses for thatching a roof like this one in 1861.

[Accounts] 1861

Nov./2

Paid Mr. [John] Stickland	£12 0s 0d
Thatcher's bill for thatching the dwelling house	£2 2s 9d
Liquor charged for ditto	8s 5d
13 rope of draining at 1/6	19s 6d
Repairing pipes for water	3s 6d
Reed for thatching the dwelling house	<u>£9 10s 0d</u>
	£25 9s 2d

Rent	£44 10s 0d
Disbursements	<u>£25 9s 2d</u>
	£19 0s 10d

Due to Mr. [Thomas] Pipe up to Michaelmas

[29 September] 1861 the sum of £19 0s 10d

We have not charged you £1 9s 3d paid at Xmas for the fire insurances we can deduct it

[over]

There has been nothing paid out this half but Mr. [John] Stickland's annuity that is twelve pounds.

No doubt but you will think it a long figure for reed, but it is very scarce and dear as people thrash principally with machines, but you know Mr. Bondfield [Bonfield] is allowed two guineas.

Pd. hundred for reed

Letter Number 41, Page 1

1861

Novr 12 Pd Mr Strickland   £ " s " d

Thatchers Bill for thatching   12 " 6 " 0

the dwelling house —   2 " 2 " 9

Liquire charged for do   8 " 5

13 rope of Draining at 1/6 p 4 19 " 6

repairing pipes for water —   8 " 6

Reed for thatching the

dwelling house &c —   9 " 10 " 0

         £ 25 " 9 " 2

Rent — 44 " 10 " 0

Disb — 25 " 9 " 2

     19 " 0 " 10

Due to Mr Pipe up to Michlemas

1861 the sum of 19 " 0 " 10

we have not charged you

£ " s " d

1 " 9 " 3 paid at Xmas for the fire

assurance we can deduct it

Letter Number 41, Page 2

There has been nothing paid out this half
but Mr Strickland's annuity that is
twelve pounds

No doubt but you will think it
a long figure for seed but it
is very scarce and dear as people
thrash principly with Machines but you
know Mr Bondfield is allowed two guineas
per hundred for Seed

Letter Number 42

Date: May 1862
Writer: William Jennings
Recipient: Thomas Pipe
Sent from: Northay Farm, Whitestaunton, Chard
              Somerset County, England
Sent to: Waupaca, Waupaca County, Wisconsin, USA

Key Ideas

- Summary of bills paid through May 7, 1862, for work at the properties.

––––––––––––––

1862   Mr. W. Jennings

Do. To Wm. Lawrence

For thatching done at Pitthayne [Pithayne Farm] and Whitehornes [Whitehorns Farm]

By order of Mr. Bonfield

Coating the Linhay Petthayne [Pithayne Farm]   40ft 3in by 16ft
                                      3 in <u>6 54</u>

At 3/- the square   19s 7d

Ridging Drawing House Whitehornes [Whitehorns]   44 by x62 64

Ridging the Linhay   44 x 62 65

Square   5 28

At 2/6 the square   13s 2d

February 1st

½ day shearing down the Old Coate and repairing the Linhay and barn   1s 0d

Mar 4th

1 day repairing and shearing the Old Coate Whitehorns linhay [Farm]   2s 0d

March 7th

½ day shearing the Drawing House Whitehorns [Farm]   1s 0d

May 7th

Paid Wm. Lawrence   £1 16s 9d

Letter Number 42

1862	Mr. W. Jennings		
	Do To Wm Lawrence		

For thatching done at Pitthayne & Whitethornes
By order of Mr Benfield

Coating the   Squr feet

Linhay Pitthayne { 40 " 3 by 16 " 3 11 " 6 " 54

At 3/0 per Square   19 7

Ridging the

Dwg House Whitethornes } 44 by 6   11   2 " 64

Ridging the Linhay   44 by 6   11   2 " 64

Squt 5 " 28

At 2/6 per Square   13 2

Febuary 1st ½ Day Shearing down the Old Coate & Repairing } 1 0
the Linhay And Barn

March 4 1 Day Repairing and Shearing the } 2 0
Old Coate Whitethornes Linhay

7 ½ Day Shearing the Dwg House Whitethornes 1 0

May 7 Paid Wm Lawrence   £   1 16 9

Letter Number 43

Date:	May 1862
	[Ellen (Nelly) was 7 years old in December 1861.]
Writer:	Elizabeth Coleman Jennings
Recipient:	Thomas Pipe
Sent from:	Northay Farm, Whitestaunton, Chard
	Somerset County, England
Sent to:	Waupaca, Waupaca County, Wisconsin, USA

Key Ideas:

- John Bradford from America is visiting. He is the brother of William Coleman's wife, Elizabeth Bradford. Their father died last March.
- Elizabeth Coleman Jennings' brother, William Coleman, may visit England this summer. He is living in Nebraska.
- Thomas Pipe's brother, William Jennings Pipe, visited William and Elizabeth Coleman Jennings about three weeks ago. He is now out of military service.
- Elizabeth Coleman Jennings states that her youngest child, Ellen (Nelly), was seven years old last December 1861.
- John Stickland asked for Thomas Pipe's address. They are living at Collieforges Farm in Yarcombe. His wife is expecting. He says if he cannot find something in Yarcombe, he will go back to Australia.
- Elizabeth Coleman Jennings was at Broadwindsor, Dorset, visiting Thomas Pipe's Aunt (Mary Ann Jennings) Dommett.
- Cousin Frank Jennings visited yesterday. He will marry Emma Dommett who lives near Bridgewater, Somerset. Frank acquired a farm three years ago in Shepton Beauchamp, Somerset.
- Uncle John's Jennings health is better.

[crosshatched]

Northay May

Dear Thomas

I suppose you think us neglectful in not sending you cash before but Mr. Bonfield has not paid it yet, but your Uncle [William] has paid it in advance as you said you wanted it in May. Bonfield has had bad luck with his cows. He has had five barrens out of his small dairy cows, and calves has been very high this spring and buying them in has made him short for a time, but we hope he will be able to meet his payments the next half year. The last two years has been rather trying for farmers. The season has been so wet. We have had a very wet March, not able to go in the land to do anything. We are later with our sowing this spring than ever we have been before. We were very sorry to get such bad

account as the last but hope now times are better with you. I should be very thankful to hear that America was once more in peace and quiet. We have had a gentleman here from America. He was here about Easter, a Mr. John Bradford, my brother Wm.'s [Coleman] wife's [Elizabeth Bradford] brother. His brother Wm. [William Bradford] came home with him. Their father died suddenly last March so they came home about their property. They will receive between five and six hundred pounds each. We received a letter from my brother Wm.[Coleman] a few weeks since, he thought of making us a visit this summer. He is still at Nebraska. He with his brother-in-law went to the gold diggings last summer. They did pretty well there. I suppose you have recently had a letter from your brother Wm. [Jennings Pipe] as he wrote for your address. He paid us a visit about three weeks ago. He is out of the army altogether. He is a very respectable gentlemanly man. I hope he will be fortunate to get in something to suit him.

[other way]

you did not say a word about your dear mother [Charlotte Jennings Pipe Pillar], I hope she is well. We received a newspaper from her a few days ago. If you see her or write to her give our united love to her. I hope to write to her soon. How many little ones have you? When you write tell us. We have two, our youngest [Ellen (Nelly)] was just seven years old last December. I was surprised you had not heard from your Stickland friend. John had your address twelve months ago to write you. They are living at Yarcombe in a little place by the name of Collieforges [Farm]. His wife is expecting an increase this month. He says if he can't get in to something different he shall go out to Australia again. I was at Broad-windsor [Dorset] last week paying your Aunt [Mary Ann Jennings] Dommett a visit. They were all well. They have a very nice place there. Their two youngest children at Taunton [Somerset] to

[other way]

School. Elizabeth [Dommett] the eldest has finished. She has a new pianoforte. She plays and sings nicely. I thought it a gay neighbour-hood round there very different to what it is here. Your cousin Frank Jennings was here yesterday. I understand he is going to be married shortly to a young lady [Emma Dommett] near Bridgwater [Somerset]. He has been in a farm at Shepton Beauchamp [Somerset] this last three years. He is getting on well. Your Uncle John's [Jennings] health is bet-ter. He directed to be remembered to you and also your Aunt [Mary Ann Jennings Dommett]. Your Uncle W. [William] and myself write in kindest love to you all hoping this will find you all well as it leaves us

From your affectionate

Aunt Elizabeth [Coleman] Jennings

Please write soon or we shall fear you did not get the cash all right

Letter Number 43, Page 1

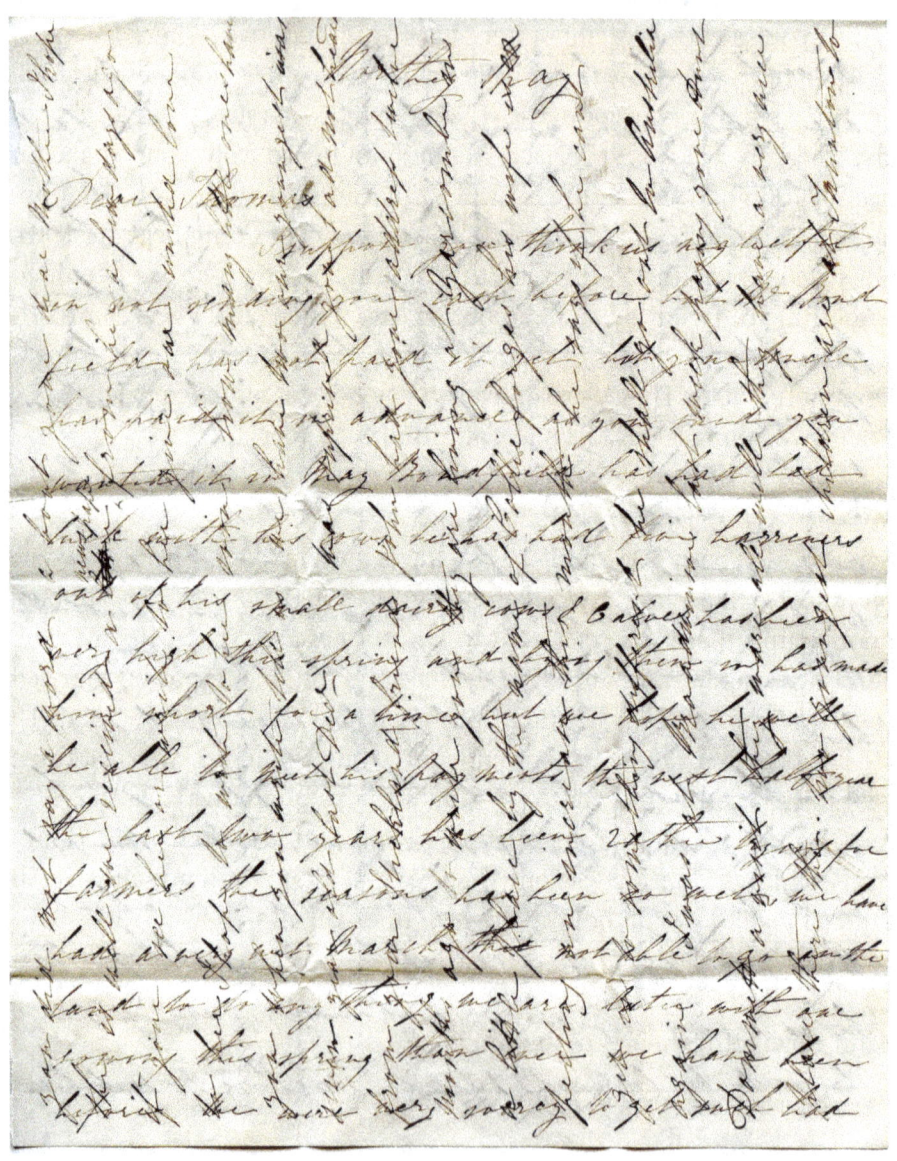

Letter Number 43, Page 2

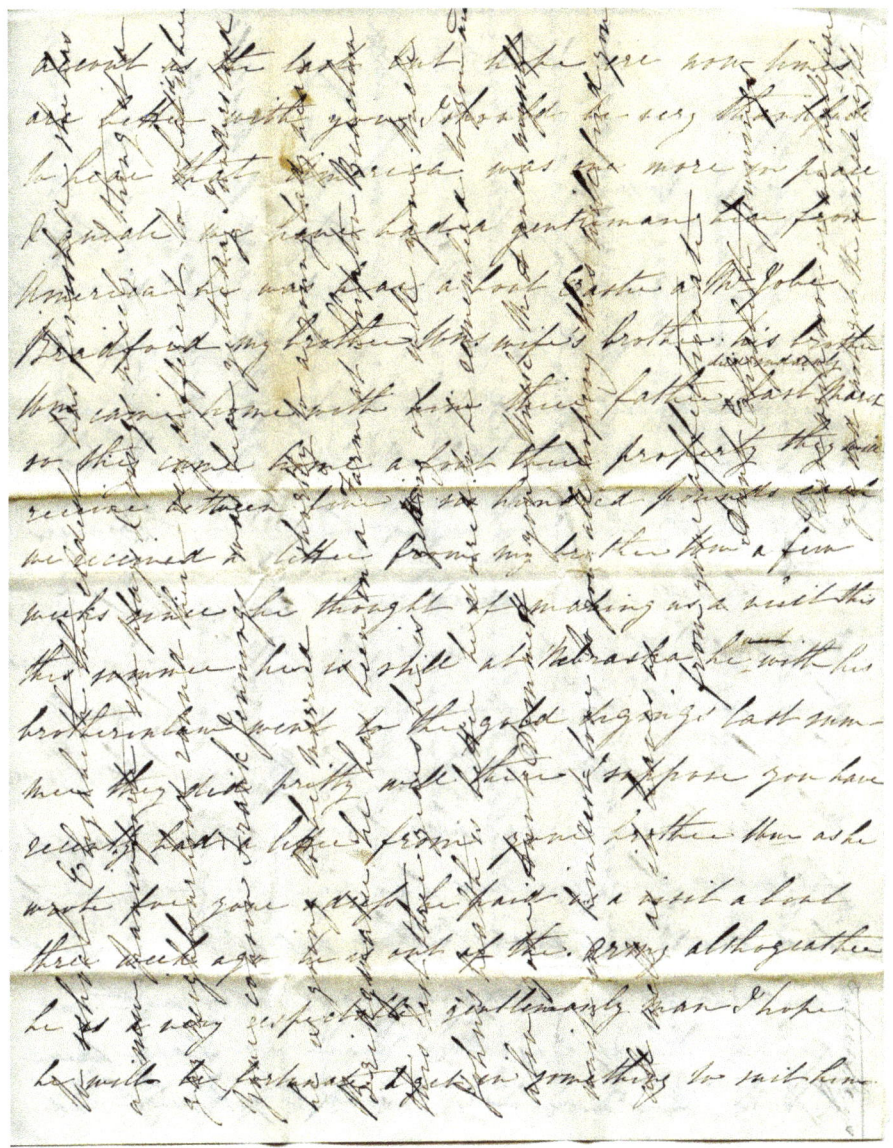

Letter Number 43, Envelope Front

Letter Number 43, Envelope Back

Letter Number 44

Date: 2 October 1862
Writer: Thomas Pipe
Recipient: William Jennings Pipe
Sent from: Waupaca, Waupaca County, Wisconsin, USA
Sent to: London, England

Key Ideas

- Thomas Pipe tells his brother William Jennings Pipe about reading his brother's letter to the James Pillar family. Jack (James Piller, Jr.) brought his letter when he visited before going into military service. Thomas Pipe had hoped that William Jennings Pipe would have come to America and joined the American army. He thought he would get a good position because he is an experienced officer.

- Thomas Pipe tells his brother his feelings about the Civil War. He says he will serve reluctantly if he has to.

- Thomas Pipe explains to William Jennings Pipe what happened to the money from Uncle Edwin's Pipe's will. According to Thomas, Uncle Edwin Pipe was onboard *Her Majesty's Ship Cornwallis* when the Treaty of Nanking was signed on August 29, 1842. The Treaty ended the First Opium War resulting , in part, with indemnities paid to the British. See https://en.wikipedia.org/wiki/HMS_Cornwallis_(1813).

- Thomas Pipe requests that his brother buy some items in London, England, and give them to Henry Minton from Vinland, Wisconsin, who will be in London on family business.

———

China War [Written in later by a descendant.]

Waupaca, Oct 2nd, 1862

My Dear Brother [William Jennings Pipe]

I had the pleasure of reading your letter to Mother [Charlotte Jennings Pipe Pillar] about three weeks ago which brother James Pillar [Jr.] brought up as he came to make us a visit before he left for the war. I promised to write to you as Mother wished me to do. She said that she would write to you soon. I was about to write to you when I heard that you had joined the army again. I thought you might have done well to have come here and joined the American Army. I thought you might have got a good position, as they have been very short of experienced soldiers for officers, but I presume that you are quite as well off where you are. I should like to know when you write what this Volunteer Rifle

Corps is, if it is a standing thing. It seems to be to be something new since I left. Is your chances good for promotion. I suppose that Mother is full of trouble again, now as John [James Pillar, Jr.] has enlisted for this war. I think this war is one of the most awful things that I ever heard of, the way they use up men and means is shocking to think of, and where the end of it will be the lord only knows. Over one half of the able-bodied men has been taken already and now talk of drafting. Should it be my lot to go I should go very reluctantly as I believe they are not half treated as soldiers or men. I think it has been truly said that this is a war of speculation. What is to be done in this part I do not know as everything that we have to buy is up to double the price it was a year ago, that is groceries and clothing.

You stated in your letter that you would like for me to state the circumstances in

relation to the [China War] prize money. It is as follows, when Uncle Edwin Pipe died, he left a will giving to me all the prize money that was due him or that might become due him from the China Wars. I received that which was due him before he started for China which I think was £44. Then I received what was due on rations which I think was 8 pounds. This amount Uncle Orlando got hold of and used up for me. There was supposed to be a good amount to come from the Chinese were to him as he was on board her Majesty's Ship Cornwallis which ship the treaty was made on. Now in relation to this I had a parchment or rather a copy of the will which I drew the money with. The first I drew from the Admiralty Office. Then I was informed that the Chinese prize money was to be drawn from the East India Company or the East India House. I forget which, to which place I forward the parchment on enquiry several times when I

had it returned stating that it was not payable yet. In the meantime, I found that my money that Uncle Orlando had was all used up and the parchment either destroyed or laid aside. I have been informed that I could collect the money as they [had?] the copy and my signature from the amount received. You would do me a great favour by looking after it for me as I have but a poor opportunity to find out any about it.

Dear brother I have one other favour to ask of you or Uncle William, that is to buy me a lot of goods and forward to me by a neighbour of mine which will call on you in London in the course of a month or five weeks from this date. He will be here in one week from today. He is coming to England after some property which belongs to his son. His name is Henery [Henry] Minton. He is a farmer of this town. I intended to write to Uncle to buy me the goods and send it to me, but as this man is coming to London, I thought it would be cheaper for him to bring it as it might have duty. Elizabeth will write

[top] to [top of first page] you and describe the articles should it not be convenient for you to attend to it. You might send Elizabeth's note to Uncle William and if you can attend to it you might send and get the money of him. I should like the amount of £10 or £12 worth as everything is so enormously dear as well as poor in this country.

[cross hatched] From your affectionate

Brother Thos. Pipe

to you and describe the artecls, Should it nat be convenén
fou you to atend to it you might Cly note to Uncle Willem
and if you can atend to it you might Send and get the
money of him I Should the amtt of £10 or £12 With as every
thing is so enormously dear as well is Poor in this Country

Rampall Octr 2, 62

My Dear Brother

                      I had the plea
sure of reading your letter to
Brother about three weeks ago,
which Brother Jat Piller brought
up as he came to make us a
visit before he left for the war
I promised to wright to you as
Mother wished me to do. She said
that She would wright to you soon
I was about wright to you when I
herd that you had joined the Army
again I thought you might here
don well to have com heer and join
the American Armey, I thought you
might here got a good position, as
they here been very Short of Experience
Soleers for Officers, but I presume
That you ar quit as well off where
you or. I Should like to know when
you wright what this Infanture Riffle

Corps is if it is a Standing thing
it simes to me to be somthing new
Since I left, is your chences good
for promotion. I Sopose that
Mother is ful of trouble againe now
as John has inlisted for this War
I think this War is one of the most
offul things that I ever herd of
the way they use up Men and Means
is Shocking to think of, and where the
end of it will be the Lord only knows
over one half of the able bodied Men
has ben taken already, and now talk
of draften, Shold it be my lot to go
I Should go very relucketntly, as I belive
they ar not half treated as Solgers or Men
I think it has ben truly said that this
is a War of Speculation, what is to be
don in this part I do not know as
evry thing that we here to buy is up
to double the price it was a year ago
that is Groceries and Clothing,
you Stated in your letter that you oald
like for me to State the curcumstinces in

Relation to the Prise Money, It is as
folows, when Uncle Edwin Pipe died he
he left a will given to me all the prise
Money that was due him or that might
become due him from the Chines Wars
I received that which was due him before he
started for China which I think was £
then I received what was due on rations
which I think was 8 pounds, this amt.
Uncle Orlando got hold of and used
up for Me, there was Soposed to be a good
amt. to Com from the Chines wer to
him as he was on Bord her Majestys
Ship Corn Walice which Ship the treaty
was Made on, Now in relation to
this I had a partchment or rether a
Coppey of the will which I drew the
Money with, the first I drew from
the Admerialty Office, then I was infor
-med that the Chines prise Money was to
drawen from the East Inda Company
or the East Inda Ibouce I forget which
to which place I fowerded the partchm
-ent on inquirey sireral times when I

China Was

had it returned Staten that it was
not peicbell yet, In the mean
time fount that thy money that uncle
Orlendo had was all used up and the
Sertehment either destroid or laid
aside, I have been informed that I
cold coleet the mony as thy the coppy
and my Signature for the amt recd,
you ould do me a great faver by looken after
it for me as I have but a poore opperta
-nity to fiend out any about it,
Dear Brother I have one other faver to ask
of you or Uncle William, that is to buy
me a bot of goods and fowerd to me by
a Neiher of mine which will Caul
on you in London in the corse of a four
or five Weeks from this date, he will leave
hier in one weke from to day, he is coming
to England after som property which belong
to his Son his name is Henery Minton,
he is a Farmer of this Town, I intinded
to wright to Uncle to buy me the goods and
send it to me, but as this man is coming to
London, I thought it ould be cheper for him to
bring it as it might save duty, Elizebeth will wright

Letter Number 45

Date: 7 November 1862
Writer: Thomas Pipe
Recipient: William Jennings
Sent from: Waupaca, Waupaca County, Wisconsin, USA
Sent to: Northay Farm, Whitestaunton, Chard
                Somerset County, England

Key Ideas

- Thomas Pipe tells William Jennings he feels disorganized and mortified for reporting the same about the times for the last four years. Times have not changed.
- Prices are high. Sales of products are low. Shipping costs are enormous.
- John Stickland wrote for the first time to Thomas and Elizabeth Stickland Pipe. John Stickland was interested in information about America.

Elizabeth continues

- Elizabeth Stickland Pipe tells William Jennings that she has received a letter from her brother, John Stickland.
- She reports that James Pillar, Jr. was drafted and is going to war.
- George Washington Sinclair has been in the war for two years. He went off to war without providing a home for his three children.
- Charlotte Jennings Pipe Pillar fetched the baby, Jonathon Phillip, and saw that the other two children, Ellen Joan and William Phillip, had a home.
- Elizabeth Stickland Pipe reports that a new church is being built. The church may be open for Christmas.

Grandpa Thomas Pipe to Uncle during Civil War [Witten later by a descendant.]

Waupaca, Nov 7th, 1862

Dear Uncle [William Jennings]

I certainly feel guilty of a gross neglect to you in not writing to you more punctually. But I assure you that my mind is so very mixed that I scarcely know how to write a letter. Through the hard times the condition of the country and the prospect ahead, I feel almost discouraged. I feel mortified when I look back and think that every letter that I have written to you for the last four years has been in the same strain. I certainly thought three years ago that a change must be for the best, but it certainly is for the worst. This cursed rebellion is an awful stroke on this part of the country especially. I think we have the worst of it at the present, as we are so far from the seat of war and the eastern market. We have to sell everything that we raise at a low price and pay the very highest for what we have to consume. That might seem strange to you, but the reason is this, we are fifteen hundred miles from the real market of the country therefore we have to pay the freight both ways which is enormous especially at the present time. I will give you a few of the prices of the different articles presently.

I think there is certain classes and certain parts of this country that is gotten rich from this war, but I think the tide will change in a little time. I received a letter from J [John] Stickland a short time since, the first that we ever had from him. He seems to be rather unsettled. He wrote for information in relation to this country. I could not give him much encouragement to come at present, although farms might be bought at almost any price. Should times get to be good this would be the time to buy. I also wrote to brother William [Jennings Pipe] two or three weeks ago. I have a neighbour of mine who has gone to London for some property. I asked William [Jennings Pipe] to buy me some goods to the amount of 10 or 12 pounds and send back to me and count on you for the amount. If you will let him have it and charge it to my account, you will do me a great favour. I had almost forgotten that I had not acknowledged the receipt of the last year's rent. I am happy to say that it came to hand in good time. I hope when I hear from you that I shall hear that your crops were good this last summer, all good prices at present. When you write please tell me how you are doing and what your old ewe sold for this year. Please tell me what kind and how much stock Mr. Bonfield keeps at Pithain [Pithayne Farm]. I will leave off for Elizabeth to finish.

[There is a hole in the middle of this letter so many words are missing.]

Dear Uncle

I suppose you think I have very neglectful in not writing you before this, but hope you will forgive me this time. I must tell you that I had a letter from my brother [John Stickland]. He said he had received a letter from Mother [Elizabeth Wall Stickland Bartlett] and Mary [Stickland] and when he wrote to us he must tell me to write to [torn, possibly mother and sister] but I think I shall not just yet for they never answer the [torn] them 4 years ago but if they write I have no objections [torn] John [Stickland] thinks he shall not stay where is a great [torn] he should emigrate but where he had not made [up his] mind. He enquired a few particulars about this country but [torn] it is a poor place to come at the present. Times are [torn] clothing very, they ask just about so much again as they did 6 months [ago]. They ask 14 pence a yard for calico. Print is 10 pence narrow width, and everything in proportion. This war is a great injury and expense to the country which is thought will never be the same as before, and no one can tell when it will be closed. They have two very hard battles and has killed and wounded a great many of our acquaintance. We had a company left this place which had been gone about 10 days and had been in four battles and those that are saved write and say it is the greatest sight they ever saw, which they never want to see again, for to carry off the wounded and bury the dead. I suppose you will be surprised to hear of James Pillar [Jr.] enlisting. He was afraid of being drafted as they intended to do, which I think a great many went that would not have gone had it not been on that account. James [Pillar Jr.] and Elizabeth [Pillar] made us a visit before he went. His brother [Thomas Pipe?] and father [James Pillar Sr.] feels very bad about his going. We had 3 funeral

1862 [Written later by a descendant.]

sermons preached on Sunday last and two of the soldiers killed at the battle. George [Washington] Sinclair is being in the army nearly 2 years. He went off without providing a home for each of his 2 [3] children. He has written to the old Mrs. [William] Sinclair, his step mother, but never askcd if they are comfortably provided for, which after he went away Thomas's mother [Charlotte Jennings Pipe Pillar] fetched the baby [Jonathon Phillip] and got a good home for all [of] them [Ellen Joan and William Phillip] but at different places, neither place have they any [torn] just one of them and they feel very proud of them [torn] ever written her a letter.

The weather here has been [torn] for a few days so as to stop the boats from running [torn] that we do not get our mail but 3 times a [torn]. We used to ever day so you can judge how cold [torn] to freeze up the river. Today it is very cold mist expect snow before a great while. We have had it already so as the ground has been covered for two three days. We shall expect sleighing before a great while. I suppose you soon think of Christmas. That is a thing that Americans do not think anything of, only the church people, and that is only preaching Christmas Eve. The church is trimmed the same as in England. There is a new church built but the seats and painting which rather think will be opened at Christmas. I must now conclude as I have a little sewing to do tonight. Hoping you and Uncle and family are well. Not knowing where there has been any increase since I last heard, but I will say we are all well. Our family are 6 children [John Stickland, Tom, Frank, Mary Elizabeth, William Edwin, Florence] which are enjoying good health.

Wishing you a merry Christmas and a Happy New Year

From your affectionate niece

E. [Elizabeth] Pipe

Please to excuse as my pen is very bad

Letter Number 45, Page 1

Grandpa Thomas Pipe to Uncle
during civil war

Wanpace Nov 7th 1862

Dear Uncle,

I certenley feel gilty of a gross neglect to you in not wrighten to you more punctnoly, But I ashure you that my mind is so very mixt that I scercley know how to wright a letter, Through the hard times the condi -tion of the Cuntrey and the prospect a head I feel almost discurriged, I feel Mortified when I look back ont think that every letter that I have writen to you for the last four years has been on the Same straine, I certenley thought three years ago that a chenge Must be for the best but it certenly is for the Worst, This cursed Rebell ion is an offul Stroke on this part of the Cuntrey espeenaly, I think we have the worst of it at the present so we or so for from the seet of War and the Eastern Morkit, We have to sell every thing that we raise at a low piese, and pay the very hiss for what we have to conenme, that might slem strange to you, but the reason is this we or fiften hundred Milts from the reel Morkit of the Cuntrey therefore we have to pay the freight bothe ways which is enermi espeenaly at the present time, I will give you a few of the prieses of the different articels presen

I think there is certain Cleses and certen perts
of this Cuntrey that is goten ritch from this
Wor. but I think the tide will change in the
of a little time, I recived a letter from J.
Stickland a short time since the first that we
ever had from him, he sums to be rathor
unsittled, he wrote for information in relation to
this Cuntrey, I cold not give him mutch inenrige
ment to com at present, although Forms might
be bought at almost any price. Should times
get to be good this vold be the time thing,
I also wrote to Brother William two or three weks
go I have a frend of mine who has gon to
London for som property, I asked William to
buy me som goods to the amount of 10 or 12
pounds and send back to me, and cant on you
for the amount. If you will let him have
it and charge it to my act you will do me
a great faver, I had almost forgoten that I
had not acknoliged the receipt of your rent
I am happy to say that it come to hand in
good time, I hope when I hear from you me.
I shall hear that your crops are good this last
Somer all good prices at present when you
wright pleas tell me how you are doing and what
your lit corn sold for this year, pleas tell me
what stock and how mutch stock Mr Bonfield
keep at Pitham I will leve of for this to finish

Letter Number 45, Page 3

Letter Number 45, Page 4

1862

[Handwritten letter, largely illegible cursive]

Sermons preached on Sunday last and 2 of them of the ...
... George ... being in the army nearly
2 years ... writing a ...
... he has written to the Old Mr. ... his ... Mother
... ask if they ... published for which
after he wrote a ... Mother ... the Baby and
got a good home for ... at different places
neither place have they any ... and
they feel very proud of them ... ever written him a letter
The Weather here has ... for a few days to as
to stop the Boats from running ... we do not get
our mail but 6 times a ... we used to every day
... cold ... to freeze up river
... day it is very cold ... expect snow before a great while
we have had it all ready so as the ground has being covered
for two or three days we shall expect sleighing before a great
while I suppose you will soon think of Christmas that is a
... that Americans do not think any thing of ... but Church
people and that is ... keeping Christmas ... the Church is
... the same as in England there is a New Church Built
... Scots ... painting which ... then he will be opened
at Christmas I was now ... as I have a little sewing to do
tonight hoping you and Uncle and family ... know of where there
has been any ... since last but Will say we are all
well ... family are 6 children which are in ... good health
wishing you a merry christmas and a happy new year
please to excuse } from   Your affectionate Niece
as my pen is   E Pipe
very bad.

Letter Number 46

Date: 6 May 1863
Writer: William & Elizabeth Coleman Jennings
Recipient: Thomas & Elizabeth Stickland Pipe
Sent from: Northay Farm, Whitestaunton, Chard
                 Somerset County, England
Sent to: Waupaca, Waupaca County, Wisconsin, USA

Key Ideas

- John Stickland signs a stamped receipt from Mr. Bonfield for paying a half year's annuity as directed in Uncle John Stickland's Will, proved 30th July 1850. (See Appendix D.)

Chard, May 6th, 1863

Received from Mr. G. Bondfield [Bonfield] half year's annuity twelve pounds

£12 0s 0d due Lady Day [25 March]

Signed John Stickland

[Written on back] Lady day [25 March] 1865

Letter Number 46

Chard May 6th 1863

Received from Mr G Bondfield
half year,s Annuity twelve pounds
12 . 0 . 0 due Lady day

John Strickland

Letter Number 47

Date: 19 June 1863
Writer: William Jennings & Mary Ann Jennings
Recipient: Thomas Pipe
Sent from: Northay Farm, Whitestaunton, Chard
Somerset County, England
Sent to: Waupaca, Waupaca County, Wisconsin, USA

Key Idea

- William Jennings reports that his wife Elizabeth Coleman Jennings had cow fever and is very unwell with rheumatism.
- William Jennings Pipe has returned and is in London. He is out of soldiering (military service).
- Cousin Mary Ann Jennings writes to her cousin, Thomas Pipe, with news. Her Uncle Frank Coleman is married to Emma Dommett of Buckland St. Mary, Somerset. He bought Yarcombe Inn and is now living there.

[page 1]

Whitestaunton, June 19, [18]63

Dear Thomas

It is a long time since I heard from you. I hope this will find you and your wife and family well. I am sorry to tell you that your Aunt [Elizabeth Coleman Jennings] is very unwell. In the first place she had the cow fever and now very bad in the rheumatic [rheumatism] not able to take no rest. William [Jennings Pipe] has been down for a week. He is now in London, going to return again in the course of a week. He is out of soldiering [military service], going to get in something else.

[page 2]

I am afraid we are going to have a wet summer. It is now raining in torrents, and it has been for this fortnight past. The corn trade is very bad particular. Wheat is not worth more than 6s a bushel. Mr. Bonfield complains the rent been so high I have consented to drop him £8 a year for the next two years and I can assure you very dear in that amount which will be £72 a year. When you write please to tell me if I am to let [rent] it after the time is up. It ought not to cost more than £60 a year but still I can get more [rent?] and wages high. I used to give 7s a week wages and now we are giving 9s. That tells quite a different tale

[page 2 crosshatched]

From your affectionate uncle Wm. Jennings

[Page 3]

Lady Day [25 March] account Michaelmas [29 September] account

Mr. [John] Stickland's annuity	£12 0s 0d
1 hundred reed	£2 0s 0d
Fire insurance	£1 15s 6d
Thatcher's bill	14s 7d
Income tax	6s 9d
	£16 16s 10d

Rent	£44 10s 0d
On the last half	£9 16s 1d
	£54 6s 1d
	£16 16s 10d
Due to Mr,??	£37 9s 3d

Mr. [John] Stickland's annuity	£12 0s 0d
Thatcher's bill	£1 16s 9d
2 hundred and 5 sheaves reed	£4 0s 0d
Insurance	£1 9s 3d
Income tax	£1 0s 3d
Paid Wm. [Jennings] Pipe for clothing	<u>£14 7s 8d</u>
	£34 13s 11d

Rent	£44 10s 0d
	<u>£34 13s 11d</u>
	<u>£9 16s 1d</u>

This account ought to have been on the top

Michaelmas [29 September] Account

[page 4]

My dear Cousin

As dear father has written Cousin Tom such a short letter, I thought I would just write a few lines to you. Although I do not remember you, yet I often think of you all and how much I should like to see you. Now I suppose I must try and tell you a bit of news. My uncle Frank [Coleman] is married to one of the Miss Dommetts [Emma] of Buckland [St. Mary, Somerset]. He had bought the Yarcombe Inn and is now living there.   [Mary Ann Jennings]

Whitestaunton
June 19 "63

Dear Thomas

It is a long
time sine I hard from you
I hope this will find you and
your wife & Family well I am
sorry to tell you that your
Aunt is very unwell in the
first place she a had the low
Feavour and now very bad
in the rhematic not able to
hath no rest William has been
down for a week he is now in
London going to return agan
in the corse of a week he is
out of the soldering going to
get in something else

I am afraid we are going to
have a wet Summer it is now
raining in torrents and it has
been for this fortnight past the
corn trade is very bad particular
wheat best not worth more than
6/s a bushel Mr Bonfield compt
and the rent been so high I have
concented to drop him £8 a year
for the next two years and I can
assure you very dear in that
amount which will be £72 a year
when you write please to tell me if
I am to let it after the time is up
It aught not to cost more than £80
a year but still I can get more
acts and wages high I use to give
7/s a week wages & now we are giving
9/s that tells quite a different tale

Lady day account

Michelmas account

Mr Stricklands annuity	12 " 0 " 0
1 Hundred Recd	2 " 0 " 0
Fire insurance	1 " 15 " 6
Thatchers Bill	" 14 " 7
Income Tax	1 6 " 9
	1 6 " 6 " 10

Rent	44 " 1 " 11
On the last half	9 " 1 6 " 1
	5 4 " 6 " 1
	1 6 " 16 " 10
Wm Widow Pipe	3 7 " 9 " 3

Mr Stricklands Annuity	12 " 0 " 0
Thatchers Bill	1 " 16 " 9
2 Hundred & 5 Shares Recd	4 " 0 " 0
Insurance	1 " 9 " 3
Income Tax	1 " 0 " 3
Paid Wm Pipe for Clothing	14 " 7 " 8
	34 " 13 " 11

Rent	44 " 16 " 0
	34 " 13 " 11
	9 " 1 6 " 1

This account aught to have been
on the top

Michelmas Account

My dear Cousin
As dear Father
has written Cousin Tom
such a short letter I thought
I would just write a few
lines to you. Although I do
not remember you, yet
I often think of you all
and how much I should
like to see you. Now I suppose
I must try and tell you
a bit of news. My Uncle
Frank is married to one
of the Miss Dommetts of
Buckland he has bought
the Yarcombe Inn and
is now living there

Looking Back

Volume 1 of this work introduces the main letter writers and recipients in the Pipe family letter collection. Both the Pipe and Stickland family roots are detailed. John Valentine and Elizabeth Stickland Pipe, their two children, and John Valentine's brother, Thomas Pipe, immigrated to America and first settled in Monroe County, New York. John Valentine Pipe traveled back to England to settle Elizabeth Stickland Pipe's inherited properties, and on his return trip, traveled the ill-fated *City of Glasgow* and was lost at sea.

Elizabeth Stickland Pipe and her two children moved to Vinland, Winnebago County, Wisconsin, where her brother-in-law, Thomas Pipe, and his mother, Charlotte Jennings Pipe Pillar, lived. They eventually married and moved to the town of Farmington, Waupaca County, Wisconsin, starting their own family. The family moved to the village of Waupaca, where Thomas operated butcher and livery business.

Looking Ahead

Volume 2 begins with letters starting in 1864. Thomas Pipe is feeling the social and economic effects of the Civil War on their everyday lives. The Jennings leave Northay Farm and eventually move to Hursey Farm in Burstock, Beaminster, Dorset.

In 1874, the Pipes learn from solicitors Dommett & Canning how William Jennings has managed their inherited properties over the last 21 years. The Pipes travel to England in 1875 for a seven-month visit with family and friends. They settle their business regarding the inherited properties. Thomas Pipe dies in 1880. Elizabeth Stickland Pipe lives another 36 years at The Pipe House with her son William's family. Elizabeth dies in January of 1918.

Appendix A

The will of John **STICKLAND**
Dated 25 February 1806 and proved 22 June 1810

THE NATIONAL ARCHIVES via Ancestry

PREROGATIVE COURT OF CANTERBURY

PROB 11/1512/370

Will of John Stickland

Dated 25th February 1806

Proved 22nd June 1810

I John Stickland of Yarcombe in the county of Devon yeoman being of sound mind

and perfect memory do this twenty fifth day of February in the year of our lord one

thousand eight hundred and six make and publish this my last will and testament in

manner following that is to say

I give unto my wife Betty the sum of £50 to be paid her in one year next after my decease

Also I give unto my said wife such part and articles of my household goods and

furniture as she shall select and choose within one year next after my death not

exceeding in value the sum of £50 according to the estimation of the same by my herein after named trustees

And I devise give and bequeath unto my son John Stickland his heirs and assigns

for ever all my messuage and lands which I have in fee simple within the parish of

Yarcombe aforesaid or elsewhere

And I constitute and ordain my friends Robert Spiller of Underdown and Henry Spiller

of Knightshayne within the said parish of Yarcombe yeomen and Robert Smith of

Stockland in the county of Dorset tallow chandler to be guardians and trustees of my

said son John and of my said messuages and lands for and on behalf of my said son

John during his minority to let protect and manage the same as in their discretion

they think best for his advantage maintenance and education

And I give and bequeath unto my two daughters Mary and Elizabeth the sum of

£300 each to be paid them on their respective attainment to the age of 21 years with

interest for the same from my decease until their arrivals to that age after the rate of

4.5% which interest or such part thereof as my hereinafter named trustees and

executors in trust shall think proper it is my will shall be applied from time to time

towards the maintenance and education of my said daughters Mary and Elizabeth

during the minority but in case either of them my said daughters shall happen to

marry before her attainment to the age of 21 years it is my desire that my executors

in trust may if they think fit immediately on such marriage pay the said legacy of

£300 to such of my said daughters or both of them so married together with such

interest as may then remain and endure for the same

And in case my said wife shall happen to be with child at the time of my decease I

then give unto such my posthumous child or children as she shall be afterwards

delivered of the sum of £250 to be paid such child or children at the age of 21 years

for interest for the same after the land and in manner so directed touching the said

Page 2

legacies of £300 given to each of my said daughters Mary and Elizabeth which said

two legacies so given to them in case my said wife shall happen to have such my

posthumous child or children and the same live to the age of 21 years shall in that

case be reduced from £300 down to £250 each, nor shall my said two daughters

Mary and Elizabeth be entitled to claim during the minority of such my posthumous

child or children only such legacies of £250 each with interest therefore after the rate

and manner before mentioned

Al the rest and remainder of my leasehold lands stock goods monies chattels and

personal estate whatsoever and wheresoever, after payment of my just debts funeral

expenses and before mentioned legacies I give and bequeath unto my said friends

Robert Spiller Henry Spiller and Robert Smith and the survivor of them his executors

administrators and assigns upon trust and for the following intents and purposes,

that is to say it is my will and I direct my said trustees to protect manage and dispose

of all my said residuary estate in the best way and manner they and the survivor of

them in their discretion can during the minority of my two sons Thomas and Robert

Stickland and to apply from time to time the rents interests and profits of the same

or such part thereof as my said trustees or the survivor them think proper towards

the decent and frugal maintenance and education of my said two sons Thomas and

Robert during their minority and on the attainment of the eldest of them to the age of

21 years it is my will that my said trustees shall then pay make assign and deliver

over unto such eldest of my said sons one full just moiety of all my said residuary

effects and the accumulated profits of the same, if any then remaining in the hands

and care of my said trustees or either of them for the use and benefit of the eldest of

my said two sons for ever

And on the attainment of the youngest of my said two sons to his age of 21 years I

then order my said trustees to pay assign and deliver over unto him the other moiety

of my residuary estate and effects with the accumulated profits of the same, if any,

then remaining in the custody of my said trustees or either of them for the sue of my

said two sons for ever

And in case either of my said two sons Thomas or Robert shall happen to die during

his minority and leave no legitimate issue I then give the survivor of them all my said

residuary estate and effect to be paid assigned and delivered over to him by my said

trustees on his attainment to the said age of 21 years save only that my said trustees

shall first pay thereout the sum of £20 unto each of my then surviving children,

except my said son John, in addition to the legacies which I have here-inbefore given

to them

And further it is my will if both my said sons shall happen to die and leave no

legitimate issue during their minority that then all my said residuary estate and

effects shall devolve and be paid by my said trustees in equal and like shares unto all my then surviving children on their respective attainments to the full age of 21

years 'and in case my said daughters Mary, Elizabeth or any posthumous child or

children shall happen to die in their minority and leave no legitimate issue and not

have been paid their respective legacies hereby given to them as I have before

directed, it is then my will that the legacy and legacies given to such decease

Page 3

daughter or daughters posthumous child or children shall devolve and be paid in

equal and like shares unto all my surviving children, except my said son John

Stickland, on their several attainments to the age of 21 years

Further it is my will and direction that my said trustees and the survivor of them his

executors administrators and assigns shall and will confide the care maintenance of

all my children during their minority unto my said wife Betty and also the direction

and superintendence of their education unless my said wife shall be her misconduct

or imprudence give my said trustees good and sufficient reason to take the care

maintenance and education of my children out of her management and power for the

security and advantage of my said children

And I hereby constitute and ordain my said friends Robert Spiller Henry Spiller and

Robert Smith joint executors in trust of this my will during the minority of said two

sons Thomas and Robert Stickland and on their attainment to the full age of 21 years

I then appoint my said two sons Thomas and Robert to be thenceforth join executors

of this my will

Also it is my will and I hereby legally authorise my said trustees and executors in

trust to pay retain and reimbursee themselves and each of them from time to time

out of my said trust estate for all their or either of their necessary trouble and

reasonable expenses in the proper execution of this my last will and the fulfilment of

my aforesaid trusts and that my said trustees and executors in trust shall not be

answerable or responsible for any more of my monies property and estate than they

or either of them shall actually receive or be in possession of, nor for any loss that

shall happen in the execution of this my will and my aforesaid trusts except the same

occur their or either of their wilful neglect or default, nor shall the one of them be

answerable or responsible for the acts and deeds of the other of them but each of

them for his own acts and deeds

In witness whereof I the said John Stickland have to the first sheet of this my last

will and testament containing two sheets of paper set my hand and to the last sheet

thereof my hand and seal the day and year first above written

Signed: John Stickland

Signed sealed published and declared by the said testator, the above erasure being

first made, as and for this last will and testament in the presence of us who at his

desire in his presence and in the presence of each other have subscribed our names

as witnesses thereto: the mark of George Flood, the mark of James Vincent and Wm

Kite

Proved at London 22 nd June 1810 before the judge by the oaths of Robert Spiller and

Henry Spiller and Robert Smith the executors till Thomas Stickland and Robert

Stickland the sons or either of them shall attain the age of 21 years having been first

sworn by common duly to administer

Citation:

Prerogative Court of Canterbury and Related Probate Jurisdictions: Will Registers. Digitized images. Records of the Prerogative Court of Canterbury, Series PROB 11. The National Archives, Kew, England; Ancestry.com. *England & Wales, Prerogative Court of Canterbury Wills, 1384-1858* [database on-line, images 826-828]. Provo, UT, USA: Ancestry.com Operations, Inc., 2013. entry for John Stickland.

Transcribed by ST Moore

Appendix B

The will of Robert **STICKLAND**
Dated 19 February 1831 and proved 19 March 1832

THE NATIONAL ARCHIVES

PREROGATIVE COURT OF CANTERBURY

PROB 11/1797/393

Will of Robert Stickland

Dated 19th February 1831

Proved 19th March 1832

This is the last will and testament of me Robert Stickland of Yarcombe in the county

of Devon yeoman

In the first place I give and bequeath the sum of £1,000 unto my cousin Thomas

Smith of Clayhidon in the said county of Devon yeoman and Robert Spiller of

Painshayne in the parish of Yarcombe aforesaid yeoman their executors

administrators and assigns to be paid within one year next after my decease with

interest after the rate of 4% from my death until so paid

Upon and for the trust intents and purposes and with under and subject to the

powers and declarations hereinafter expressed concerning the same, that is to say

upon trust that they the said Thomas Smith and Robert Spiller and the survivor of

them and the executors administrators and assigns of such survivor do and shall as

soon as they or he conveniently can lay out and invest the same in their or his

names or name in the purchase of parliamentary stocks or funds of Great Britain or

on good and sufficient real security or securities with full power from time to time to

vary the same at their or his discretion

And do and shall during the natural life of my dear mother Elizabeth Stickland as

from time to time received pay all the interests dividends and proceeds of the said

sum of £1,000 unto her my said mother Elizabeth her agent or assigns for her own

absolute use and benefit

And from and after the decease of my said mother Elizabeth upon trust that they the

said Thomas Smith and Robert Spiller and the survivor of them or the executors

administrators or assigns of such survivor do and shall pay transfer and assign the

sum of £500 part of the said sum of £1,000 unto my brother Thomas Stickland if he

be then living otherwise unto and amongst all his then surviving children if more than

one in equal and similar shares and portions but if only one such child then the

whole to that one

And also from and after the death of my said mother upon trust to pay transfer and

assign the sum of £200 part of the said £1,000 unto John the son of my said brother

Thomas and £100 unto Elizabeth his daughter if they have then respectively attained

the age of 21 years otherwise on their respective attainments to that age and in the

interim from the death of my said mother until he my said nephew and niece shall

attain their said ages of 21 years it is my will that the interest and proceeds of the

said legacies of £200 and £100 shall be paid unto my said brother Thomas or his

representative towards the education and maintenance of my said nephew and niece

Page 2

And further it is my will and I declare if either of them my said nephew or niece shall

happen to die during his or her minority and leave no legitimate issue that then the

legacy of him or her so dying without issue hall devolved and be paid unto and

amongst all the then surviving children of my said brother Thomas if more than one

in similar shares, but if only one survivor then the whole to that one

And upon further trust to pay transfer and assign upon and from the death of my said mother the remaining sum of £200 part of the said sum of £1000 unto my brother

John Stickleand as a vested legacy provided always and it is my will and I do hereby

direct that it shall and may be lawful to an for my said trustees and each of them and

every of their executors and administrators by and out of the said trust money

hereinbefore mentioned to deduct and reimburse himself of themselves and to allow

to each other from time to time all such costs damages journeys charges and

expenses as they every or either of them shall be put unto pay or sustain by reason

of any of the trusts hereby in them reposed or in the execution thereof or by reason

of any other matter or thing relating thereto as between solicitor and client

And that none of my trustees shall be answerable for any more money than what

they shall respectively receive nor be charged or chargeable for the receipt or

receipts of the other of them but each for his own receipt acts deeds wilful defaults

only nor shall they or either of them be accountable for any involuntary loss or losses

of all or any part of the said trust money but shall be saved harmless in respet of all

acts and things done by them or either of them in the execution of the trusts hereby

in them reposed and also stand indemnified of and from all such involutary loss and

losses unless the same happen through their or his wilful neglect or default

And I give my said brother Thomas the sum of £100 to be paid my within one year

net after my decease

All the rest residue and remainder of my stock goods monies securities for money

mortgages in fee otherwise chattels and personal estate whatsoever, charged in the

first place with the payment of all my just debts funeral and testamentary expenses

and before mentioned legacies thereout, I give and bequeath unto my said brother

John Stickland his executors administrators and assigns and him my said brother

John I constitute and appoint executor of this my will

In witness whereof I have to the first sheet of this my last will and testament

containing two sheets of paper set my hand and to this the second and last sheet my

hand and seal this 19 th day of February in the year of our lord 1831

Signed: Robert Stickland

Signed sealed published and declared by the said Robert Stickland the testator as

and for his last will and testament in the presence of us who at his request and in his

presence and in the presence of each other have subscribed our names as witnesses the words 'all or such involuntary loss and losses' having been first

interned

Wits: Martha Pitts, Robt Spiller, Wm Kite

Probate granted to John Stickland brother and sole executor

Citation:

Prerogative Court of Canterbury and Related Probate Jurisdictions: Will Registers. Digitized images. Records of the Prerogative Court of Canterbury, Series PROB 11. The National Archives, Kew, England; Ancestry.com. *England & Wales, Prerogative Court of Canterbury Wills, 1384-1858* [database on-line, images 708-709]. Provo, UT, USA: Ancestry.com Operations, Inc., 2013. entry for Robert Stickland.

Transcribed by ST Moore

Appendix C

The will of John **JENNINGS**, of Birch Oak in the parish of Membury Devon yeoman
Dated 9 May 1837 and proved 7 February 1838

THE NATIONAL ARCHIVES

PREROGATIVE COURT OF CANTERBURY

PROB 11/1890/425

Will of John Jennings of Birch Oak in the parish of Membury Devon yeoman
Dated 9th May 1837

Proved 7th February 1838

I John Jennings of Birch Oak in the parish of Membury in the county of Devon yeoman do make ordain publish and declare this to be my last will and testament in manner following, that is to say

First I give and bequeath unto **my grandson John Pipe son of my daughter Charlotte now the wife of John Pipe** the sum of o£10 of lawful money current in England to be raised out of all and every of my effects and paid to him on his attainment of age of 21 years by my executrix hereafter named

Also I give and bequeath to **my daughter Charlotte Pipe** and to each of her children that shall be living at the time of my death one decent suit of mourning the same to be ordered and selected and paid for from and out of my effects by my executrix

And whereas **my two sons Edmund Jennings and Thomas Jennings** and my said **daughter Charlotte wife of the said John** Pipe have been already provided for as to the part or share of my property which would have been theirs had no such provision for them been made therefore my will is and I hereby order and direct that no further provision for them shall be made from and out of my live and dead stock and other my effects nor shall they or either of them be entitled to ay part or share or proportion thereof

Also I give and bequeath unto **my wife Mary Jennings and my other three children namely John William and Mary Ann Jennings** all and every my household goods money book debts live and dead stock farming utensils and all other my effects of what kind and nature soever and wheresoever to hold the same to her my said wife for and during the term of her natural life with impeachment of waste except willful or malicious waste subject nevertheless to the payment of the said sum of £10 to **my said grandson John Pipe** here before given and all other expenses that may be lawfully incurred in and towards the fulfilling the purposes of this my will and all other my just debts funeral and testamentary expenses

And from and immediately after the death of my said wife Mary then I give and bequeath the same household goods money book debts live and dead stock farming utensils and all other my effects unto my said three children namely John William and Mary Ann Jennings the same to be divided among and between them in equal portions share and share alike and for the purpose of effecting such distribution in the manner and for the purposes aforesaid

And for carrying this my will into effect in all respects I hereby authorise and empower my brother in law John Bond of Ilton in the county of Somerset gentleman and my son Edmund Jennings of the same place yeoman their executors or administrators to the fulfilment in all respects of the contents of this my will

And for this purpose I hereby empower them the said John Bond and Edmund Jennings their executors or administrators with the consent of my said wife and three children namely John William and Mary Ann Jennings to call in and compel payment of any monies that may be due unto me at the time of my death

And I hereby further authorise and empower the said John Bond and Edmund Jennings to take an inventory of all and every of my effects al and every of my effects at the time of my death or as soon as conveniently can be afterwards and to inspect into and look to the same when and as often as is necessary during the lifetime of my said wife and to see that the same is not diminished in value by any fraud or wilful waste and t pay himself and themselves all reasonable expenses her or they may be at or put to in the discharge of the trusts hereby in him and them reposed

And I hereby constitute ordain and appoint my said wife Mary Jennings sole executrix of this my last will and testament

In witness whereof I the said John Jennings the testator have to this my last will and testament set my hand and seal the 9th day of May 1837

Signed: John Jannings

Signed sealed published and declared by the said testator the interlineations being first made in the presence of us who in his presence at his request and in the presence of each other have subscribed as witnesses:

John Dommett, John Hayes

Proved at London 7th February 1838 before the judge by the oath of Mary Jennings widow the relict and sole executrix to whom administration was granted having been first sworn by commission duly to administer

Citation:

Prerogative Court of Canterbury and Related Probate Jurisdictions: Will Registers. Digitized images. Records of the Prerogative Court of Canterbury, Series PROB 11. The National Archives, Kew, England; Ancestry.com. *England & Wales, Prerogative Court of Canterbury Wills, 1384-1858* [database on-line, images 828-829]. Provo, UT, USA: Ancestry.com Operations, Inc., 2013.entry for John Jennings.

Transcribed by ST Moore

Appendix D

The will of John **STICKLAND**
of Yarcombe co Devon yeoman
Dated 28 February 1848 and proved 30 July 1850

THE NATIONAL ARCHIVES

PREROGATIVE COURT OF CANTERBURY

PROB 11/2117/70

Will of John Stickland of Yarcombe co Devon yeoman
Dated 28th February 1848

Proved 30th July 1850

This is the last will and testament of me John Stickland of Yarcombe in the county of Devon yeoman

First I charge all my real and personal estate of what nature or kind so-ever with the payment of all my debts funeral expenses and legacies as well such as I hereby give and also such as I may hereafter give by any codicil or codicils to this my will

I do appoint Robert Spiller of Pounds Farm in the parish of Yarcombe aforesaid yeoman and Robert Smith of Dunkeswell in the county of Devon yeoman my trustees and executors of this my will

I give unto **my dear wife Ann Stickland** the sum of £1,000 to be paid to her within twelve calendar months after my decease and as hereinafter mentioned I also give and bequeath to my said wife all my household goods plate glass furniture and other effects in and upon the dwelling house outhouses and premises where I now live or which I might occupy at my decease together with all my dairy goods farming utensils horses waggons carts agricultural implements cider and casks with the live and dead stock upon the farms which I may occupy at my decease

I direct that my wife shall be at liberty to continue in the occupation of any dwelling house land and premises which I may occupy at my decease for twelve calendar months hereafter without paying any rent for such occupation

And I also direct that in the event of my death happening at a time when it will not be practicable for my said wife conveniently to remove the crops in ground during the twelve calendar months aforesaid it shall be lawful for my said wife to continue in the occupation of such dwelling house land and premises for such additional time as may be necessary for her to do so, she paying such sum by way of rent for such additional occupation as my trustees shall in their and his discretion think fit

I direct that the fixtures in and upon the dwelling house in which I reside and particularly the ancient back in the fire place in my general siting room dated 1554 together with the cider press and apple mill and things which are generally considered fixtures shall remain attached to the freehold of the premises

I also direct my trustees for the time being of this my will to pay the legacy of £1,000 hereinbefore given to my wife out of any moneys due to me at my decease upon bonds notes debts or other personal securities, except mortgages for terms of years. And in the event of such personal securities being insufficient to pay the said legacy I direct that my wife shall be at liberty to elect to take any mortgage belonging to me not exceeding a security for £1,000 either in a discharge of such legacy or to make up the deficiency of such personal security and in the event of my wife's declining of such mortgage and there should be no such personal securities as aforesaid sufficient to discharge the said legacy owing to me then I direct that my said trustees to pay the said legacy out of my general personal estate

I give to **my niece Elizabeth the wife of John Pipe of Membury** in the county of Devon yeoman the sum of £300 to be paid to her within twelve calendar months from my decease

I give to **my niece Mary Stickland** the sum of £300 to be paid to her with twelve calendar months after my decease

I give to **Dan Pym of Buckland St Mary** in the county of Somerset yeoman the sum of £100 and in the event of his dying before me I direct that the legacy so given to him shall be divided equally amongst his children and the issue of any deceased child of the said Dan Pym such issue to take his or her parents share

I give to **Page Shire the elder of Buckland** aforesaid the sun of £100 and in the event of his dying before me I direct that the legacy so given shall be divided equally amongst his children and the issue of any decease child of the said Page Shire, such issue to take his or her parents share

I give to **Sidney Doble Levi Doble and Edwin Doble** sons of Robert Doble of Buckland aforesaid yeoman the sum of £19 19s each

Also I give to **Temperance Greedy the wife of James Greedy of Curland** in the county of Somerset yeoman and **Edith Wyatt the wife of Walter Wyatt o**f Buckland St Mary aforesaid yeoman the sum of £19 19s each

I give to my executors **Robert Spiller and Robert Smith** the sum of £50 each for their trouble in the execution of the trusts of this my will

I give and bequeath unto the said Robert Spiller and Robert Smith their executors administrators and assigns all estate vested in me as trustee for any person or persons upon trust to hold the same upon the trusts thereof

I do charge all that and those my estate and estates farms lands hereditaments and premises called **Much Hill Farm in the parish of Yarcombe** aforesaid occupied by Joel King, **Combes's Pithayne** and **the allotment in Mannings Common in Yarcombe** aforesaid now in my own occupation **Whithorns otherwise Bardscombe** situate at Membury aforesaid and now in my own occupation and also **Peacross** in Membury aforesaid occupied by John Dening with the annual sum of £30 to my nephew John Stickland during his life

And I direct such annual sum to be paid to my said **nephew John Stickland** by quarterly payments in each year during his life the first quarterly payment to be made at the expiration of three calendar months next after my decease

And I give power to my said **nephew John Stickland** to recover the annuity when in arrears for more than twenty eight days and all costs and charges of such recovery by distress and sale in like manner as rack rents are recoverable by law

And as to all my said estates called **Much Hill Farm Combes's Pithayne with the allotment on Mannings Common Whithorns otherwise Bardscombe and Peacross** I give devise and bequeath the same unto the said Robert Spiller and Robert Smith their heirs executors administrators and assigns upon the trusts and to and for the several uses and intents and purposes hereinafter expressed and declared concerning the same, that is to say

To the use and behoof of my **nephew Thomas Stickland son of my late brother Thomas Stickland** and his assigns for and during the term of his natural life without impeachment of waste except voluntary waste in houses and other buildings and from and after the determination of that estate to the use and behoof of the said Robert Spiller and Robert Smith their heirs and assigns during the natural life of my said nephew Thomas Stickland upon trust to preserve and support the contingent uses and estates hereinafter limited from being defeated or destroyed and for that purpose to make entries and bring actions as the case shall require but nevertheless to permit and suffer my said nephew Thomas Stickland and his assigns to hold and enjoy the said premises and to receive and take the rents issues and profits thereof to his and their own use and benefit during the term of his natural life

And from and after the death of my said nephew Thomas Stickland to the use of the first and every other son of his body lawfully to be begotten severally and successively according to their several securities in tail general and in default of such issue to the use of all and every the daughters and daughter of the body of my said nephew Thomas Stickland lawfully to be begotten to be divided between them if more than one in equal shares as tenants in common and the heirs of the respective bodies of all and every such daughters and daughter issuing and if there shall be but one such daughter then to the use of such only daughter and the heirs of her body lawfully issuing and in default of such issue of my said nephew Thomas Stickland then as to my said estates called Combe Pithayne and the allotment in Mannings Common Whitehorns otherwise Boundscombe and Peacross to the use and behoof of my said niece Elizabeth Pipe and her assigns for and during the term of her natural life without impeachment of waste except as aforesaid and from and after the determination of that estate to the use of the said Robert Spiller and Robert smith and their heirs for and during the natural life of my said niece Elizabeth Pipe upon trust to support the contingent uses hereinafter limited from being defeated or destroyed and for that purpose to make entries and bring actions as the case shall require

But nevertheless to permit and suffer **my said niece Elizabeth Pipe** and her assigns during her life to receive and take the rents and profits of the same hereditaments for her and their own use and benefit and from and after the decease of my said niece Elizabeth Pipe to the use of all and every the children and child of my said niece Elizabeth Pipe lawfully to be begotten who being a son or sons shall attain the age of 21 years or die under that age leaving issue of his her their body or being a daughter or daughters shall attain the said age or marry under that age with the consent of her or their guardian for the time being to be equally divided between or amongst them if more than one in equal shares as tenants in common, and if there shall be but one such child then to the use of that one or only child

And in default of such issue of my said niece Elizabeth Pipe then to the use of **my niece Mary Stickland** her heirs and assigns for ever

And as to my said estate called **Much Hill** I give and devise the same in default of such issue of my said **nephew Thomas Stickland** to the use and behoof of such issue of **my said niece Mary Stickland** and her assigns for and during the term of her natural life without impeachment of waste except as aforesaid and from and after the determination of that estate to the use of the said Robert Spiller and Robert Smith and their heirs for and during the natural life of my said niece Mary Stickland upon trust to support the contingent uses hereinafter limited from being defeated or destroyed and for that purpose to make entries and bring actions as the case shall require but nevertheless to permit and suffer my said niece

Mary Stickland and her assigns during her life to receive and take the rents and profits of the same hereditaments for her and their own use and benefit

And from and after the decease of my said niece Mary Stickland to the use of all and every children and child of my said niece Mary Stickland lawfully be begotten who being a son or sons shall attain the age of 21 years or die under that age leaving issue of his or their body or being a daughter or daughters shall attain the said age or marry under that age with the consent of her or their guardian for the time being to be equally divided between or amongst them if more than one in equal shares as tenants in common and if there shall be but one such child then to the use of that one or only child

And in default of such issue of my said niece Mary Stickland then to the use of my niece Elizabeth Pipe her heirs and assigns for ever

And as to all the rest residue and remainder of my residuary real and personal estate and effect of what nature kind or quality soever and wheresoever situate subject to the payment of my debts funeral expenses and in legacies I give devise and bequeath the sae and every part thereof unto and to the use of my **said nephew Thomas Stickland** his heirs executors administrators and assigns for his and their own absolute use and benefit

And I hereby expressly declare that my will to be that any sale mortgage or charge on any other disposition in the way of anticipation which **my said nephew John Stickland** in regard to his annuity or which **my said Thomas Stickland or my nieces Elizabeth Pipe and Mary Stickland** or either of the in regard to any estate or interest for life which they or either of them may at any time take in any part of my real and personal estate shall make or attempt or agree to make of the said annuity or estates for life respectively shall to all intents and purposes be absolutely void

And I do hereby declare that any legacies hereinbefore by me given to ay person who may be married women shall be paid to them for their separate use and benefit independently and exclusively of any husband or husbands to whom they may be married and without being in anywise subject to their debts claims or demands and that the receipts of the married women respectively notwithstanding their respective covertures shall be good and effectual discharges for the same

And I do hereby declare that the receipt or receipts of the said Robert Spiller and Robert Smith or the survivor of them or the executors or administrators of such survivor for any sum or sums of money payable to them or him or by virtue of the trusts I this will shall be a sufficient and effectual discharge or sufficient or effectual discharges for the same respectively or so much thereof respectively as in such receipt of receipts thereof respectively shall be expressed or acknowledged to so received, and that the person or persons not whom they same shall be given his her or their executors administrators assigns shall not afterwards be answerable or accountable for any losses misapplication nor non-application or be obliged or concerned to see to the application of the money therein mentioned and acknowledged to be received or any part thereof provided always and I hereby declare that if the trustees appointed for this my will or be appointed under the present provision of any of them or their or any of their executors administrators and assigns shall die or be desirous of being discharged from or refuse or decline or be incapable to act in the trusts thereby in them reposed as aforesaid before the same shall be fully executed then and in every such case it shall and may be lawful to and for the said trustees or the surviving or continuing trustee appointed under this my will whether they or he shall accept the trusts thereof or shall renounce the same or for the trustees or for the surviving or continuing trustee to be appointed under this present provision or the executors or administrators of such last surviving or continuing trusteed by any deed or deeds instrument or instruments in writing to be by them him or her sealed and delivered in the presence of and attested by two or more credible witnesses from time to time to nominate and appoint any fit person or persons to be a trustee or trustees in the room or place of the trustee or trustees so dying or desiring to be discharged or becoming unwilling or incapable to act as aforesaid, and that when and so often as any new trustee shall be nominated and appointed as aforesaid all the trust estates monies and premises or such of them as shall then be subject to the trusts and provisions as aforesaid which shall have vested in such trustee or trustees so dying desiring to be discharged or becoming unwilling or incapable to act as aforesaid shall be thereupon with all convenient speed conveyed assigns or transferred so and in such manner as that the same shall and may be loyally and effectually vested in the person or persons so to be appointed as aforesaid either solely or jointly with the surviving or continuing trustees or trustee as occasion shall require, to the use and upon and for the trusts intents and purposes hereinbefore expressed or declared or such of them as shall be then subsisting undetermined and capable of taking effect and the person or persons so to be appointed as aforesaid I shall have and be entitle to exercise the same powers and authorities as if he or they had been appointed a trustee or trustees of this my will provided always and I do hereby further declare that the trustees of this my will hereby appointed and to be appointed as aforesaid and each and every of them his heirs executors and administrators shall be charged and chargeable for such monies only as they respectively shall actually receive by virtue of the trusts hereby in them reposed notwithstanding their or any of their giving or jointly in giving any receipt or receipts for the sake of conformity

And I direct that none of them shall be answerable or accountable for any banker or broker with who the said trust monies and premises shall be place for safe custody or for any default tor neglect of the others or other of them or for involuntary losses

And also that it shall and may be lawful for them with and out of the monies which shall come to their respective hands by virtue of the trusts aforesaid to retain and reimburse themselves respectively and also to allow their respective co-trustees or co-trustee all costs charges damages expenses and fees to counsel for advice which they or any of them shall or may sustain expend or disburse in or about the execution of the aforesaid trusts or in relation thereto

In witness whereof I have to the first eight sheets of this my last will and testament affixed my hand and to the ninth and last sheet thereof my hand and seal this 28th day of February 1848

Signed: John Stickland

Signed by the said John Stickland the testator as and for his last will and testament in the presence of each of us present at the same time who at his request in his presence and in the presence of each other have hereunto subscribed our names as witnesses the erasures and alterations against which we have placed our initial having first bee made

Signed: H. Dommett solicitor, Chard

H. Kinsman his clerk

Proved at London 30ᵗʰ July 1850 before the judge by the oaths of Robert Spiller and Robert Smith the executors to whom administration was granted having been first sworn by commission duly to administer

Citation:

Prerogative Court of Canterbury and Related Probate Jurisdictions: Will Registers. Digitized images. Records of the Prerogative Court of Canterbury, Series PROB 11. The National Archives, Kew, England; Ancestry.com. *England & Wales, Prerogative Court of Canterbury Wills, 1384-1858* [database on-line, images 72-74]. Provo, UT, USA: Ancestry.com Operations, Inc., 2013. entry for John Stickland.

Transcribed by ST Moore

YARCOMBE PARISH

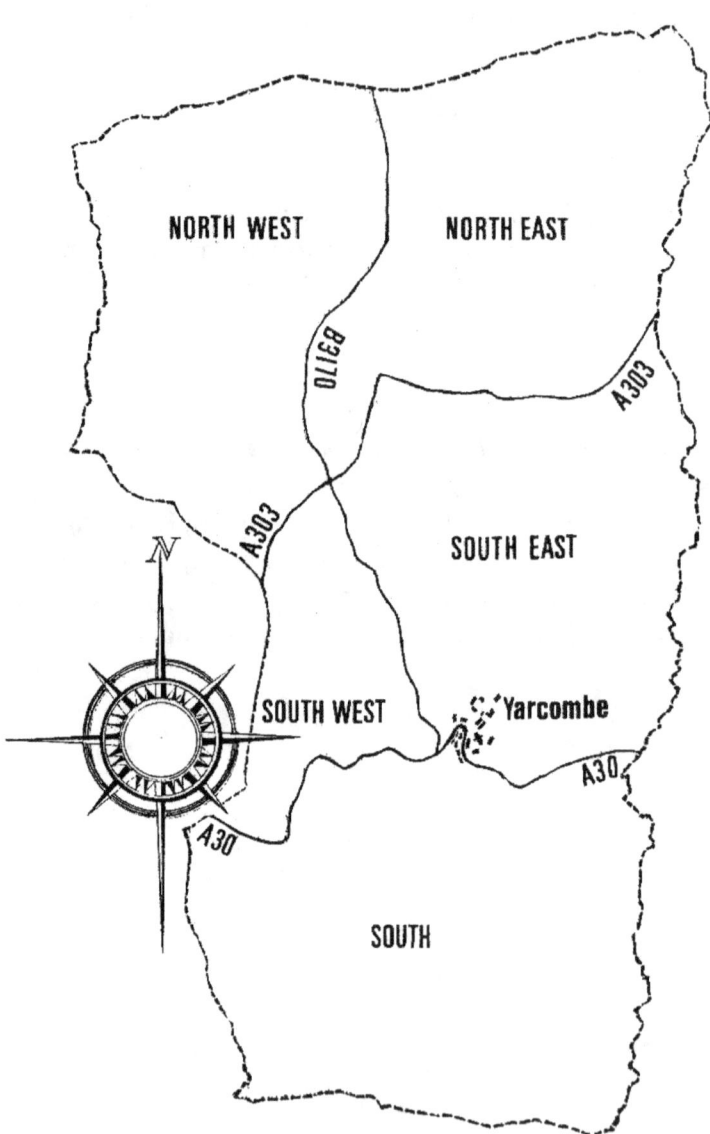

Yarcombe Parish map is found on page 29 of Ruth Everitt's 1999 *From Monks to the Millennium*. The "Gazetteer" shows the parish in 5 geographical areas. Everett's book can be found on the Yarcombe Home page at http://www.yarcombe.net/Ancestral-Searches.html.

SOUTH EAST

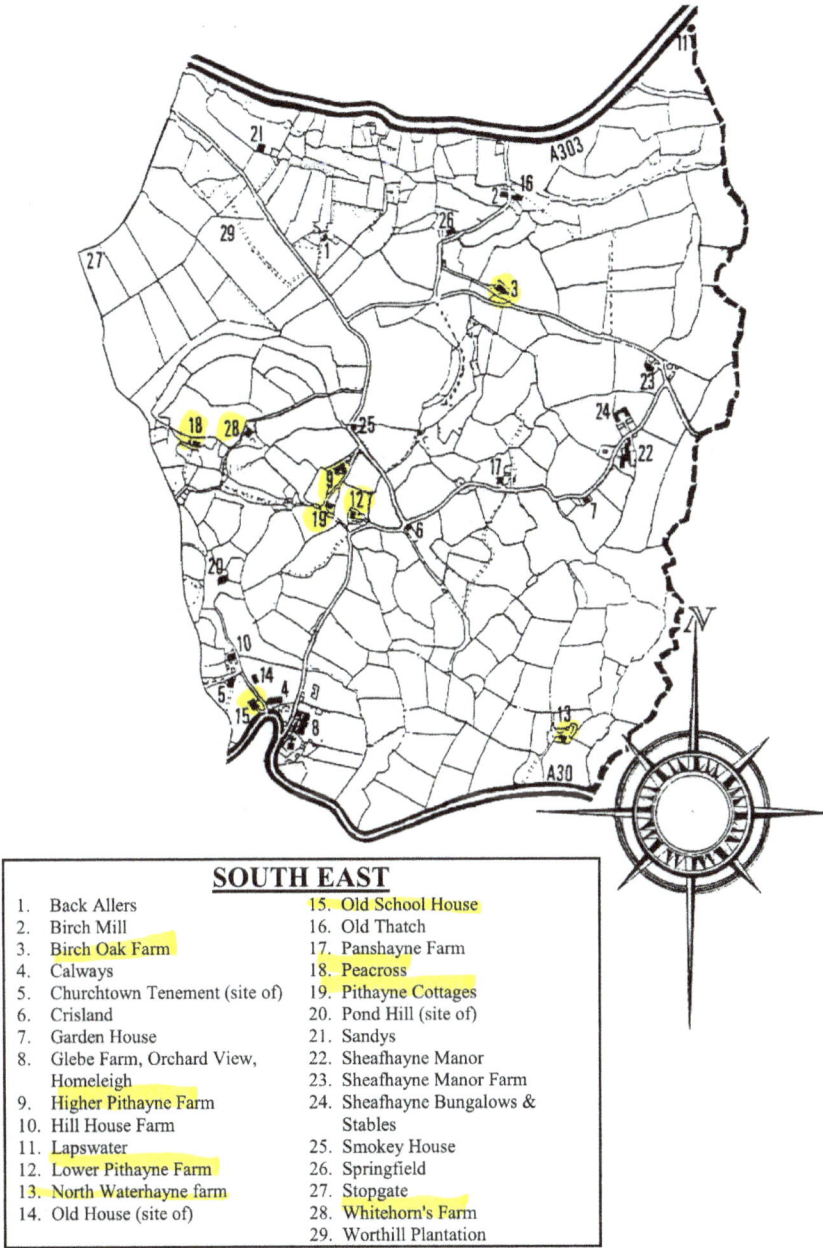

SOUTH EAST

1.	Back Allers	15.	Old School House
2.	Birch Mill	16.	Old Thatch
3.	Birch Oak Farm	17.	Panshayne Farm
4.	Calways	18.	Peacross
5.	Churchtown Tenement (site of)	19.	Pithayne Cottages
6.	Crisland	20.	Pond Hill (site of)
7.	Garden House	21.	Sandys
8.	Glebe Farm, Orchard View, Homeleigh	22.	Sheafhayne Manor
		23.	Sheafhayne Manor Farm
9.	Higher Pithayne Farm	24.	Sheafhayne Bungalows & Stables
10.	Hill House Farm		
11.	Lapswater	25.	Smokey House
12.	Lower Pithayne Farm	26.	Springfield
13.	North Waterhayne farm	27.	Stopgate
14.	Old House (site of)	28.	Whitehorn's Farm
		29.	Worthill Plantation

Many of the farms mentioned in the letter collection are located on the Southeast Yarcombe map. The highlighted names and locations show the proximity of these properties. The map is found on page 68 in Everett's book.

Appendix E

The will of John **BOND** of Atherstone, gent.
Dated 20 January 1854 and proved 18 May 1854

THE NATIONAL ARCHIVES

PREROGATIVE COURT OF CANTERBURY

PROB 11/2190/391

Will of John Bond of Atherstone gent
Dated 20th January 1854

Proved 18th May 1854

This is the last will and testament of me John Bond of Atherstone in the parish of Whitelackington in the county of Somerset gentleman

I give to my **nephew William Bond son of my last brother William** £350

I give to my **niece Letitia the wife of George Wakely** £150

I give to my **niece Elizabeth Bond daughter of my late brother Isaac Bond** £150

I give to my **niece Harriet the wife of Joseph Hayne** £150

I give to my niece **Mary Ann Dommett daughter of my late sister Mary Jennings** £150

I give to my nephew **John Jennings son of my said late sister Mary Jennings** £200

I give to my **nephew William Jennings another son of my said late sister Mary Jennings** £100

I give to **nephew Thomas Jennings another son of my said late sister Mary Jennings** £100

I give to **nephew Edwin Jennings another son of my said late sister Mary Jennings** £400

I give to my **niece Charlotte another daughter of my said late sister Mary Jennings** £50

I give to **my nephew Nicholas Bradley son of my sister Ann Bradley** £100

I give to my **nephew Edmund Bradley another son of my said sister Ann Bradley** £100

I give to my **niece Mary the wife of James Wyatt** £100

I give to my **niece Ann the wife of Frederick Bond** £500

I direct all the previous pecuniary legacies to be paid within one year next after my decease and with interest after the rate of four pounds per centum per annum from the time of my death to the time of the payment of the same respectively

I direct the legacies of such of the said pecuniary legatees as at the time of the actual payment thereof respectively shall be married women to be paid into their respective proper hands in order that the same may be enjoyed and disposed of as their separated property free form marital control and for which legacies their respective receipts shall be discharges

I give to **Edwin Francis Jennings the son of Edward Jennings by his late wife Fanny whose maiden name was Fanny Stephens**, £500 when he shall attain the age of 21 years and I direct that the said legacy shall not vest in him nor be paid unless he shall attain that age, but if the said Edwin Francis Jennings should die under the age of 21 years then one moiety of the said sum of £500 shall on his death be paid to his father the said Edwin Jennings and the other moiety thereon shall lapse to or for the benefit of my nephew John Bond the executor of this my will and if the said Edwin Francis Jennings shall be under the age of 21 years at the time of my decease then I direct that a sum equal to the interest of £500 at the rate of four pounds per centum per annum commencing from the time of my decease shall during the minority of the said Edwin

Francis Jennings or if he shall die under the age of 21 years until his death be paid and applied by my executor in such manner as he in his discretion shall think fit in or towards the maintenances education and bringing up of the said Edwin Francis Jennings

I hereby direct that in case any or either of my legatees hereinbefore named shall at the time of my decease be indebted to me in any sum or sums of money secured by bond or promissory note that the legacy given to each legatee so being indebted or so much of such legacy as shall be equal to the amount due on his or other said bond or note may be retained by my executor and applied in discharge or in part discharge of the amount due on the bond or note of the legatee from whom the same shall be retained

I also give to my said **nephew Thomas Jennings** my gig and the horse which at the time of my decease shall be used in bearing the same and also all my wearing apparel

I also give to my said **niece Ann the wife of Frederick Bond** my phaeton

I give my print "Thomas Oldaker" and my silver cup inscribed "E Abraham Esq: to **John Bond** as a token of respect / set/ to my nephew John Bond son of my said late brother Isaac Bond, for his sue and after his decease to my said nephew Frederick Bond and after the survivor of them **to John Bond son of my said nephew Frederick Bond**

I give to each of my friends Mrs Chapman, wife of William Coward Chapman, Miss Eliza Buncombe, Mrs Stephens wife of John Stephens, Mrs Budge the wife of Mr Geroge Budge, Miss Rebecca Stephens and Mrs Grabham wife of James Grabham a mourning ring of the value of £2

I give to each of my male and female farm labourers above the age of 21 years who shall have worked for me for one whole year next immediately before my decease £1 to be paid as soon after my decease as may be

I give to each domestic servant who shall be living with me at the time of my decease a suit of mourning

I desire and request my executor to erect as soon after my decease as conveniently may be a substantial tomb to the memory of myself and family in the church yard of Ilton in the said county of somerset and enclose and fence in the said tomb with iron palings

I give all my cash monies securities for money all terms and interest to which hi shall be entitled in any messuages lands or tenements as lessee or assign at the time of my decease and all the rest residue and remainder of my goods chattels estate and effects of what nature or kind soever they may be unto my said **nephew John Bond son of my said late brother Isaac Bond** who is now living and has lived for many years with me for his own soe and absolute use and benefit subject to repayment and discharge of all the aforesaid legacies as above specified and to the payment of my debts funeral and testamentary expenses and I give all estates which now are or herein may become and be at the time of my decease vested in me upon any trusts or by way of mortgage unto my said nephew John Bond his heirs executors and administrators respectively subject to the equities and upon the trusts affecting the same respectively

And I also give to my **said nephew John Bond** his heirs and assigns all real estates and interest which I have hereafter purchase or acquire and I appoint my said nephew John Bond whole and sole executor of this my will

I revoke all former wills by me made

In witness whereof I have to this my will contained in two sheets of paper set my hand and sealed, to wit my hand at the bottom of the first sheet and my hand and seal to this last sheet the 30th day of January 1854

Signed: John Bond

In witness contained in this and the previous sheet of paper was signed and sealed by the above hand John Bond the testator and by him declared to be his will in the presence of us present at the same time who at his request in his presence and in the presence of each other have hereunto set our names as witnesses

William Denman, John Rutter

Proved at London 18th May 1854 before the worshipful Samuel Fowkes Warnbey doctor of laws and surrogate by the oath of John Bond the nephew the sole executor to whom administration was granted having been first sworn duly to administer'

Citation:

Prerogative Court of Canterbury and Related Probate Jurisdictions: Will Registers. Digitized images. Records of the Prerogative Court of Canterbury, Series PROB 11. The National Archives, Kew, England; Ancestry.com. *England & Wales, Prerogative Court of Canterbury Wills, 1384-1858* [database on-line, images 325-326]. Provo, UT, USA: Ancestry.com Operations, Inc., 2013. entry for John Bond.

Transcribed by ST Moore

Appendix F

Estate Duty copy of will of James **PIPE** of Donyatt, yeoman
Dated 11 September 1833 and proved 18 October 1834

SOMERSET HERITAGE CENTRE

DD/ED/1834/206.

Estate Duty copy of will of James PIPE of Donyatt, Yeoman.

Dated 11 Sep 1833.

Proved: 18 Oct 1834

To son James Pipe annuity of £10 a year for life chargeable upon my dwelling house

and appurtenances called Wheadons now in my occupation with powers of distress

and entry for recovery thereof to be paid half yearly the first payment to made in the

six calendar months next after my decease

To son John Pipe £5 to paid within 12 months of my decease

To daughter Elizabeth Pipe for her life my dwelling house and garden called Lesseys

with the orchard and close of pasture or meadow called Home Close, one close of

pasture land called The Drying Close or Yarnhay, and also all that house by the river

side near Donyatt Bridge called the Bucking House, all within the parish of Donyatt

After death to her children

If Elizabeth dies without children then to my grandson James Pipe, son of my son

Joseph Pipe forever

To daughter Elizabeth Pipe all my household goods and furniture

To sons Joseph Pipe and Edward Pipe 20s each to be paid within one month after

my decease

Residue to son Orlando Pipe and daughter Mary Pipe

Friend Ralph Horsey of Taunton gent to make inventory of all my goods and chattels

Son Orlando and daughter Mary Pipe to be joint executors

Signed: Jas Pipe

Wits: Richard Cannicott, Mary Lang, John Cannicot

Probate granted to Orlando Pipe and Mary Pipe spinster both of Donyatt

Value of estate under £800

Will of James Pipe, Page 1

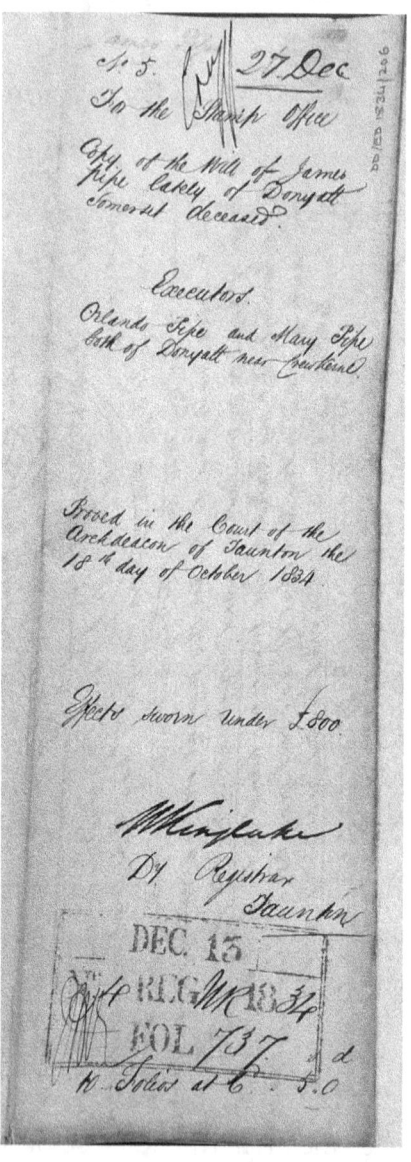

Citation:

Estate Duty copy of will of James PIPE of Donyatt, yeoman, Somerset Heritage Centre, Somerset, England.

Transcribed by ST Moore.

Will of James Pipe, Page 2

my estate and effects be taken and made within one month after my inter-
ment – And I hereby request authorise and empower my good friend Ralph
Horsey of Taunton gentleman to see to the making of such inventory and
valuation of my said estate and effects so given and devised to my said
children Orlando and Mary and that an equal division be made thereof between
them and of the third part of my household goods and furniture so as aforesaid
given to my said daughter Elizabeth and in all other respects to see to and
assist in the execution of this my will and that he shall reimburse himself
out of my said estate and effects so as aforesaid given to my said children
Orlando and Mary all costs and expences he may incur in the execution of
the trust hereby in him reposed – And I do hereby constitute and appoint my
said son Orlando Pipe and my said daughter Mary Pipe joint executor and
executrix of this my will And I hereby revoke all other wills by me at any
time heretofore made and do declare this present writing contained in two
sheets of paper to be my last will and testament – In witness whereof I
have hereunto set my hand & seal to wit my hand to the first sheet and
my hand and seal to this last sheet the day and year first above written –
＿＿＿ Jas Pipe (Ls) ＿＿＿＿ Signed sealed published and declared by
the said James Pipe the testator as and for his last will and testament
in the presence of us who in his presence and in the presence of each other
have subscribed our names as witnesses thereto ＿ Rich'd Cannicott ＿＿
＿ Mary Lang ＿＿＿ John Cannicott ＿＿＿＿＿＿＿＿＿＿＿

This and the foregoing sheet contain a true copy of the original will
the same having been examined therewith this ninth day of December
1834 by us –

         R H Liverlake

         Jno Chorley Junr

Appendix G

*Deed of Confirmation between Mrs. Elizabeth **PIPE***
*and Sir Francis George Augustus Fuller Elliot **DRAKE***
Dated 1874

Deed of Confirmation

Dated 1874

Mrs Elizabeth Pipe

To

Sir Francis Geo A. F E. Drake baronet

This Indenture made the [blank] day of [blank] one thousand eight hundred and seventy four **between Elizabeth Pipe** of Greece in the county of Monroe in the state of New York in the United States of America widow of the one part and **Sir Francis George Augustus Fuller Elliott Drake** of Nutwell Court Woodbury in the county of Devon baronet of the other

Whereas by an indenture dated the [blank] day of [blank] one thousand eight hundred and seventy three and made between Thomas Pipe and Elizabeth his wife therein after referred to by and comprehended in the designation of "The Lessors" of the one part and the said Sir Francis George Augustus Fuller Elliott Drake who was thereinafter referred to by and comprehended in the designation of "The Lessee" of the other part

It is witnessed that for the consideration therein mentioned they the said Thomas Pipe and Elizabeth his wife **did** and each of them **did** by the now reciting presents demise and to farm let unto the said lessee

All those messuages or dwelling houses commonly called or known as "Whitehorns" situate in the parish of Membury within the county of Devon and "Pithayne" within the parish of Yarcombe in the said county of Devon with the barns stables outhouses yards gardens and appurtenances thereto respectively belonging

And also all those several closes or pieces of land arable meadow and pasture or orchard land or ground adjoining or lying near or contiguous thereto respectively and then or theretofore held and enjoyed therewith and containing together sixty three acres or thereabouts, be the same more or less

And also all that allotment or close of land situate in and forming part of Mannings Common in the parish of Yarcombe aforesaid heretofore in the

[page 2] occupation of George Bondfield [Bonfield] deceased and then and late of Susan Bondfield [Bonfield] deceased his widow and containing by estimation three acres more or less with their and every of their appurtenances

And also the exclusive right of shooting and sporting over the same except all timber and trees whatsoever and all mines minerals gravel pits and quarries thereon

To hold the same, subject as thereinafter mentioned, unto the said before lessee his executors administrators and assigns for the term of ten years from the twenty fifth of March then last under the yearly rent of one hundred pounds payable on the four usual quarterly days of payment without deduction except Property Tax and the further yearly rent of fifteen pounds by equal quarterly payments on the days therein aforesaid for every acre and so in proportion for every less quantity than an acre of the Meadow ground thereby demised with the said lessee should plough up or convert into tillage without the previous consent in writing of the lessors their heirs and assigns

And by the indenture now in recital the said lessee for himself his executors administrators and assigns covenanted with the lessor their his and her heirs and assigns that the lessee would during the said term duly pay the said rent thereby reserved as and when the same respectively became due

And also to pay all rates and taxes in respect of the demised premises

And to keep the same premises in sufficient repair on being allowed rough timber and two pounds per hundred for reed except the main walls and roof of the farm house and buildings and outer doors thereof which were

[page 3] to be kept in repair by the lessors and also the barn of White-horns which it was thereby agreed might be let down and also except injury by accidental fire

And at the expiration of the term to so deliver up the same to the lessors their heirs or assigns

And that it should be lawful for the lessors their heirs or assigns and their his or her agents at all reasonable times during the said term to enter upon the demised land view and examine the condition thereof and to leave notice of any wants of reparation which the said lessee his executors administrators or assigns would within three months after every such notice repair and make good accordingly

And also to use and manage the demised premises in a good and husbandlike manner and in a due and regular course of husbandry

And also should not carry off any hay straw or manure from the said premises but in and upon the same would spend use lay and employ all the hay straw swedes turnips mangoldwurzels [beets] fodder dung soil muck manure and compost that should from time to time arise come grow or be made in and upon the same premises

And also should leave upon the demised premises all the manure that should be produce thereof during the last year of the said term without requiring any recompense for the same

And not to break up or convert into tillage any of the meadow or pasture lands

And that it should be lawful for the lessors their heirs or assigns at Michaelmas next before the expiration of the said term to enter upon and plough up all such parts of the said demised lands as should the preceding year have been sown with winter corn or grain

And it is by the now reciting indenture provided and agreed

[page 4] that if the said rents thereby reserved or any part thereof should be unpaid for twenty one days after any of the said days whereon the same ought to have been paid, although no formal demand thereof

should have been made, or in case of the breach or non-performance of any of the covenants and agreements therein contained by the said lessor their executors administrators or assigns then that it should be lawful for the said lessors their heirs or assigns attorney or agent into the demised premises to re-enter

And by the now reciting indenture the said Thomas Pipe for himself his heirs executors and administrators and for the said Elizabeth his wife her heirs executors administrators covenanted with the said lessee that he and they paying the rents and observing performing and keeping the covenants thereinbefore on his and their parts contained should peaceably hold occupy and enjoy the demised premises with their appurtenances for the said term and to keep the buildings of the premises in repair except in such matters as were thereinbefore covenanted and agreed to be demised and performed by the said lessee

And it was thereby declared and agreed that the yearly rent thereinbefore reserved was so reserved and should be taken and be in the proportions and manner following, that is to say the yearly sum of eighty five pounds as and for the annual value of the hereditaments thereby demised and that the sum of fifteen pounds the balance of the said yearly rent as consideration for the omission from the now reciting demise of the usual reservation

[page 5] to lessors of the right of hunting shooting and sporting over the demised premises

And whereas the hereinbefore recited indenture was executed by William Jennings in the names and as the attorney of the said Thomas Pipe and Elizabeth his wife and it has since been made known to the said Sir Francis George Augustus Fuller Elliott Drake that the marriage of the said Elizabeth Pipe with the said Thomas Pipe was informal and void and he has requested and it has been arranged and agreed that the said Elizabeth Pipe should confirm the said least in manner hereinafter mentioned and enter into the covenants hereinafter contained

Now this indenture witnesseth that in pursuance of such request and arrangement and agreement and in consideration of the premises and of ten shillings now in hand paid by the said Sir Francis George Augustus Fuller Elliott Drake to the said Elizabeth Pipe the receipt whereof she does acknowledge, **she** the said Elizabeth Pipe **Doth** by these presents demise lease and to farm let unto the said Sir Francis George Augustus Fuller Elliott Drake

All and singular the said messuage farm and lands and all and every the hereditaments described comprised or referred to in the hereinbefore recited indenture with their and every of their appurtenances

To hold the same unto the said Sir Francis George Augustus Fuller Elliott Drake his

[page 6] executors administrators and assigns for the residue of the said term of ten years if she the said Elizabeth Pipe shall so long live nevertheless upon the conditions and subject to the provisos and agreements contained in the hereinbefore recited indenture

And the said Elizabeth Pipe for herself her heirs executors and administrators doth hereby covenant agree and declare with the said Sir Francis George Augustus Fuller Elliott Drake his executors administrators and assigns that the said hereinbefore recited indenture of lease shall be deemed and taken to be good valid and effectual to all intents and purposes for all the residue of the said term of ten years if the said Elizabeth Pipe shall so long live

And that during such term she the said Elizabeth Pipe her heirs executors or administrators shall and will uphold the same

And that the said Sir Francis George Augustus Fuller Elliott Drake his executors administrators and assigns paying the said yearly rent of one hundred pounds hereinbefore mentioned to be reserved in and by the hereinbefore in part recited indenture of lease and duly performing the same indenture on his and their parts to be performed shall

[page 7] and may peaceably and quietly hold possess and enjoy the said premises during the said term thereby granted without any eviction or disturbance by the said Elizabeth Pipe her heirs or assigns or any person or persons lawfully or equitably claiming by from or under her

In witness whereof the said parties to these presents have hereunto set their hands and seals the day and year first above written

Signed sealed and delivered

By the above named Elizabeth Pipe

In the presence of

A.B.

Add address and description, (with title)

C.D.

Add address and description

After enquiry Mrs Pipe to please place her finger on the seal and say "I deliver this as my act and Deed"

Citation:

Privately held by Elizabeth Pipe Hansen [ADDRESS FOR PRIVATE USE,] Amherst, Wisconsin, 2025.

Transcribed by ST Moore

Deed of Confirmation, Cover

Dated   1874

Mrs Elizabeth Pipe

— to —

Sir Francis Geo A F E
Drake Baronet

Deed
of
Confirmation

Deed of Confirmation, Page 1

This Indenture made the   day of
One thousand eight hundred and seventy
four **Between Elizabeth Pipe** of Greece in the
County of Monroe in the State of New York in the
United States of America Widow of the one part and
Sir Francis George Augustus Fuller Elliott Drake of
Nutwell Court Woodbury in the County of Devon &c
Baronet of the other part **Whereas** by an Indenture
dated the   day of   One thousand &c
eight hundred and seventy three and made between
Thomas Pipe and Elizabeth his Wife thereinafter &c
referred to by and comprehended in the designation
of "The Lessors" of the one part and the said Sir Francis
George Augustus Fuller Elliott Drake who was thereinafter referred
to by and comprehended in the designation of "The Lessee"
of the other part **It is witnessed** that for the   &c
considerations therein mentioned they the said Thomas
Pipe and Elizabeth his wife **Did** and each of them &c
Did by the now reciting presents demise and to farm
let unto the said Lessee **All those** Messuages or &c
Dwellinghouses commonly called or known as "Whitehorns"
situate in the parish of Membury within the County of
Devon and "Pithayne" within the parish of Yarcombe in
the said County of Devon with the Barns Stables &c
Outhouses Yards Gardens and appurtenances thereto
respectively belonging **And also** all those several &c
closes or pieces of Land arable Meadow and pasture
or Orchard land or ground adjoining or lying near
or contiguous thereto respectively and then or heretofore
held and enjoyed therewith and containing together
Sixty three acres or thereabouts (be the same more or less)
And also all that allotment or close of land situate
in and forming part of Mannings Common in the
parish of Yarcombe aforesaid heretofore in the &c

Deed of Confirmation, Page 2

occupation of George Bondfield deceased and then and late of Susan Bondfield deceased his Widow and containing by estimation three acres more or less with their and every of their appurtenances *ee* **And also** the exclusive right of shooting and *ee* sporting over the same except all timber and trees whatsoever and all mines minerals Gravel pits and quarries thereon **To hold** the same subject as *eee* thereinafter mentioned unto the said Lessee his executors Administrators and assigns for the term of Ten Years from the twenty fifth of March then last under the yearly rent of One hundred pounds *eeee* payable on the four usual quarterly days of payment without deduction except property Tax and the further yearly rent of fifteen pounds by equal quarterly payments on the days therein aforesaid for every acre and so in proportion for every less quantity than an acre of the meadow ground thereby demised which the said Lessee *eee* should plough up or convert into tillage without the previous consent in writing of the Lessors their Heirs and assigns **and** by the Indenture now in recital the said Lessee for himself his executors *ee* administrators and assigns Covenanted with the *ee* Lessors their his and her Heirs and assigns that the Lessee would during the said term duly pay the said rents thereby reserved as and when the same respectively became due **and also** to pay all rates and taxes in respect of the demised premises **and** to keep the same premises in sufficient repair on being ~~being~~ allowed rough Timber and Two pounds per hundred for Reed *eee* except the main walls and roof of the Farm House and Buildings and outer Doors thereof which were

Deed of Confirmation, Page 3

to be kept in repair by the Lesors and also the Barn
at Whitehorns which it was thereby agreed might
be let down and also except injury by accidental fire
and at the expiration of the term to so deliver up
the same to the Lesors their Heirs or assigns and
that it should be lawful for the Lesors their heirs or
assigns and their his or her agents at all reasonable
times during the said Term to enter upon the demised
and view and examine the condition thereof and to
leave notice of any wants of reparation which the said
Lesee his Executors Administrators or assigns would
within three months after every such Notice repair
and make good accordingly and also to use and
manage the demised premises in a good and lee
husbandlike manner and in a due and regular
course of husbandry and also should not carry off
any hay straw or manure from the said premises
but in and upon the same would spend use lay
and employ all the hay straw Swedes turnips eee
mangold Wurtzell fodder dung soil muck manure
and compost that should from time to time arise come
grow or be made in and upon the same premises
and also should leave upon the demised premises
all the manure that should be produced thereon
during the last year of the said term without eee
requiring any recompense for the same and not to
break up or convert into Tillage any of the Meadow
or pasture Land and that it should be lawful
for the Lesors their heirs or assigns at Michaelmas
next before the expiration of the said Term to enter
upon and plough up all such parts of the said eee
demised lands as should the preceding year have
been sown with Winter Corn or Grain and it is
by the now reciting Indenture provided and agreed

Deed of Confirmation, Page 4

that if the said rents thereby reserved or any part ee
thereof should be unpaid for Twenty one days after
any of the said days whereon the same ought to
have been paid (although no formal demand thereof
should have been made) or in case of the Breach or
nonperformance of any of the Covenants and eeeee
agreements therein contained by the said Lessee his
executors Administrators or assigns then that it should
be lawful for the said Lessors their heirs or assigns
Attorney or Agent unto the demised premises to eee
reenter __and__ by the now reciting Indenture
the said Thomas Pipe for himself his heirs eeee
executors and administrators and for the
said Elizabeth his wife her heirs executors
and administrators, with the said Lessee that he
and they paying the rents and observing eeee
performing and keeping the covenants thereinbefore
on his ~~and their~~ and their parts contained should
peaceably hold occupy and enjoy the demised
premises with their appurtenances for the said
Term __and to__ keep the Buildings of the premises
in repair except in such matters as were
thereinbefore covenanted and agreed to be done
and performed by the said Lessee __and__ it was
thereby declared and agreed that the yearly rent
thereinbefore reserved was so reserved and should
be taken and be in the proportions and manner
following that was to say the yearly sum
of eighty five pounds as and for the annual
value of the hereditaments thereby demised
and that the sum of fifteen pounds the
balance of the said yearly rent as a eeee
consideration for the omission from the now
reciting demise of the usual Reservation

Deed of Confirmation, Page 5

to Lessors of the right of hunting shooting
and Sporting over the demised premises
__and Whereas__ the hereinbefore recited eeeee
Indenture was Executed By William Jennings
in the names and as the attorney of the said
Thomas Pipe and Elizabeth his Wife and it
has since been made known to the said eee
Sir Francis George Augustus Fuller Elliott Drake
that the marriage of the said Elizabeth Pipe
with the said Thomas Pipe was informal ee
and void and he has requested and it has
been arranged and agreed that the said ee
Elizabeth pipe should confirm the said lease
in manner hereinafter mentioned and eee
enter into the Covenants hereinafter contained
__Now this Indenture Witnesseth__ that in
pursuance of such request and arrangement
and agreement and in consideration of
the premises and of Ten shillings now in
hand paid by the said Sir Francis George
Augustus Fuller Elliott Drake to the said
Elizabeth Pipe the receipt whereof she doth hereby
she doth hereby acknowledge __She__ the said
Elizabeth Pipe __Doth__ by these presents eee
demise and to farm let unto the said
Sir Francis George Augustus Fuller eee
Elliott Drake __All__ and singular the said
Messuage Farm and lands and all and
every the hereditaments described comprised
or referred to in the hereinbefore eeee
recited Indenture with their and every
of their appurtenances __To hold__ the same
unto the said Sir Francis George eee
Augustus Fuller Elliott Drake his ee

Deed of Confirmation, Page 6

executors administrators and assigns for
the residue of the said Term of Ten years
if she the said Elizabeth Pipe shall so
long live nevertheless upon the conditions and
subject to the provisoes and agreements
contained in the hereinbefore recited
Indenture **and** the said Elizabeth Pipe
for herself her heirs executors and
administrators **Doth** hereby Covenant agree
and declare with the said Sir Francis
George Augustus Fuller Elliott Drake
his executors administrators and assigns
That the said hereinbefore recited Indenture
of Lease shall be deemed and taken to be
good valid and effectual to all intents
and purposes for all the residue of the
said Term of ten years if the said
Elizabeth Pipe shall so long live **and that**
during such term she the said Elizabeth
Pipe her heirs executors or administrators
shall and will uphold the same **and
that** the said Sir Francis George Augustus
Fuller Elliott Drake his executors
administrators and assigns paying the said
yearly rent of **One** hundred pounds hereinbefore
mentioned to be reserved in and by the
hereinbefore in part recited Indenture of Lease
and duly performing the several Covenants
contained in the same Indenture on his
and their parts to be performed shall and

Deed of Confirmation, Page 7

may peaceably and quietly hold poßeß and
enjoy the said premises during the ~~said~~ term
thereby granted without any eviction or disturbance
by the said Elizabeth Pipe her heirs or assigns ee
or any person or persons lawfully or equitably
claiming by from or under her *In Witness* ee
whereof the said parties to these presents have
hereunto set their hands and seals the day ee
and year first *above* written ♯ eeeeeeeee

Signed Sealed and delivered
by the above named Elizabeth Pipe
in the presence of

A. B.
of &c

add: d ddreß and description (with Title)

C. D
of &c

add addreß and description

† after asking Mrs Pipe will please
place her finger on the seal and say
"I deliver this as my act and Deed"

Note: *The bibliography pertaining to this series resides at the conclusion of Volume 2.*

Indexes

Origin & Destination	Letter Number
Birch Oak Farm, Membury, Devon County, England (later Yarcombe County)	11,20
Brydon, Highampton, Devon County, England	80
Buckland St. Mary, Somerset County, England	12,13
Calkin's Place, Farmington, Waupaca County, Wisconsin, USA	30
Cataract House, Greece Center, Monroe County, New York, USA	7
Chard, Somerset County, England	68,69,71,72,76,79, 81,82,83,84,88,89, 90
Chard, Whitestaunton, Somerset County, England	86,87
Chicago, Cook County, Illinois, USA (103 West Madison Street)	73
Dunfermline, Fife County, Scotland (37 Rose Street)	100
Exchange & Savings Bank, Waupaca, Waupaca County, Wisconsin, USA	74
Farmington, Waupaca County, Wisconsin, USA	28,29,31,32,33,34, 35,53
Fort Manoel, Manoel Island, Gżira, Republic of Malta	6
Forton, Chard, Somerset County, England	63,64
Frizinghall, Bradford, West Yorkshire, England (16 Ferndale Grove)	102
Greece, Monroe County, New York, USA	18
Greece Center, Monroe County, New York, USA	8,9,10,19
Hilgay near Downham, Norfolk County, England	82
Hursey, Broadwindsor, Dorset County, England	76,77,78,80,92

Origin & Destination	Letter Number
Hursey, Burstock, Beaminster, Dorsetshire County, England	65,66,67,70
Kirby House, Milwaukee, Milwaukee County, Wisconsin, USA (Corner of East Water & Mason Streets)	96
London, England	38,44
Manchester, Lancashire County, England	81,84,86
Manitowoc, Manitowoc County, Wisconsin, USA (South Eighth Street)	104
Neenah, Winnebago County, Wisconsin, USA	75,85
New York, New York, USA (111 Broadway)	74
North American Hotel, State Street, Rochester, Monroe County, New York, USA	14,17
North Greece, Monroe County, New York, USA	4
Northay Farm, Whitestaunton, Chard, Somerset County, England	1,2,3,4,5,6,7,8,13,14, 15,16,17,18,19,22,23, 24,25,26,27,28,29, 30,31,32,33,34,35, 36,37,39,40,41,42, 43,45,46,47,48,49, 50,51,52,53,54,55, 56,57,58,59,60,61,62
Oxford Junction, Jones County, Iowa, USA	95,97,98,99
Pipe House, Lanark, Portage County, Wisconsin, USA [Sheridan, Waupaca County, Wisconsin, USA, Post Office]	73,78,83,90,91,92, 93,94,95,96,97,98, 99,100,102,103,104, 105
Rochester, Monroe County, New York, USA	1,2,3,5
Stawell, Victoria, Borung County, Australia	77,91
Stevens Point, Portage County, Wisconsin, USA	93
Stevens Point, Portage County, Wisconsin, USA (413 Normal Avenue)	103
Stoford near Yeovil, Somerset County, England	16

Origin & Destination	Letter Number
Taunton, Somerset County, England (Stamp Office)	12
Thorncombe, Dorset County, England	75
Unknown	101,105
Vinland, Winnebago County, Wisconsin, USA	10,11,20,22,23,24, 25,26,27,36
Waupaca, Waupaca County, Wisconsin, USA	37,38,39,40,41,42, 43,44,45,46,47,48, 49,50,51,52,54,55, 56,57,58,59,60,61, 62,63,64,65,66,67, 68,69,70,71,72,79, 88,94
West Liverpool, Lancashire County, England (8 Gloucester Street)	15
Whitestaunton, Somerset County, England (Post Office)	89
Winsham, Somerset County, England	85
Woodville, Calumet County, Wisconsin, USA	87
Yarcombe, Devon County, England	9

Writer & Recipient	Letter Number
Kite, Thos.	12
McCunn, Ethel	102
McCunn, Florence	100
McCunn, Florence Pipe	90,92
Mead, H.C.	74
Messer, Thomas	95,97,98,99
Pillar, Charlotte Jennings Pipe	11,36,83
Pipe, Amelia Woodnorth	88
Pipe, Elizabeth Johnson	103
Pipe, Elizabeth Stickland	4,7,8,14,17,19,22,24, 26,28,29,31,33,35, 38,41,46,48,51,55, 56,58,59,60,61,63, 65,66,68,70,71,72, 77,78,79,80,81,83, 84,86,88,90,92,96, 100,102
Pipe, John Valentine	4,7,9,10,13
Pipe, Mary Agnes Messer	99,103
Pipe, Thomas	10,18,20,23,24,25, 26,27,28,29,30,31, 32,33 33,34,35,37, 39,40,41,42,43,44, 45,46,47,48,49,50, 52,53,54,55,56,57, 58,59,60,61,62,63, 64,65,66,67,69,70, 73,75,76,77,78,79, 80,82,83,85,87,88, 89,90, 91,92,93
Pipe, Thomas (estate)	94
Pipe, Tom Jr.	79,88
Pipe, William Edwin	95,97,98,104
Pipe, William Jennings	6,38,44,77,91
Poll, Alfred	82

Writer & Recipient	Letter Number
Rendell, Giles	73
Roberts, Elizabeth Jones	87
Scranton, Edwin	1,2,3,5
Spiller, Robert	9
Stickland, Anna	80
Stickland, Mary	81,84,86
Unknown	21,101,105
Woodnorth, Mary Elizabeth Pipe	78,90,92,96,101
Woodnorth, Frank	96
Wyatt, William	12,13

About the Author

Joan Naomi Steiner was born and raised on her grandfather's farm in Calumet County, Wisconsin. She graduated from Chilton High School. She earned her doctorate at New York University and her Master of Science in Teaching English and Bachelor of Science degrees from the University of Wisconsin-Stevens Point.

Dr. Steiner's professional career includes teaching high school students for twenty-five years and administrating in school districts for seventeen years. She has also taught at the university level and worked as a consultant for more than forty school districts in Wisconsin.

Dr. Joan Naomi Steiner

Dr. Steiner has known the Pipe family descendants for most of her life. Recently, her son invited her to visit his cousins, who inherited the Pipe family portraits and letter collection. Her research has uncovered not only records, but also family history told by ancestors in their own words.

Dr. Steiner has also written *A German Bohemian Immigration: The Population Shift from Western Bohemia to Calumet County, Wisconsin,* which has been translated into German and Czech languages. Dr. Steiner's website is a database of findings and a repository for records and resources for immigrants from Great Britian, Germany, and today's Czech Republic. You can find it at https://germanbohemianwisconsin.com/.